COACHING
RELATIONSHIPS

COACHING RELATIONSHIPS

THE RELATIONAL COACHING FIELD BOOK

EDITED BY ERIK DE HAAN
& CHARLOTTE SILLS

First published in 2012 by Libri Publishing

Copyright © Libri Publishing

Authors retain copyright of individual chapters.

The right of Erik de Haan and Charlotte Sills to be identified as the editors of this work has been asserted in accordance with the Copyright, Designs and Patents Act, 1988.

ISBN 978 1 907471 28 5

A CIP catalogue record for this book is available from The British Library

Design by Carnegie Publishing

Printed in the UK by Halstan Printing Ltd

Libri Publishing
Brunel House
Volunteer Way
Faringdon
Oxfordshire
SN7 7YR

Tel: +44 (0)845 873 3837

www.libripublishing.co.uk

CONTENTS

CONTENTS

INTRODUCTION

1. THE RELATIONAL TURN IN EXECUTIVE COACHING

A FIELD OF RIVALLING IDEAS

The field of executive coaching and adjacent fields like counselling and consulting are, in principle, 'all about the client' and his or her development. However, until recent years, coaching theory and methodology have shown a strange bias towards models, approaches and techniques – in other words, the focus has been more on what the coach does than on the client. Even where models have emerged to understand the client and his personality or patterns, the emphasis quickly turns to what the coach should do and how she or he should intervene. Perhaps it is quite natural and understandable that executive coaches have written mostly about themselves and what methods they prefer, but there are other powerful reasons for this bias:

- *Historical motives* – When introducing new ideas, authors tend to emphasise the difference of these from existing ideas and approaches; they have to amplify these differences if they want to gain an audience and a representation in the field. This starts off a coach-centred literature base, with ever-more authors studying the proposed methods and responding from their own experience and convictions.

- *Commercial motives* – When coaches advertise their services and attempt to win clients, they feel pulled to talk about what they have to offer, their methods and how they are great and different. Clients contribute to this fallacy of 'buying a coach' – whereas 'buying a process' or 'starting a commitment' are descriptions nearer the truth.

1

- *Motives of allegiance* – When a coach gets educated and trained, and particularly when this schooling (or self-study) is successful, he or she doesn't learn only about coaching; he or she doesn't learn only about clients, him or herself, and methodology: he or she also learns to embrace an approach, a system, a role model and/or a school of thought. Factors of allegiance and even dogmatism have long been underestimated in the development of coaches and consultants.

These factors do not conspire only to create a very self-conscious and coach-centred profession; they also contribute to making the field even more rivalrous than a field of knowledge-intensive service provision would otherwise be.

There is a further motive for focussing chiefly on the coach's behaviour and it concerns our existential anxiety about uncertainty. It is so much easier to think of coaching just in terms of what you offer and what you do, rather than inquiring into the unknown and quite independent perspective of what the client might be bringing to the table and what the client might be contributing to the session's methodology and philosophy. If we begin to recognise the fact that the coaching engagement involves an interplay between two people's frames of reference, desires, beliefs and assumptions as well as their habitual ways of being in the world, we are faced with an unpredictability that is both exciting and unsettling. It is this perspective on the coaching relationship that this book aims to address.

A UNIFYING FORCE

In recent years, we have seen a significant shift in the technical, philosophical, theoretical and methodological emphasis of coaching. There has been a countervailing movement away from the focus on the coach and the coach's models, towards a focus on the relationship between them as a central vehicle for change. This "relational turn", as it is known (Mills 2005; De Haan 2008c), has mirrored similar movements in all fields of psychological work as well as in organisational theory, sociology and the arts. It has involved a change of emphasis from a focus on coach techniques and interventions, goal-setting and action planning, towards an appreciation of and engagement with patterns of relating. Thus it places relationship, to self and to others, including the coach, at the heart of the coaching work.

BACKGROUND TO THE RELATIONAL APPROACH

Why has the world seen such a profound emphasis on the importance of relating? Firstly, there have been remarkable and synchronistic developments in the areas of 'post-modern' philosophy, neurobiology and the study of human development. Research in these three areas has revealed an interconnectedness between human beings that was hitherto only recognised in some philosophies and spiritual traditions. Since the Renaissance and in particular the Enlightenment ages, men (and women) committed themselves to positivist, evidence-based, logical ways of understanding the world that led to huge leaps in understanding and development but left little room for mysteries such as intuition, intersubjectivity and unconscious mutuality. This has gradually given way to a focus on difference, plurality and context. Recent discoveries in affective neuroscience have provided, and are continuing to provide, significant evidence (Rizzolatti & Craighero 2004; Panskepp 1998; Schore 2003; etc.) that underscores the centrality of relatedness in human development and behaviour. In organisational thinking, chaos and complexity theory, which recognises how small gestures can amplify into large-scale pattern shifts, is encouraging us to think of an organisation, and even a society, simply as a collection of interactive processes rather than a structure (see Bill Critchley's chapter in this volume). What is more, though perhaps we guessed it, the loving relationship between mother and infant has been shown to be crucial in developing the brain and the sense of identity, while in later life, an accepting and supportive relationship can also facilitate changes in neural patterns and sense of self in the world (Schore 2003; Allen 2011).

The findings of all these disciplines coincided with a revolution in epistemology offered by feminist psychologists of the 1980s, such as Jean Baker Miller, Joyce Fletcher and Carol Gilligan, who challenged "the gendered nature of knowledge creation" (King 2004 and see Kathleen King's chapter in this volume). They pointed out that traditional child developmental theories (for example, Piaget, Erikson and Freud), all of which stressed the importance of ego strength, autonomy and separateness, stemmed from a psychological research base that was the exclusive province of men. These feminist thinkers offered another understanding of health and maturity, which involved interdependence, co-operation and the "relational skills" of support and empathy.

Finally, a confluence of ideas in the world of psychology and psychotherapy has given birth to an approach to psychological work (be it coaching, therapy or counselling) that has brought the different schools or traditions together in a previously-unheard-of integration. Part of this emergence has been the findings of over seventy years of psychotherapy outcome research, which is being convincingly replicated by increasing amounts of coaching research. We explore these findings in more detail below.

The relational focus in coaching is not only a result of these developments. It has also arisen out of a need to understand something that could not be explained or comprehended within existing psychological or coaching theories and to respond to increasingly complex client systems. Seen through this lens, relational coaching – rather than being a formally organised school or system of beliefs – can be thought of as a framework or way of thinking about the client, the coach, the relationships, the organisation – and about how coaching works. This perspective says that actually client, coach and organisation are intimately interlinked and that for anything to grow or change it is essential that the links grow and change as well. Moreover, growth and change will occur only in the presence of links that are or become nurturing, supportive and challenging. So what could be more helpful than focusing on the link, the connection, the *relationship* itself while it emerges and evolves?

2. PERSUASIVE EVIDENCE

Perhaps the most powerful force for directing our attention to relationships and back to our diverse and wonderful clients is the force of the high-level, in-depth effectiveness studies coming largely out of the adjacent field of psychotherapy. These studies could only have been conducted to that breath and rigour in that particular field, because the large institutions that pay for up to 80 per cent of those services (such as the National Health Service in Britain, the government in some other European countries and the large medical insurance companies in the U.S.) have been able and willing to pour millions of dollars into rigorous quantitative research. They do this for the simple reason that the potential savings made by having hard data about effectiveness are enormous. Only after stacking large amounts of randomised control trial studies together, a procedure known as meta-analysis, has it been possible to achieve clear and unambiguous conclusions about effectiveness and active ingredients of therapy, which have gradually found broad agreement among therapists and others. While coaching and therapy are two different activities, they have enough in common – in the sense that they both involve the intentional use of a relationship to further the development of a client – to make these conclusions highly relevant for practitioners in both fields. It is this research that has helped great numbers of professional practitioners to look again at their effectiveness and at finding a new way of practising that hones precisely that which is now known to be more effective.

COMMON FACTORS: THE ONES THAT COUNT

This 'great psychotherapy debate', neatly summarised in Wampold's book (2001) of that name, has demonstrated essentially that (1) psychotherapy is highly effective, on a par with psychiatric medicine; (2) none of the main psychotherapy approaches studied enjoys enhanced effectiveness by comparison to the others; (3) in consequence, all of the specific active ingredients identified are *common* to all professional approaches. These are the so-called *common factors*.

Common factors have to do with the setting (meeting at regular intervals, providing an expectation that things may get better), with a client's desire to be helped (the client's expectations, preferences and support networks), with the coach (warmth, quality of listening) and finally with the relationship (quality of communication, trust, agreement about the shared endeavour).

THE THREE MAIN COMMON FACTORS THAT COUNT TOWARDS EFFECTIVENESS:

I. CLIENT PERSONALITY AND CONTEXT

Without doubt, the single most important effective 'ingredient' in therapy is a factor which, by definition, therapy cannot influence – namely the support, assistance, trials and tribulations experienced by the client *outside* the therapeutic relationship. In most cases, the time spent outside therapy is more than 99 per cent of the time available, so it is not surprising that much happens there that is of greater importance in terms of change than what takes place or what is said during the therapy. Estimates of the effect of external factors are as high as 40 per cent of the explained variation (Lambert 1992), i.e. an effect size of as much as $d = 1.65$. In other words, clients with support outside therapy will do better on average than 95 per cent of the group without such support.

One other important client-related factor is hope, or having positive expectations of therapy, which according to Lambert (1992) carries an estimated effect size of $d = 0.85$.

II. THERAPIST PERSONALITY

Using the outcome of therapy as a measure of the quality of the therapist, vast quantities of raw research data have been re-analysed in order to establish how variability due to therapists can be compared with the variability of different approaches. It emerges that therapist-related variability is many times greater than the variability due to different approaches. In fact, therapist variability fully explains the small residual effect size due to differences between approaches ($d = 0.20$).

On the basis of the variability between therapists, we can also estimate an effect size associated with the person of the therapist, i.e. how much effect a good therapist produces on average compared with a less-good therapist. It appears to be between $d = 0.50$ and $d = 0.65$ (6 per cent of the variability in

Project MATCH Research Group (1998) and 9 per cent of the variability in Crits-Christoph & Mintz (1991)), i.e. of the same order of magnitude as the effect resulting from the quality of the relationship between therapist and client.

However, there are a number of personal characteristics of therapists which have been shown by statistical research to have a favourable effect on the outcome of psychotherapy:

- Empathy, understanding, respect, warmth and authenticity – the criteria already emphasised by Carl Rogers (Rogers 1957; Lambert & Bergin 1994)

- Being attractive(!), inspiring confidence and appearing competent, in that order (McNeal, May & Lee 1987)

- The therapist's own mental health (Beutler, Crago & Arizmendi 1986)

- The ability to let go of one's own system of values and to communicate within the other person's value system (see Norcross 1993; Beutler, Machado & Neufeldt 1994).

In apparent contrast with the last finding above, one aspect of the person of the therapist that appears to be particularly essential to a good outcome is the degree of 'ideological commitment' of the therapist. The evidence that there is no significant difference in outcome between approaches might suggest that the therapist need not espouse any approach. On the contrary, however, it is important that they do have a coherent theory/model and that they are strongly committed to and believe in it. The only rider – which is both subtle and important – is that they should not be unwavering in their adherence to the model but flexibly responsive to client characteristics and preferences, which includes inquiring regularly into what the client is finding helpful and what not (Norcross 2011).

III. RELATIONSHIP FACTORS

The third significant common factor is the quality of the relationship between therapist and client as experienced by the client. If you ask the client to score these or similar aspects, and also independently measure the outcome of therapy using one of the standard instruments, the correlation found between those scores is, on average, as much as 0.26 (with a negligible chance, $p < 0.001$, that the two do not correlate). This corresponds, under certain assumptions, to an effect size of $d = 0.54$ – i.e. a moderate effect (see Horvath & Symonds 1991; Martin, Garske & Davis 2000). It was noticed in this respect that the scores awarded by clients and independent observers correlate strongly and, taken together, are the best predictors of outcome one can find. Scores for the working alliance given by the therapists correlate much less well with the outcome. Another interesting finding is that it doesn't matter *when* the working alliance is scored: the initial working alliance is just as good a predictor as the working alliance at the end of the therapy.

RESEARCH INTO EXECUTIVE COACHING OUTCOME

The research evidence for effectiveness in psychotherapy has accumulated over more than seventy years; its findings are persuasive and cannot be ignored. The activity called coaching is a much newer profession and there is much less published research. However, the body is growing and it is important to examine the existing coaching outcome literature, to see whether the findings are comparable.

We define executive coaching as a form of leadership development that takes place through a series of contracted one-to-one conversations in a relationship with a qualified 'coach' or 'mentor'. Executive coaching aspires to be that part of leadership development that leads to the highest occurrence of appropriate, actionable and 'just-in-time' outcomes for executives, as the learning during the sessions is completely tailored to the individual and their practice. In coaching, the client learns and grows through reflecting on their own experiences and intuition via thought-provoking and insightful inquiry from the coach, in a trusting and supportive environment.

We have found only a small number of quantitative studies on coaching and mentoring effectiveness; hence we think they are worthy of careful reading and we summarise them here. Most empirical research into executive coaching is concerned with the value of coaching from the perspective of the client, with the research taking the form of an extensive evaluation of customer satisfaction including, on occasion, clients being asked to estimate how much their coaching has contributed to the bottom line of their organisation in financial terms (e.g. McGovern et al. 2001). Fewer still are the studies that explore the effectiveness of coaching by looking at effects other than client satisfaction. Olivero et al. (1997) studied managers who had taken part in a three-day educational training course, followed by eight weeks of coaching. They found that both the training and the coaching increased productivity considerably, with the bulk of the increase attributable to the coaching. In the case of Thach (2002), managers underwent a 360° feedback process before and after their coaching. They found an average increase in 'leadership effectiveness', both in terms of self-perception as well as perception by others.

A significant impact of executive coaching has also been found by Peterson (1993) and Evers, Brouwers & Tomic (2006). Evers, Brouwers &

Tomic measured self-efficacy beliefs and outcome expectancies, on each of three dimensions. Their study compared a pre-intervention and post-intervention measurement and also involved a control group. Whilst their sample was not very large (30 managers in both the experimental and the control group) they did find some objective evidence for a positive outcome of the coaching intervention with a significant increment for the coached group over the control group for one of the three dimensions in both self-efficacy beliefs ("setting one's own goals") and outcome expectancies ("acting in a balanced way").

One of the most thorough studies into the impact of executive coaching was undertaken by Smither et al. (2003) who worked with a control group and based their conclusions on a more objective criterion than evaluations by the clients. Similar to Peterson (1993) before them, Smither et al. included evaluations by independent researchers and by the clients' superiors, colleagues and staff (360° feedback). The research was conducted among 1,202 senior managers in a multinational organisation and involved two consecutive years of 360° feedback results. The researchers found that managers who work with an executive coach are significantly more likely than other managers to (1) set specific goals; (2) solicit ideas for improvements from their superiors; and (3) obtain higher ratings from direct reports and superiors.

The findings above are supported in the more extensive *mentoring* outcome literature, which is reviewed in Allen et al. (2004), through a meta-analysis comprising 43 outcome studies of mentoring in the organisational/workplace domain. Taking only the studies with control groups, they found generally small but significant effect sizes, e.g. for effect of mentoring on number of promotions: 10% explained proportion of variance; and for career satisfaction 4% explained proportion of variance. They also found the criterion measuring the mentoring relationship ("satisfaction with mentor") to be the best predictor of career outcomes (14% explained proportion of variance for career mentoring and 38% for psychosocial mentoring). One thorough study of mentoring outcomes that was included by Allen et al. (2004) is Ragins, Cotton & Miller (2000) who studied a group of 1,162 professionals from many organisations and looked at the effect of formal/informal mentoring relationships on a range of work and career attitudes. Of the respondents, 44% had an informal mentor, 9% a formal mentor as part of a mentoring programme and 47% no mentor (the control group). Their results show that the crucial factor in effectiveness is the client's satisfaction with the mentoring *relationship*. In the absence of that factor, there were no demonstrable differences between professionals who were mentored and those who were not. If client satisfaction with the relationship is present, however, professionals clearly demonstrate more positive attitudes towards themselves (self-confidence), their work, promotion prospects, their organisation and their career. The group that produced Allen et al. (2004) later confirmed the results summarised above in a much larger meta-analysis, with $N > 10,000$ and including workplace, youth and academic domains (Eby et al. 2008).

In the small but growing body of outcome-research literature on coaching, we have found the following recent articles exploring the question of *what sort* of coaching is effective; in other words, *which* coaching models, qualities of coaches, matching characteristics or coaching behaviours make a difference to clients?

Scoular & Linley (2006) have looked at how both (1) a 'goal-setting' intervention at the beginning of the conversation and (2) personality (dis-) similarities between coach and client, as measured by MBTI, impact on perceived effectiveness. Due to the limited sample size, no difference resulted between outcome measurements at two and eight weeks after the session between 'goal-setting' and 'no goal-setting'; but they did demonstrate that when coach and client differed more on some aspects of the personality instrument (the MBTI 'temperaments') the outcome scores were significantly higher.

Stewart et al. (2008) have looked at how both client personality and client self-efficacy predict coaching outcome. They measured the so-called 'big-five' personality factors (Digman 1990) and general self-efficacy (see Schwarzer, Mueller & Greenglass 1999) for 110 clients and correlated these personality factors with coaching outcome. They found moderate positive effects for conscientiousness, openness, emotional stability and general self-efficacy, but they warned that other factors are likely to play a role as well.

Boyce, Jackson & Neal (2010) studied 74 coach–client relationships in the context of a U.S. military academy, where clients were cadets and coaches were senior military leaders who had had some training in executive coaching. The study analysed the impact of relationship aspects (rapport, trust and commitment) and matching criteria (demographic commonality, behavioural compatibility and coach credibility) on coaching outcome. Their main findings were that matching had no significant impact on outcome, whilst relationship, as assessed by both clients (explained proportion of variance around 50 per cent) and coaches (explained proportion of variance around 25 per cent), affected outcomes significantly.

With a sample of internal coaches working alongside a leadership development programme within a manufacturing company involving 30 coach–client pairs, Baron & Morin (2009) were able to show that *working alliance* as a measure of the coaching relationship, when rated by clients, predicted coaching outcomes (explained proportion of variance around 25 per cent) whilst coaches' ratings of working alliance do not predict outcomes significantly.

De Haan et al. (2011) examine how various executive coaching interventions make a difference to clients. 71 coaching clients, from as many organisations, reported on the various interventions of their coaches and all strengths of interventions were compared with their evaluations. In that work, De Haan et al. found no distinction among specific coach interventions of coaches, leading to the conclusion that helpfulness, as in psychotherapy, is much less predicted by technique or approach as it is by factors common to all coaching, such as the relationship, empathic understanding, positive expectations and so forth.

In summary, we note that outcome research in coaching is still in its infancy and that the holy grail of executive coaching – "what determines outcome for clients?" – is still there to be sought. There is no agreed research standard like the randomised control trials used in psychotherapy outcome research (Wampold 2001). What is also striking is that the first four research papers above (Peterson 1993; Olivero et al. 1997; McGovern et al. 2001; and Thach 2002) which did not make use of a control group, found very large effects (generally larger than those found in psychotherapy), whilst the more rigorous studies involving control groups discussed next (Allen et al. 2004; Smither et al. 2003; and Evers et al. 2006) all found only small effects, generally smaller than those found in psychotherapy (Wampold 2001). It seems that if the client alone is the focus of the study, the outcome tends to be very positive, whereas if one controls for perceptual and research artefacts this effect is much smaller though still positive.

THE IMPLICATIONS FOR COACHING PRACTICE

This extensive body of evidence from both psychotherapy and coaching research offers some very strong pointers to the coach as to the key features of successful coaching:

- A relationship, as experienced by the client, of respect and empathy combined with a shared agreement about goals and the nature of the work

- An authentic meeting where the coach shows a clear allegiance to an approach, but holds it lightly while responding to the preferences and frame of reference of the client

- Client factors including motivation and 'hope' as well as supportive family, friends and the organisational context

- Practitioner qualities such as attractiveness, flexibility and warmth

- An opportunity for the client to explore himself and his thoughts and feelings, as well as try out new behaviour

- Seeking feedback from the client about what they experience as helpful

- No attempt to match, for example, the coach's gender, race or religion with client's unless the client strongly requests this – but an offer of curiosity and interest into the client's culture and views.

Of course, some of the common factors with the highest impact on outcome are beyond the control of coach and client. For example, it is not immediately possible to change either the client's or the coach's characteristics! However, some are definitely within the coach's influence and it seems a good idea for coaches to begin radically supporting their clients with them.

COMMON FACTORS WITHIN OUR CONTROL:
MOTIVATION AND HOPE

Many writers and practitioners have emphasised the importance of motivation and hope in clients – from psychoanalysts such as Yalom (1970) to positive psychologists (Fredrickson 2003). The meta-analyses of randomised control studies show that there is a rather high outcome for hope (being on a waiting list), placebo (being in conversation, but not a therapeutic one) and self-help (working on one's own with the help of a manual). Clients will often ask "What will this bring me?" or "What can I expect from doing this?" or just generally "Can you help me?" or "How am I doing as a client?" These can be seen as opportunities for coaches at least not to diminish their motivation and to consider working explicitly on self-confidence and self-motivation by giving active support, a compliment, or a 'hopeful' view such as "Coaching is usually very effective with this issue" or "This is exactly the sort of problem that we can address in coaching". In fact, we think this factor may be linked to the issue of allegiance we described above. This common factor concerns how convinced the coach is that his/her own approach (ideology, methods and technique) is the right one, even though they are ready to modify it flexibly in response to the client. We presume that this is one of the elements that builds the client's motivation and trust in their coach's competence.

This is the client's allegiance to the process, the sessions and the work, something we might strengthen explicitly or by demonstrating our own allegiance and trust.

COLLABORATIVE COMMUNICATION

The coach is willing to be in authentic relationship and, specifically, to ask for feedback from the client into their experience – what is working, what is useful, how the relationship is going – and to give feedback.

EXTERNAL FACTORS

Clearly the coach cannot have much influence over the client's life and circumstances external to the coaching. However, if he/she bears in mind the huge significance of this factor in the outcome, it will be important to hold it as an area of inquiry. He/she can ask questions about who the client can talk to, what support he has in his organisation – and if there is little support, what networks he could establish. What could the client be doing to enhance the quality of his work and work-life balance? Is there anything the coach and/or client can be doing to develop a 'coaching culture' that will support the client's attempts to change?

TAILORING THE APPROACH TO CLIENT 'STYLE'

While the research continues to show that no individual approaches work better than any others (of the commonly recognised models), it also has shown the importance of an approach that suits the style of the client and is tailored to his needs. For example, a client who is resistant to rules and authority responds better to a method that gives him control, where the coach is non-directive but may use humour or paradoxical interventions. A client who works well with guidance may respond better to more of a directive, action-orientated style. This would suggest the usefulness of a coaching approach that can successfully integrate a number of theoretical and methodological viewpoints and is not a rigid 'recipe' format.

RELATIONSHIP

The only other common factor that is fully in the hands of the client and coach working together is the *relationship*. Coaching and consulting are relational practices and the relationship gets built up solely by two (or more) people agreeing to work together and building an alliance and mutual commitment.

Relationship has been shown to be the single best predictor of outcome of therapy, in such a way that it is not only the quality of the relationship in the final session that is a good predictor of final outcome (which would be a trivial finding) but the quality of the relationship in the early sessions as well, provided the relationship is assessed by the client. The fact that relationship has received such a boost in the quantitative research results has helped a wide range of professionals to explore whether they can work more explicitly on their relationship with their clients as it is co-created in the room.

Different theoretical and philosophical views of human beings create their own areas of interest in the relationship. The development of relational approaches has brought a great unifying, integrating force to bear on coaching and consulting, as for example approaches as apparently divergent as person centred and psychoanalytic find an important meeting place.

3. ROOTS IN THE PSYCHOLOGICAL THERAPIES

While only named "relational" in the last thirty years or so, this perspective has been evolving for many years in the theories and methods of both psychoanalytic and humanistic psychology and psychotherapy and, more recently, coaching. It has major roots in object relations theory in the UK (for example, Fairbairn 1952; Winnicott 1965; Klein 1963; Balint 1968; Bowlby 1977) and, in the US, with interpersonal psychoanalysis (Sullivan 1953) and relational psychoanalysis (Mitchell 1988). Building upon, and to some extent away from, Freud's original psychoanalytic theory, the early object relations psychotherapists placed relationship at the very heart of what it is to be human. In a similar departure, the early interpersonal analysts suggested that a person's learned patterns of relating are at the root of his/her psychological problems and believed that paying attention to these patterns, as they emerged in the therapy, was likely to change them.

The second important psychological root of relational psychotherapy is the humanistic (and existential humanistic) psychotherapy movement (see, for example, Moreno 1945; Rogers 1951; Maslow 1943; May 1983), with its aspirational focus on human growth and the meaning and process of living in society. The interest here was on phenomenology, individual truth and intersubjectivity; and its methodology of authentic relating, empathic attunement and respect for the intrinsic value of being human quickly became its hallmark. Inspired by the likes of Buber (1958), Perls (1951), Goulding & Goulding (1979), Jacobs (1989) and Hycner & Jacobs (1995), humanistic psychotherapy saw an increasing recognition of the importance of here and now relating and the significance of experience in facilitating change.

INTEGRATION

The coaching relationship is the perfect vehicle for integrating these major psychological traditions in a new paradigm. It brings the psychoanalytic world's rigorous attention to the unconscious, inner world of "implicit knowing" and relating together with the humanistic recognition that human beings exist in relationship and that real connection with another is the source of well-being and growth. It also leaves room for incorporating the pragmatic, collaborative goal-orientated investigation of the (cognitive) behavioural tradition.

We believe that, in order to focus our attention on the relationship with our clients, coaches must appreciate explicitly that:

I. Human beings are deeply motivated to be in relationship with others, so part of what we (client and coach) anticipate from this relationship might be to repeat our other relationships and, ideally, to create better ones, both within and outside the coaching room

II. All content of coaching can be seen as relational, i.e. clients are continually, even if subliminally, linking relationships elsewhere (real and imagined) to this relationship

III. This coaching relationship is worth exploring at all times, for the learning contained within it

IV. This coaching relationship is worth strengthening (in the eyes of the client).

On the one hand, nobody can really deny that there is such a thing as a relationship in our work nor that it is worth strengthening this 'rapport', 'working alliance' or whichever term used for it; on the other hand, focusing entirely on the relationship as it evolves from moment to moment is a very radical new proposition.

The relational turn is a bit like a Fourier transformation in physics: suddenly you don't see all the bits and the pieces, the issues and the comments anymore, and you start looking at a *field* which stretches all through the remarks, comments, issues and detailed information, a field which is all to do with the conversation itself, with the feel of what is present this very moment, and with the quality of our relationship whilst we are talking, listening, advising, challenging and so on.

4. THE BIG QUESTIONS IN RELATIONAL COACHING

We identify three big questions which are still open and undecided within this new field of relational coaching, three questions which constantly challenge relational practitioners:

I. If we know the relationship in the eyes of the client is likely to be the best predictor of successful outcome, how then do we strengthen that (view of the) relationship? The points given above are some rough ideas. It may turn out that swapping funny stories and not formally attending to the relationship at all is the optimal way to strengthen the relationship for most clients!

II. Knowing that it is the relationship that counts, as the client experiences it, is there anything to be gained from making the relationship more mutual, more shared? Is 'transparency', or equality, likely to be a strength of the sessions? In other words, does the coach's disclosure of his own responses and feelings contribute to effectiveness? And if so, when? Research seems to suggest that some therapist self-disclosure can be helpful (Norcross 2011) but this is not yet definitely clarified.

III. To what degree is it useful to make this relationship, here and now, explicit? It is common practice in relational coaching to focus explicitly, and in collaboration with the client, on the coaching relationship itself, in order to raise awareness of patterns of relating that may be echoes of the past and unhelpful in the present. Could this form part of the client's raised understanding of himself and education about 'useful' ways of being, which is another identified benefit (Asay & Lambert 1999). Again, this is still being researched and there is insufficient evidence so far.

These questions and others raised by taking a focus on the coaching relationship are the topic of this book. We have sketched the background to relational coaching and one way into it, through quantitative research outcomes. The chapters of the book pick up and explore some of the other issues.

AND FINALLY…

We believe that if we as coaches are entirely honest with ourselves we would admit that we have always been preoccupied by our coaching relationships and by our own feelings about the relationship. Now there is a way of thinking that gives us full permission to attend fully to the relationships we are in and to what happens at that relational level. We welcome this opportunity to deepen our understanding of human beings and their lives.

5. OVERVIEW OF THE CHAPTERS IN THIS VOLUME

The title of the book has preserved the multiple meanings of relational coaching: a focus on the nature of coaching relationships, a focus on the importance of here-and-now relating, as it evolves, and a focus on relationships in the 'material' that the client brings. The five sections of the book encompass these different lenses. These five 'acts' of the book also play out the 'drama' of the relational turn, telling the story of the proud arrival of this radical view of coaching (act 1), of how this view expands our understanding of relationships (act 2), showing what it means for the contracting and supervision that coaches undertake (act 3), how it opens our eyes to deeper vulnerabilities within the relationship (act 4) and, finally, how it defines a new way of doing research into coaching effectiveness (act 5).

All five parts of the book are fully focused on executive coaching practice as it really happens. Part I explores three different theoretical and philosophical 'allegiances' in ways of working in and with the relationship. Part II introduces some more radical ways of thinking that have been opened up by the relational turn – Chapter 4 focuses on the 'mutuality' of a relational perspective, Chapter 5 hones spirituality in the coaching relationship and Chapter 6 describes a cognitive-behavioural approach to the relationship. The third part of the book highlights some consequences of the relational turn for how coaches may approach contracting and supervision. Chapter 7 introduces relational contracting and then Chapter 8 describes the vicissitudes of multi-party contracting in coaching. Chapter 9 defines what it means to supervise coaches relationally. The Part IV of the book inquires more deeply into the coaching relationship under various aspects. Chapter 10 explores the multi-layered character of coaching relationships, Chapter 11 looks at 'shame' in organisational life and in the coaching relationship and Chapter 12 focuses on language and in particular on working across a language divide. The fifth and final part of the book contains three descriptions of robust pieces of research into what works in coaching. The compatibility of the findings, the demonstrated effectiveness of the quality of the coaching relationship and the support that these results from three different countries (the U.S., Canada and the U.K.) give to each other make, we think, a very rich conclusion to the book.

Many thanks should go to Liz Ainslie for her invaluable editorial help. Liz handled most of our communication with the authors, produced the final edit and managed to process all the references in the book electronically so that they could be double checked easily. We also thank Paul Jervis and all at Libri publishing house. Finally, we proudly highlight the fact that parts 1, 2 and 3 of the book each have a chapter from a graduate of our very own Ashridge Master's in Executive Coaching (AMEC), an MSc-study that is entirely based on relational principles. We thank Rob Watling (AMEC 2), David Skinner (AMEC 2) and Jane Cox (AMEC 1) for their powerful and highly personal ideas. All three chapters are ultimately based on their respective AMEC dissertations.

PART I

INTRODUCING RELATIONAL COACHING IN PRACTICE

This section of the book contains the following chapters:

Chapter 1 – Bill Critchley – Relational coaching: dancing on the edge

Chapter 2 – Andrew Day – Working with unconscious relational process in coaching

Chapter 3 – Rob Watling – Learning and re-learning: putting relationships at the centre of executive coaching

The relational turn in executive coaching has brought the focus right back to the client. Relational coaching has created a space for coaches of very diverse backgrounds to renew their focus on the client and on interventions that make a real difference to coaching relationships. Relational coaching is often misunderstood. Firstly, the term has no opposite: there is no coaching without a relationship, there is in that sense no 'non-relational' coaching. Secondly, the term is sometimes taken to signify a form of 'mediation', an intervention that improves relationships between people. In this section, three experienced practitioners from very different backgrounds describe what is meant by 'relational' and write about what convinced them to be relational coaches and what it means to them.

In the unfolding journey of this book, this part represents the exposition – in other words, a 'big bang' moment that heralds the relational turn in the field of coaching and underlines its profound impact on clients and practitioners.

CHAPTER 1

RELATIONAL COACHING: DANCING ON THE EDGE

BILL CRITCHLEY

INTRODUCTION

The purpose of this chapter is to expand on what we mean by the term 'relational' coaching, and what if anything might be 'edgy' about coaching in this way. On the face of it, coaching is clearly relational as it involves two people sitting in a room talking to one another. What is there not to understand about 'relational' in that context? Indeed social existence is nothing if not relational. However, we – that is I and my colleagues at Ashridge Consulting* – mean something rather specific by 'relational', which is not just qualitative. In other words we are not just talking about a 'good' relationship, where people observe the social conventions of politeness and consideration or, going further, listen well to one another, take the ethics of mutual respect, diversity, justice and so forth really seriously. Of course such ethical principles are important – and it is usually important to be polite – but sometimes it is useful to provoke, to go beyond the limits of social conventions and say something which may surprise and disturb our client.

This article elaborates on how we are using this word 'relational' in the particular context of coaching 'practice' by working through a number of perspectives, some practical and some theoretical. It intends thereby to explain the somewhat radical nature of this approach to coaching.

I start with the psychological perspective of John Bowlby, as it seems important to 'ground' a discussion about a process which usually takes a

---

* Ashridge Consulting developed a programme called 'Coaching for Organisation Consultants' which at the time of writing has been running for some six years and has also been developed into a Master's Programme. Both these programmes are based on the argument that coaching is inherently relational.

dyadic form, in a basic understanding of human need, human personality and human interdependence. This is itself radical in the sense that coaching is normally located in a business context, or at least one where efficiency and effectiveness take precedence over psychological considerations.

BOWLBY AND ATTACHMENT THEORY

John Bowlby argues (Bowlby 1988, p. 5) that certain 'basic' types of behaviour, such as sexual behaviour, exploratory behaviour, eating behaviour and, of particular interest to this article, attachment behaviour (and its reciprocal, parenting behaviour) are to some extent pre-programmed and biologically rooted, but also to a large extent 'learned'. In outlining this position he observes that keeping these types of behaviour conceptually distinct from each other is in contrast with traditional libido theory that treats most types of behaviour as the "varying expressions of a single drive" (ibid.). On the same page he observes that "the modern view of behavioural development contrasts sharply with both of the older paradigms, one of which, invoking instinct, over-emphasises the pre-programmed component and the other of which, reacting against instinct, overemphasised the learning component" (ibid.). He thus collapses the nature-versus-nurture argument, helpfully in my view, which continues to polarise much discussion about the extent to which coaching and other 'helping' professions can really make a difference, and observes of parenting behaviour that, while it has strong biological roots, "all the detail is learned, some of it during interaction with babies and children, much of it through observation of how other parents behave" (ibid.).

Bowlby is arguing that human beings have a primary need for attachment, in both the physical and the psychological sense. He says:

> A feature of attachment behaviour of the greatest importance clinically, and present irrespective of the age of the individual concerned, is the intensity of the emotion that accompanies it, the kind of emotion aroused depending on how the relationship between the individual attached and the attachment figure is faring. If it goes well, there is joy and a sense of security. If it is threatened there is jealousy, anxiety and anger. If broken there is grief and depression...
>
> (Ibid., p. 4)

He is asserting that attachment, or relational needs, will always configure in one way or another how we live our lives; and I am suggesting that this primary need is bound to configure a coaching relationship – for when a coaching client meets his or her coach, he/she brings into the encounter, both consciously and unconsciously, their experience of primary relationships, their expectations of someone who is supposed to be 'there for them'.

By analogy with parenting it seems reasonable to suggest that a skilled coaching process developed from a profound understanding of relational needs is capable of contributing to human growth. It also seems safe to suggest that coaching which does not take account of the relational dynamics inherent in the coaching process may well be ineffectual and, at the worst, potentially harmful.

Bowlby's ideas, although radical and controversial at the time he proposed them, have become fairly mainstream in psychotherapy and are taken as more or less incontrovertible. However, they still seem fairly controversial in the field of coaching, as evidenced by the number of times during the course of our coaching programmes we are asked to define the boundary between coaching and psychotherapy. This question is predicated on the assumption that there either *is* or *should be* a clear boundary between the two, and a means of knowing when to 'refer' a client to a psychotherapist.

It seems to me to follow from Bowlby's assertions that to make such a distinction is impossible. Clearly coaching and psychotherapy have different purposes and take place in different contexts, but in both cases the relational dynamics will configure outcome and this is unavoidable. This is evidenced by psychotherapy research into 'common factors' and recent coaching research into effective outcomes. Of all the variables having an effect on outcome, by far the largest impact comes from the relationship itself rather than from any particular method or technique (see the research section of this volume).

A CASE STUDY

I was recently working with a client – a new client who worked in the field of media production. He came because he felt unconfident in his work, rarely able to articulate his views unless directly asked for an opinion, and stifled by his fear of making any kind of social impact.

I noticed that as he sat opposite me attempting to tell me why he had come, he was mumbling and muttering, mainly looking away from me, to his right and down. Usually at first meetings I aim to gather some biographical detail and explore my client's work context, so that I have some sense of his wider 'field' or context, and in my experience the 'figure' or focus of the work usually emerges from this inquiry.

In this case, I was finding it hard to hear him, let alone understand what he was saying. I stayed with this, attempting to make some sort of sense for about twenty minutes until finally I said; "you know you tend to look at the floor and mumble when talking; are you aware you do this?" He said he was aware of it,

> yes. I continued, "If you and I are to work together, I'm going to have to ask you
> to make an effort to speak to me so I can hear." When the session, which was
> our introductory meeting, ended, I asked how he had experienced our
> encounter and whether he wanted to continue working with me. "Yes," he said,
> "No-one has ever said anything about my speaking before."

This may not sound like rocket science and, as an intervention, it does not really 'fit' into any of the standard models – for example, it does not appear to be particularly empathetic, deploying skilled listening and questioning skills – but it drew attention in a very direct (and in this case necessarily pragmatic) way to what was going on between us. It requires a certain courage to do this, as it breaks with most norms of social intercourse.

Some time after we finished meeting he wrote me an e-mail in which he said: "The course of coaching that I undertook with you has had a profound effect on me, and I think about it all the time". In Bowlby's terms, I think I became a significant attachment figure and my first intervention signalled to him that here was someone who wanted to have a relationship with him and was going to make some demands on him so that he could be both seen (I insisted that he make eye contact rather than look away and down) and heard. At the core of all relational practice, in my view, is the simple but profound need of our clients to be seen and heard and accepted, however hard they may try to disguise it, or send us up numerous alleys and byways sign-posted 'performance improvement'!

GESTALT AND SOCIAL CONSTRUCTIVISM

I continue this exploration of 'relationship' in the coaching process with two related perspectives, Gestalt and Social Constructivism, which are at the same time practical and philosophical. Along with the theme of 'relationality' these constitute the core informing themes that run through the coaching programme at Ashridge.

'Gestalt' is a largely untranslatable German word that tends to be broadly associated with the notion of 'wholeness'. It was originated by a group of psychologists (Koffka 1935; Köhler 1969; Wertheimmer 1944) who were disenchanted with the scientific 'atomistic' and reductionist methodology which largely prevailed at that time (and still does to a great extent). They advocated a more 'phenomenological' methodology with the purpose of discovering the 'wholeness' of things. They also studied the nature of perception and discovered that individuals tend to seek *pattern* in perceived phenomena, and hence fill in the gaps when presented with an 'incomplete' pattern.

This discovery that people make meaning by *creating* pattern is of profound philosophical significance: it challenges the positivist assumption that 'reality' can be determined by systematic and rigorous observation by a detached observer. Instead, it appears that people make their own reality through interacting with the phenomena they encounter. To some extent we literally make our own worlds and thus it is in our interacting or relating with our environment that we create meaning. So meaning emerges *in relationship*. Hitherto I have been arguing that relationship is core to the coaching process from a psychological perspective. Now I am suggesting that relationship is also core from an epistemological perspective.

This discovery presaged the development of the world view known as Social Constructivism (Glasersfeld 1995; Vygotsky & Cole 1978). Broadly speaking, Social Constructivism takes the epistemological position that nothing can be objectively known because we inevitably bring our subjective categories of knowing to the phenomena we encounter. Within this broad epistemological church there are a range of ontologies, from the Limited Realism of the cognitive psychologists (Ellis 1998; Beck 1976) to the Social Constructionism and the primacy of the relational of Gergen (Gergen 1999 and 2009).

While it is not the purpose of this chapter to explore Social Constructivism as an epistemology, it is important to emphasise that among those who advocate this world view there is much argument as to whether an objective reality actually exists out there to be known, or whether we are actively creating 'reality' through our own participation in it. The former view, which sees reality existing independently of human agency, is closer to received wisdom; the latter view, which sees reality as a dynamic, emerging, participative *process* which humans both create and are created by, is a much more radical perspective. Either way, all parties to this argument agree on one key thing, that 'reality' cannot be known objectively because human beings bring their categories of knowledge, their experience, their subjectivity to their knowing.

This philosophical underpinning to the word 'relational' has fundamental implications for coaching: it implies that coach and client are in a sense creating one another; meaning arises in the process of relating so the coach does not 'act upon' the client, does not act as an instrument in service of the client. Coach and client are engaged in a process of reciprocal influence. Thus the person of the coach must be fully involved; to attempt to withhold him or herself in the interests of impartiality or detachment merely attenuates the creative possibility inherent in the process of fully relating.

Thus the coach puts him or her*self* fully at risk in a process of *mutual* influence. This way of working has a very different quality from the rather dry and instrumental coaching process that is often practiced in the name of 'performance improvement', and keeps both parties relatively safe and protected from the risk of fully embodied relational engagement.

This 'relational' approach requires the coach to be capable of self-awareness and reflexivity, to allow him or herself to be *subject* to the process of relating, rather than to be in control of it, and hence to be open to being changed by the interaction. It is also risky in the sense that precise outcomes cannot be forecast. Working fully in the relationship increases the possibility of emergent novelty at the necessary expense of predictability.

GESTALT PRINCIPLES

The work of these early Gestalt psychologists was taken up by some pioneering psychotherapists, most notably Fritz Perls (Perls et al. 1951) who, with his colleagues, translated and developed it into a psychotherapeutic method. What are of interest to the coach are four key interdependent principles of this method and their relevance to coaching.

PRINCIPLE 1

The first principle flows directly from the constructivist position, namely that change occurs in the crucible of a relationship – or in *dialogue*, to use their preferred term. The dialogic approach of the early Gestaltists contrasted significantly from the somewhat-impassive stance adopted by classically trained psychoanalysts, who were usually seated behind a couch on which their patient was lying. Indeed, Fritz Perls, who had trained in the psychoanalytic school, was very sceptical about the nature of the relationship they tended to create, the potential power it gives to the analyst and the dependency it can bring about. The psychoanalysts sought to offer interpretations of a patient's free associations in their presence, and hence put themselves in some authority over the meaning to be ascribed to their outpourings. The Gestaltists sought a more mutual and reciprocal relationship as I have described above.

Nowadays of course, few coaches seek explicitly to arrange the coaching encounter so as to maximise their power. Nevertheless it is possible, by taking up an 'objective' and 'detached' stance, by seeking to solve the client's problem or by offering them advice, unwittingly to adopt a stance which takes power over the client.

The dialogic relationship is one in which power and influence is fluid, being continuously negotiated both consciously and unconsciously. The implication for coaches is that they need to pay continuous attention to the dynamics of the relationship they and their client are creating. To do this, they need to understand the dynamics of relating, to be aware of their own patterns and habits and to take the risk of reflecting on these dynamics *with their client*.

PRINCIPLE 2

The second principle is the principle of *awareness*. Perls took the view that psychoanalysis, in particular, overly privileged cognitive insight as the primary means of change, whereas our sensing is the source of all our knowing; it is our sensory contact with our environment that provides the material for our propositional knowing and it is easy for those of us who live in an environment which values rationality to lose touch with our bodily awareness. This has similarities with John Heron's (Heron 1996) construct of a 'four-level epistemology', which starts with experiential knowing, then moves to presentational knowing, and then to propositional knowing and finally to practical knowing. The implication is that unless knowing is fully grounded in sensory experience, it will be impoverished at the subsequent levels.

The Gestalt 'method' is to heighten our embodied awareness so that we become more aware of what we are sensing in our bodies, how we are feeling, what we are *noticing* in the process of relating to the 'other'. Through increasing our awareness we become more fully alive and more fully 'present'.

PRINCIPLE 3

The third principle is the focus on *the present*. This emphasises the utility of paying attention to what is happening *'now'*, rather than what happened 'then'. It does not deny the influence of our past experiences and conditioning but is primarily interested in how these experiences are being manifested in the present interaction, on the basis that we cannot change the past but we can change the present. Clearly the most present thing going on in the room in an encounter between coach and client is the relationship between them, and this is another powerful reason for paying attention to it.

PRINCIPLE 4

Contact describes the process of entering into an encounter with another person, and Gestaltists do use the concept normatively: we talk of 'good contact' and poor contact. Good contact involves the reciprocal experience of a full exchange between two people, where each is shuttling between the internal and external loci of attention, where I am noticing you and noticing myself simultaneously. Good contact is giving full attention to this particular relational encounter in the here and now, and allowing the 'next' to emerge, rather than striving for it.

These principles are easy to say and not so easy to do; it takes courage: the following vignette may bring to life what I mean.

A MOMENT OF COURAGE

I was coaching the director of a government body. He was a senior figure who had recently been knighted and was entering the final stage of his career as leader of this organisation. On the surface he was a confident, articulate, charming and powerful man, with considerable interpersonal skills; rather an archetypal, male leadership figure. I had worked with him over a number of years, and had always been rather in awe of him. I was eager for his approval and tried not to show it; I guess he attracted my paternal transference.

I had previously worked fairly extensively with him and his various leadership teams, and this coaching assignment was a departure from the usual form of my relationship with him. He had asked for a year's coaching in order to help him change his leadership style. He knew people found him intimidating and wanted to grow his subordinates rather than scare them, and to make a significant shift in the leadership culture of the organisation.

He paid me in advance, and wanted to hold the sessions in his London flat. We were on about the third session; I had been 'trying hard' to reflect back, notice themes – all good coaching stuff, but I did not feel I was making an ha'pporth of difference. Everything I said he appeared to have already thought of, and at this particular moment he had been saying: "You know, I don't know why people think I'm intimidating; I think I listen rather better than most people." I said: "Yes, you are a very skilled listener, as indeed you are a very persuasive talker. But let me tell you how I experience you; either way, whether you are listening or persuading, you are so skilful, that I feel I have absolutely no impact on you. I do not feel I can influence you, surprise you, offer you anything new at all, because you appear to already know or have anticipated anything I say." "What?" he said. "I don't understand." He looked rather bemused. I knew in that moment by the change in his demeanour that I had discombobulated him. I had taken a personal risk with this 'big' man, whom I so wanted to impress. It changed the dynamic of our relationship and, while I could have no idea whether it would change his leadership, I knew from his confusion that this was a moment of important learning for him.

In that moment I took the risk of paying attention to what I thought was going on between us. This is something we can all learn to do but it requires us to take a risk. There are in my experience usually three elements to this kind of intervention: first I make an observation that is fairly factual; secondly I declare my experience; and thirdly I may offer a hypothesis. For example, I might say: "I notice you have been telling me about a number of your problems, and that I have been doing my best to offer you possible solutions [observation]. I am beginning to sense that none of my attempts quite hit the spot, and I am feeling a little ineffectual [my experience – takes courage to say this!]. Maybe you don't really believe that I can help you, or possibly that anyone can help you?' [Hypothesis – more courage required!]

This orientation puts the dynamics and quality of the relationship at the forefront of the coach's attention. Most coaches tend to be preoccupied with their client's story and problems, which are clearly important, while the relational dynamics sometimes pass without notice and are rarely commented on. What I am proposing is that 'the relationship' between coach and client is at least as important and is often the means to the most important learning and change.

The next perspective on which I propose to draw both elaborates the philosophy of Social Constructivism and complements Gestalt principles. This is the principle of communication as described by George Mead, a sociologist writing in the 1930s. The Gestaltists discovered the way human beings make meaning by creating patterns and hence *creating* reality. Mead investigated in close detail how *social* meaning in particular emerges in the process of communicative interaction. If we are to be effective as coaches in consciously working with relationship, it behoves us to understand how 'relating' works.

COMMUNICATIVE INTERACTION

George Herbert Mead described this process of communicative interaction rather succinctly by saying that "The meaning of a gesture by one organism is found in the response of another organism" (Mead & Morris 1967, p. 147).

He used the word 'gesture' to mean any communicative move, verbal or physical, towards another. While as humans we gesture with intention – for example, I want to convey some information to you, ask you to do something, scare you, convince you or whatever – it is only in your response that the 'meaning' of the interaction emerges. Imagine that I move to shake your hand at the end of a quarrel, but you respond to it as an aggressive gesture and move away, and I run after you... so in a series of gestures and responses, patterns of meaning emerge. This is a spontaneous dance of meaning-making in which neither party can predict the other's response. They can anticipate but not predict, and in a conversation of gestures during which each party is well attuned to the other, the gesturer will be modifying her gesture even as she gestures and notices the respondent's shift in expression, or body posture.

This way of understanding the basic communicative process seems to resonate with most people's lived experience. The most important proposition to get our heads round is that this process, while it may appear otherwise, is *non-linear*. One person does not transmit a message to another person like a broadcasting signal. The process is simultaneous: as one gestures, the other is making meaning *at the same time* and the first gesturer is also simultaneously responding so that meaning emerges in the interaction.

This non-linear process is complex – witness the myriads of misunderstandings and surprises that arise in any conversation – and we have to contend with two further important factors. The first factor is particularly important for the coach, namely, that much of the gesturing and responding is influenced by 'unconscious motivation'. We cannot always take a gesture at face value and neither can we take our own response at face value.

There is not space in this chapter for a full discussion of unconscious motivation, but most of us are familiar with the notion that oftentimes patterns of behaviour and feeling, which are conditioned to some extent by early experience in our families, schools and so on, are triggered in response to certain here-and-now situations (in other words, we act out the past in the present). While we may understand this as a consequence of being human, we are usually unaware of it at the time a particular pattern or response is evoked. This is a rather simplified version of what is generally meant by 'unconscious process', but it will suffice: a coach who practises relationally needs to have some understanding of the nature and implications of unconscious process.

The second factor, by which I mean the 'relational context', has much broader implications.

THE RELATIONAL CONTEXT OF COACHING

This is the realisation that this complex process of communicative interaction *is clearly uncontrollable by any one person*. The implication of this, for a coach in a dyadic coaching relationship, has already been substantially covered in this chapter; but what about the implications for organisations? This is the context in which most of our clients live and what we are suggesting is that the core communicative process is uncontrollable in the conventional sense of managers 'being in control' of their organisation. Such a proposition may be anathema to many managers.

"WE ARE ALL PARTICIPANTS"

What I am suggesting is quite radical: that an organisation is not a fixed entity or thing, but a constant, self-referencing process of gestures and responses between people. The members of this process of organising are all participants in creating a social process which continuously evolves into an unknown future. We cannot, by definition, get outside it; as participants we simultaneously create and are created by the process of engaging together in joint action. You ask your subordinate to do something and she responds in some way which will inevitably be informed by her values, assumptions, preconceptions and interpretations of your 'gesture'. She will not respond like a robot; she will make her own meaning of your request.

The interactions that we have with each other simply create more interactions. Our interactions do not add up to a *whole* because they continuously evolve. Neither is any stable or bigger *thing* behind people's interactions. There is not *the company* that does something to people: there are only individual people relating to each other. Managers may perceive themselves as standing 'objectively' outside of *the system* in order to work *on it*, but this is an illusion, as there is no system to be outside. Power differentials are of course constructed between manager and subordinate, but there is no *away from* the constant process of relating; we are all participants in it all of the time. We are not standing outside of the river watching it go by; we are swimming in the river being part of its constant flow by forming it and at the same time being formed by it.

People in organisations (and, of course, in society at large) achieve very complex tasks by co-ordination and co-operation which is possible due to our ability to communicate with each other through language and other symbols (e.g. bodily gestures, writing). Thus, the organisation is not a purposeful *entity that enables* this joint action, but the joint action itself *is* the organisation (Stacey, Griffin & Shaw 2000, p. 187).

What generally prevents social processes from spiralling out of control is that as interdependent humans, attempting to live together in the world, we evolve 'rules' whereby we can go along together. Because we *need* other human beings in order to survive we are inevitably constrained by each other's needs and wants so we are simultaneously free and not free. What we are learning from complexity science is that there appears to be a self-organising principle in nature whereby order emerges from apparent disorder. The order cannot be predicted from the initial starting conditions but pattern emerges through interaction.

The implication for society is that it is in itself a self-organising process. Living in tighter-knit communities like organisations, this self-organisation manifests itself as 'rules' which emerge over time and are constantly evolving, taking the form of hierarchy, systems and procedures, and all the informal codes and conventions which constitute an organisational 'culture'. Often these 'rules' feel, to those lower down in the hierarchy, imposed and rather impervious to influence. In practice they have emerged over time in the on-going process of communicative interaction; they did not come down as 'tablets of stone' from any mountain.

I notice how many times in the above paragraphs I have used the word 'relating'. What I am suggesting is that 'relating' is *the core social process* and hence coaching is not just relational in itself, but it is part of a wider relational process which is the essence of what constitutes organisational life.

CONCLUSION

In this article, through drawing on John Bowlby's pioneering psychological work and with some examples from my own practice, I have attempted to show how, in a psychological sense, coaching is a profoundly relational process. I have suggested that effective coaching depends on understanding and having the competence to work with the relational dimension. Drawing on Gestalt psychology and constructivist epistemology, I went on to suggest that change and learning emerge in the crucible of the relationship and that, paradoxically, while the aim of the coach must be to create a relationship *in the service of* the client, it is nevertheless an intersubjective and interdependent relationship in which coach and client participate.

I then drew on the ideas of George Mead, a sociologist, to explore the dynamic of communication as a simultaneous movement of 'gesture and response' in which meaning is *created* in a communicative dance by two people, giving further weight to the proposition that coaching is inherently a non-linear, non-instrumental, dynamic relational process. Finally, I drew on some ideas from complexity theory to suggest that the organisations in which clients work are 'processes of communicative interaction' in which 'relating', in its broadest sense, is the core process. I suggest that organisations are social through and through and that coaching is thus not just relational in itself, but is part of a broad web of relating which constitutes what we have come to call organisation.

I think this relational perspective has important implications for the contracting and evaluation of coaching assignments, for the competence coaches need to acquire, and for the development of coaching practice.

CHAPTER 2

WORKING WITH UNCONSCIOUS RELATIONAL PROCESS IN COACHING

Andrew Day

INTRODUCTION

The purpose of this chapter is to explore how a psychoanalytic framework can help coaches to work with the client from a relational perspective. I describe below a conceptual framework for understanding the client and the unconscious dynamics in an organisation, and discuss how it is possible to understand the client's participation in these dynamics.

THE IMPORTANCE OF WORKING WITH UNCONSCIOUS MATERIAL

In its essence, coaching is a relationship between two people in which one of them, the coach, takes up a helping role with respect to the other, the client, who is performing a role in a larger system of relationships, the organisation. The client brings to this relationship a 'concern', which they have been unable to resolve and at one level can be understood as relating to their participation in this wider system of relationships. 'Concerns' include such things as difficult relationships, problems in bringing about strategic or organisational change and questions around how to motivate people or issues of leadership. It is not uncommon to find the client engaged in 'repetitive interactions' which maintain their 'concern'. These 'repetitive interactions' often reflect unconscious feelings, emotions or assumptions. The coach helps if they can provide a space where the client is able to symbolise, or put into words, this unconscious struggle in the organisation. This happens when the client is able to understand how they relate to others in their role, the unconscious dynamics in the organisation and how they participate in these dynamics. It is through understanding what was previously unconscious that the client is able to take up a different position in the organisational dynamics and from this position resolve their 'concern'.

UNDERSTANDING THE CLIENT: A RELATIONAL VIEW

Contemporary psychoanalytic theory and, to a large degree, the classical paradigm consider relationships (internal and external, real and imagined, past and present) to be central to understanding the person in their context (Mitchell 2000). This theoretical position has evolved from object relations theory (e.g. Fairbairn 1952; Klein 1963), interpersonal theories (e.g. Sullivan 1953) and self psychology (Kohut & Wolf 1978). Relatedness with other human beings is considered to be the central motive behind mental life (Greenberg & Mitchell 1983). The term 'individual' therefore has little meaning as a concept except in relationship to others.

Our sense of self is formed through our early relationships with our caregivers (i.e. parents etc.) and other authority figures. We internalise these early relational experiences to create internalised self–other representations which influence both our self-experience and our experience of others throughout our lives (Bowlby 1977). These representations are affectively charged memories which guide our interactions with others. Our early modes of connection with people, also known as attachments (Bowlby 1977), become our preferred modes of connection with people throughout our lives. Mitchell (2002) observes how:

> We populate our inner, subjective, private world, our innermost sense of self, with early relationships and experiences, and we naturally anticipate that in our daily encounters with adult reality we run into the same characters and situations.

Our sense of self can be thought of as a complex set of multiple images of self in relation to others. We hold images of our idealised self as seen by others or ourselves, images of 'me', 'bad me', 'good me' or 'not me'. These images shape how we perceive and react to others and influence what we strive for in our relationships and our work. From this perspective, self–other experience is at the heart of the human experience.

These self–other representations give rise to *repetitive interactive patterns* which can be understood as mirroring earlier relational patterns. When this occurs we externalise our internal object relations seeing others as representing our earlier internalised images of others.

Whilst being respected for running a high performing business unit for a number of years, Peter was frustrated at not being promoted and had been given feedback that he needed to change how he managed relationships with the senior leadership of the business. During our work, we uncovered that when presenting himself in interactions with them he would repeatedly challenge them on the decisions they made and how they led the organisation. He was unaware of how this influenced their view of him. Over several sessions, we started to understand that he experienced their decisions as a pressure on him to conform to something he did not want to be. Further exploration revealed he held an image of them as wanting him to be different and of pressuring him to do something that he would not want to do. He saw himself as not being who they wanted him to be. His interpretations of them and his fears of how they wanted him to be led him to rebel and emphasise in interactions that he was who he was and he was not prepared to change. Much of his interactions with them could be understood as much as a response to an image he held in his mind of 'them', those in positions of power over him. The leadership did seem to want him to change but this appeared to reflect a wish that he would chal-lenge them less and be more diplomatic in how he expressed his concerns about issues. He was therefore caught up in creating a response from them that confirmed his image of them. This established a repetitive interaction from which he was unable to unhook himself.

Such *interactive patterns* often emerge during coaching relationships in what has become known as the transference relationship. We can think of transference as the client's way of making sense and emotionally reacting to what is happening (Wachtel 2008). In this respect, the client–coach dynamic parallels the client's internal world and invites the coach to participate in a repetition of their internal world. Whether the coach takes up this invitation is often dependent of their internal relational world. By attending to how the client relates to them, the coach can understand the position the client takes up in relationships with others and its impact. For instance, I worked with a client who I felt was constantly trying to obtain my approval for her ideas and actions. I had the sense that she held an image of me as being very knowledgeable and confident whilst she held an image of herself as lacking confidence and being seen by others as lacking competence. This became a central pattern in how she related to me and others in her work.

This way of thinking about a person gives rise to a number of important questions about the coaching client and how they relate to others. These include:

- How does this person orientate themselves in relationships (including with the coach)? What are the images that they hold of these people?

- Who are the important people in their story to whom they tell their 'concerns'? Who might these represent for the person?

- How do they want to be seen by others? What fantasies lie behind their interactions with others? What anxieties does this give rise to in the client?

- What is the image they hold of themselves? What consequence does this have for how they interact with others?

The coach can bring these self–other images and representations into the client's awareness by noticing and interpreting what lies behind the client's experience of their relationships, their language and discourse and their behaviour and interactions with others.

UNDERSTANDING UNCONSCIOUS DYNAMICS IN ORGANISATION: A RELATIONAL VIEW

The meaning a client assigns to their 'concern' is dependent upon the wider relational field which constitutes their organisation (Lewin 1952). This relational field can be understood as consisting of on-going intersubjective interactions between people as a consequence of psychological and social processes. These interactions are often unconscious in nature and emerge from the wide psychosocial context. This is made up of the interplay of psychological, social, economic, power and political processes in the organisation's environment (Holti 1997). It gives rise to on-going conflicts between the interests of individuals and groups inside and outside of the organisation. These conflicts evoke unconscious anxieties and powerful emotions which are the source of unconscious dynamics and patterns of interaction. The interactions between members of the organisation therefore shape and are shaped by the emotional life of organisations, in a recursive and iterative process. Such unconscious dynamics are amplified during significant periods of disruption in the subjective experience of members of the organisation, for instance during economic crisis or as a result of changes in the organisation's leadership, during periods of organisational transitions and change or during periods of organisational growth.

To keep such anxieties and emotions out of conscious awareness, individuals and groups develop psychological and behavioural defence mechanisms, or social defences (Jacques 1955; Menzies 1960). These social defences manifest themselves in the organisation's structure, its rituals and routines, working practices and behavioural patterns. They function to enable members of the organisation to avoid anxiety. The classic study of social defences against anxiety was carried out by Isabel Menzies (1960) in the exploration of the nursing system of a teaching hospital. In this study she showed how the nursing system was structured and partly functioned to evade the anxiety of caring for patients, many of whom were in distress and in pain, or who were dying. Defences in this context included: depersonalisation and the denial of the significance of the individual; detachment and denial of feelings; splitting up the nurse–patient relationship so that a patient was cared for by a number of nurses and no one nurse in particularly was responsible for any patient and reducing the weight and responsibility of decision making by constant checks and counter checks. These defences had a secondary impact of reducing the nurses' satisfaction in their work.

Unconscious organisational dynamics can be understood as arising from a number of psychological processes, including introjections[*], projection[†], identification[‡] and denial, operating at the individual, group and intergroup levels. They interact in such a way that individuals and groups can be left 'holding' the threatening, difficult or painful emotions which belong to other groups or individuals. Different groups are therefore left to 'carry' conflicting aspects of the pressures impinging upon the organisation (Neumann 1999) so that they are each protected from facing its dilemmas and contractions. Such processes result in groups blaming others for the hostile and threatening ideas that they represent. This is particularly the case if the work of the organisation evokes anxieties in its members or if the organisation is undergoing a period of change.

> A manager in a child-care service of a local authority experienced bullying and attacks from her management in the organisation. She was left feeling that it was risky to speak up in meetings or to raise difficult issues without the risk of attack. Her experience was one of seeing individuals in power as threatening and persecutory and she was left feeling vulnerable and exposed. This dynamic mirrored the dynamic that her team encountered when it performed its work in the local community, where they worked to protect young children who were at risk or had been abused by their parents or carers. An organisation dynamic was set up in the organisation whereby individuals in less powerful positions were subjected to blame from those in power and were therefore left to carry the 'bad' feelings, anger and feelings of 'not being good enough' in the system. At the same time, the managers were made out to represent the 'bad', abusive powerful other that representing the 'abuser' in the client system.

---

[*]   Introjection is the unconscious adoption of other's ideas and feelings by an individual or group, 'as if' it were their own.

[†]   Projection is the unconscious transfer of one's own or a group's feelings to other persons or groups.

[‡]   Identification involves a person or group assimilating an emotion, property or attribute of another person or group and being transformed as a result.

To understand the relational dynamics in the client's broader system, the coach needs to explore the following questions:

- What emotions and anxieties are present in the organisation?

- How to they manifest themselves in behaviour, actions, routines and structures of the organisation?

- What emotions or feelings are held by different groups? What is the source of these emotions? How do they relate to the work of the organisation?

- What is the role the client takes up in these relationships? What are they picking up about the organisation?

UNDERSTANDING THE CLIENT'S PARTICIPATION IN ORGANISATION DYNAMICS

From a psychoanalytic perspective, we all play a role or part in creating our experience of organisations. This experience will, in some way, relate to the underlying emotional experiences of the organisation (Armstrong 1979). How we participate in this emotional life is influenced by how we interpret our experiences, the reactions we provoke in others and the roles we take up in relational processes (Bion 1961).

The client will often bring their relational experience in the organisation into the coaching relationship. This phenomenon is known as parallel process (Searles 1955). It describes how unconscious relational dynamics in one context, or system, can be replicated in relationships in another system, especially where there are overlapping structural and dynamic similarities between the different relationships (Geidman & Wolkenfeld 1980) such as between employee and employer, manager and team member. Parallel process was first identified by the psychoanalyst Harold Searles (1955) who observed that: "the processes at work currently in the relationship between patient and therapist are often reflected in the relationship between the therapist and supervisor" (p. 135). Mothersole (1999) observes that parallel process seems to occur in situations that involve issues of authority. He believes it involves a communication of unconscious material, through a web of co-created relationships in a system, which establishes the participants in complementary or reciprocal roles to each other. Krantz & Gilmore (1990) argue that the phenomenon arises from the process of *projective identification** which leaves the consultant holding feelings that belong to the client system.

---

* *Projective identification* involves the individual or group unconsciously identifying with the emotional material that is projected onto them.

Coaches, and supervisors of coaches, frequently report this phenomenon occurring in the consulting room. For instance, a client who is trying to bring about change in the organisation may experience a response from his colleagues of 'yes, but' whereby any suggestions for movement are rationalised away leaving the client feeling frustrated and helpless. This becomes a parallel process when the client starts to response with 'yes, but' to suggestions from the coach to act. It may even be replicated in the supervisor–coach relationship if the coach takes on the 'yes, but' role and the supervisor starts to experience helplessness and frustration with the coach.

Careful examination of the relations the coach has with the client can lead to a deeper understanding of the covert and unconscious elements of group and individual processes in organisations (Petriglieri & Wood 2003). Coaching supervision supports the coach in this process by providing a space for them to reflect on the coaching relationship and to explore and make sense of whether any parallel process may be present. Frequently, the parallel process will emerge in the relationship between the coach and the supervisor (Hawkins & Shohet 1989). In these interactions the coach has identified with the client and through their interaction with the supervisor invites them to take up a similar role to the coach in their work. The roles become reversed which if explored can help the coach to understand the client's unconscious material.

> When coaching a finance director in a global business, I experienced myself feeling very stuck with him. Over a number of sessions, I noticed that I became increasingly powerless, frustrated and angry with him as nothing I did seemed to have an influence. It was only after several months of working together that I saw a connection between his stuckness in his relationship with his boss and other members of the leadership team. He felt powerless and angry because he felt unable to influence them. By sharing my feelings of helplessness and frustration with our work, I was able to help him become aware of similar feelings that he held in his role. Through exploring his feelings of frustration and helplessness we were able to identify how our feelings represented feelings of powerlessness that were being disowned in the organisation and projected onto his function and him in the capacity of its leader.

WORKING WITH UNCONSCIOUS RELATIONAL PROCESS

The coaching relationship is as an interactive system in which both coach and client influence each other in a reciprocal process (DeYoung 2003; Orange, Atwood & Stolorow 1997) in the wider relational context of the organisation. Both client and coach are active contributors in co-creating the dynamics that emerge between them. They read and respond to each other's unconscious, knowingly and unknowingly, to create a relational unconscious (Gerson 2004). The client will attempt to structure the coaching relationship in a manner that is consistent with their attachment style. We can understand the client's interactions with the coach as a communication of unconscious material which they are struggling to put into words. The coach's own preference for relating to others will facilitate, inhibit and interrupt this process. A client may, for instance, relate to the coach 'as if' he were their critical, distant father and the coach finds himself feeling judgmental and critical of them. This reflects both the coach's identification with critical and distant authority figures as well as a response to the client's positioning of themselves in the coaching relationship.

As discussed above, the dynamics that emerge between the coach and client can also be seen as a repetition of how the client unconsciously participates in relational dynamics in their organisation (i.e. a parallel process). This unconscious material emerges in the experiential, affective material of the relationship. It is by naming the dynamic and through its collaborative exploration that the coach can raise the client's awareness of their unconscious participation in relational processes. Relational coaching therefore centres on the working through of relational entanglements and a struggle to help the client create something new in the relationships in the organisation.

Exploring unconscious material and anxieties is challenging for clients as it confronts them with material that they would typically keep out of conscious awareness. The coaching relationship therefore needs to hold a paradox of helping the client feel safe whilst experiencing unsafe material. This requires an 'optimum tension' is maintained between these two polarities. The coach establishes a relationship of trust with the client by being reliable, consistent and empathic whilst not avoiding what is most troubling for the client. If the client feels threatened or pushed then they are likely to retreat from sensitive material or avoid bringing material that is reflective of their deeper anxieties.

THE COACH'S USE OF SELF

The coach's subjective experience, including their dreams, fantasies, thoughts, feelings and physical reactions, often reflects unconscious material in the coaching relationship. Clients will often project onto the coach the feelings or emotions that they find unacceptable or are unable to manage for themselves (Krantz & Gilmore 1990). Petriglieri & Wood (2003) argue that whenever we feel lost, confused, disappointed, guilty or ashamed, it is useful to pause and reflect, as this can lead to a deeper understanding of covert and unconscious processes. Intense or unusual feelings, the experience of being manipulated or bodily sensations can be used by the coach to help the client become aware of unconscious material. The coach's selective disclosure of what is going on for them in the relationship may help to surface unconscious emotions in the work.

> *I was coaching a manager of a large manufacturing site who had just been told a major investment programme was not going to proceed for his site. My client wanted to explore the implications of this decision for the site and how to share the news with the management team and the employees. As the session proceeded I had a growing sensation of anger emerging from inside me. In stark contrast, my client seemed affectless in his presentation. Drawing on my emotional response, I offered an interpretation that perhaps my client was experiencing some anger in response to feeling let down by his management's decision. This helped my client to connect with his anger about the decision and his feeling of being let down. In exploring his feelings, we made connections with how his response was likely to represent the emotional reaction of the plant as a whole.*

Conclusion

Clients can find themselves caught up in dynamics in organisations where they are unable to see or understand how they participate in maintaining the very problem they want to resolve. Unconscious relational dynamics cannot be understood through rational and cognitive exploration; they emerge in the affective, experiential level of the client's and the coach's experience. Often this aspect of experience represents thoughts, feelings or emotions that are experienced as threatening or anxiety provoking for the client. Coaches can help their clients to become aware of their feelings and emotions and help them understand how these might be evoked by the images that they hold of significant others in the organisation and how they position themselves in relation to these figures. By working with the 'here and now' coaching relationship, the coach helps the client to access such material and to consider whether and how it reflects their participation in an organisation dynamic.

Working in this way, requires the coach to have the capacity both to participate in the coaching relationship and to stand outside of it and reflect critically on what is taking place between them and the client. They need to be able to recognise and own their contributions to the unconscious dynamics of the coaching relationship. This requires an openness to listen to their self-experience and embodied reactions, including their more disturbing or intense reactions. They equally need to develop the capacity to see connections between what is happening inside the coaching relationship and the client's organisation. I am conscious that many of the examples from my practice in this chapter read 'as if' unconscious process can be readily understood and seen. In the reality of practice, we are never sure and in many instances have to struggle to make sense of intense or apparently contradictory feelings and sensations. In many instances, moments of insight emerge days or weeks after a session. It is in this struggle to understand that the work takes place between the coach and the client.

CHAPTER 3

LEARNING AND RE-LEARNING: PUTTING RELATIONSHIPS AT THE CENTRE OF EXECUTIVE COACHING

ROB WATLING

I am sitting in a business centre, waiting for 'Sita' to arrive for our first coaching session. We have spoken briefly on the phone and exchanged emails but never met. I know very little about her, having declined the chance to read her CV in advance. I said I would prefer to learn about her when we meet. We are expecting to work together for four sessions over the next ten weeks – a schedule determined largely by her employer, though it is she herself who has arranged for the coaching. The organisation is fairly relaxed about the content, style and focus of the work we do together – their main intention is that the coaching supports her in her current and future practice as a senior public-service leader.

My phone rings. She has arrived a little early, so I go to meet her in the busy reception area. I am dressed plainly – somewhere between smart and casual. I'm looking forward to meeting her, but I am also a little apprehensive. I would like to get off to a good start. There is a short, slightly awkward moment when we need to work out if we have found the right person. We say each other's names as if they are questions. "Sita?" "Rob?" I am immediately struck by her professional demeanour – smart, sharply dressed but relaxed. She is younger than I had expected. Her handshake is firm but natural. We exchange pleas-antries and go through to a quiet area where I order tea. In the next 15 minutes we learn a little more about each other's work, and talk about coaching in general and my approach in particular, before we go to the small meeting room I have reserved for our first session. I already feel confident that we will be able

> *to work together. She is warm, open, alert, intelligent, engaged and curious about the things around her. I feel relaxed in her company and eager to learn more about her work.*

(Reflective journal entry)

And so another coaching relationship begins. Or rather, it has already begun. We have both prepared ourselves personally and professionally for this meeting; presented ourselves carefully; established some explicit and implicit ground rules for coaching (timing, purpose, confidentiality, friendliness, humour, links to practice, expectations...); we have started to read each other's body language; made some assumptions about each other; made some things possible; and probably ruled some things out. And I see it as part of my job to foster and monitor this relationship in the interest of my client. By the end of the session she had trusted me enough to explore a profoundly hurtful recent event with senior colleagues and had used the space of our discussion to see things in a wider perspective, acknowledging for the first time that she was playing her own part in the problem and beginning to identify a better, more constructive way forward. And I was confident enough to refer specifically to our relationship during the session itself and explore the extent to which it was helping her to make these moves.

It wasn't always like this. In my early days as a coach I was far less aware of relationships, and rather clumsy with them. And that seems strange to me now. Not just because I have learnt to pay so much more attention to key aspects of these relationships, but because I had previously done so in other areas of my professional life. In fact I have always taken pride in my ability to establish rapport with a wide range of people, and use that as the basis of establishing strong, useful, constructive working relationships. So this chapter is largely an exploration of how, why and when I have had to relearn these skills as I have worked as a coach. It is also an exploration of how I am still learning them.

The chapter begins by revisiting the ways relationships have been important to me in different parts of my career. It then explores a number of lessons I have learnt by paying progressively closer attention to coaching relationships in particular. Using anonymised notes from my reflective journal, brief references to the coaching literature and observations about my own practice, I explore the ways in which I have come to notice, refer to and harness the significance of relationships in my coaching.

RELATIONSHIPS IN MY EARLIER CAREER

Relationships have always been central to my professional practice. I remember my first 'proper' job, working in a residential community for adolescents who had all been excluded from school, isolated from their families, often in trouble with the law and struggling to find warmth or love in the world. My role was as a drama therapist, using drama and video as part of the educational and social programmes of the community. There was little prescribed structure to my work, so I spent a lot of time with the young people in and out of school. Ken, one of the residential social workers, pointed out that the task for each of us, in the end, was to build and develop relationships with some of the youngsters (we could never be expected to work closely with all of them) and to leave those relationships deliberately malleable and unfinished. The young people, he said, will then choose whether to develop those relationships with us further and perhaps even use them in a process of negotiating their own recovery. This would involve us being taken for granted sometimes. At other times we would be needed. We would often be ignored. We could expect to be loved, respected, hated, revered, confused... These relationships, he said, were often the only healthy ones in their lives and he taught me to pay close attention to them. I worked there for nearly four years and met scores of young people, yet I think I only made a significant difference to the lives of two or three people in that time. In each case there was a powerful, contested, and sometimes turbulent relationship which I encouraged, supported and offered to the young person to do with as they felt fit. I was, in the end, 'there for them'.

Later, as a University Lecturer of Media Studies and Education, I adopted an enabling role with the students that I was working with, trying to be less the authoritative instructor, and more the facilitator of others' learning. I didn't want the relationship to be based on fear or the expectation of automatic respect (like so many of the relationships I had had with my own teachers) but a mutual exploration of common interests. I still know that the best lessons I ran were those where I learnt as much as the students. When I moved on to work in larger organisations, leading teams and managing projects, I learnt how important it was to develop and support the relationships between people, as well as to look at the systems, structures and tasks that we were engaged in. Later still, as an academic studying aspects of education and social justice, I developed a wider interest in the links between knowledge, power and ethics. I learnt, above all, that such phenomena are not *properties* of individuals, but *relationships* between them.

So when I began coaching (first as a member of an internal team for a large organisation and later as an independent executive coach) it seemed only natural that I should do much of my training and development at Ashridge, where the faculty place so much emphasis on the quality and the understanding of the relationship between coach and client. This is, they point out, the single most important element of coaching – more so than specific techniques, how the process is managed, the theoretical underpinnings of the individual coach, or even the professional context of the coachee (see, for example, De Haan (2008) and the introduction and research section of this volume).

All this chimed with my belief in social construction and my professional practice to date. So how was it that, as someone who held with this world view and had been aware of the need to establish, develop and maintain professional relationships, I still found my early steps as a 'relational coach' so clumsy? I think there were many interconnected reasons. There are several such lessons or themes I want to explore in this chapter. I am sure this not an exhaustive list. And I explore them here as lessons that I have had to remember, revisit and remind myself of constantly. I am not sure that I will ever finally learn them (in the way that I learnt my times tables, a sequence of events, names, definitions, or the parts of a mechanism). But I am learning to attend to them more often and in more detail – like features of a landscape I want to explore repeatedly, with curiosity and with affection.

RELATIONSHIPS ARE NOT AUTONOMOUS

They are not 'out there somewhere', separate from us and accessible by the sort of investigation we might apply to other, more physical aspects of our world. Although we can assess and even quantify certain aspects of them using recordings and inventories, I find it far more valuable to try and notice them, to be curious about them and constantly seek to understand them better. This sits much more comfortably with my experience of developing and applying qualitative research methods and my firm belief that our world is socially constructed. And yet, as I try to concentrate on the relationships I have with my clients, I sometimes find myself behaving and thinking as if the relationships *are* out there somewhere, as if they *are* somehow separate from me. I do this despite my knowledge and belief that they are co-created and negotiated by us at every turn. Nor are relationships just something *between* us. They include us and affect us. I constantly have to remind myself of this in order to stop distancing myself from the relationship and thinking that my practice is somehow all about my clients and their reactions to their worlds.

THERE IS MORE THAN ONE CONCEPT OF RELATIONSHIPS

Our understanding of relationships is shaped, in part, by our everyday experience of them, but also by those who write, think, reflect and talk about them – particularly if we go through a formal programme of learning such as a coaching course or read a volume such as this. And, as with all areas of theory, not everyone agrees on what constitutes a relationship, how they operate or how they can successfully be managed.

As Anthony Goddard has shown in his recent review of the literature on coaching relationships (Goddard 2010), even the extent of what it is generally thought to be included in a professional relationship is disputed. This appears to be as true for coaching relationships as it is for therapeutic ones (about which there is a more extensive literature). Goddard points out that most accounts of these professional relationships refer to something like the three inter-linked elements originally identified by Bordin (1979): the participants' agreement on the goals of the intervention; the assignment of tasks and responsibilities; and the development of bonds. As the therapist/coach and client work together on goals and tasks, so the bonds between them develop and deepen. My opening story about the first meeting with Sita illustrates all three of these elements.

Goddard argues that, although the notion of the working alliance has transferred fairly quickly from the world of therapy to that of coaching, there is not necessarily any more agreement about what the term should mean. Goddard himself settles on a definition from O'Broin and Palmer:

> The Coaching Alliance reflects the quality of the coachee's and coach's engagement in collaborative, purposive work within the coaching relationship, and is jointly negotiated, and renegotiated throughout the coaching process over time.

> (O'Broin & Palmer 2010)

Goddard's review is also helpful as a reminder that the elements deemed significant by professionals are not always the same as those identified by their clients. Clients' definitions of the working alliance, he argues, are more likely to include aspects such as the therapeutic setting and the specific techniques employed (Bedi, Davis & Williams 2005), while coaches might concentrate on the quality of the relationship itself. Since coaching values the perspective of the client as much as that of the coach, we need to acknowledge this. Our clients do not come into coaching unformed and ignorant about relationships, but skilled, interested and with their own similarly imperfect understanding of how they work.

RELATIONSHIPS ARE MORE THAN RAPPORT – BUT RAPPORT IS A GREAT PLACE TO BEGIN

When we start to train as coaches it is tempting to concentrate on techniques. The literature we are introduced to is full of descriptions of processes which seem new to us and we can soon be taken firmly into 'conscious incompetence'. We are aware that we don't have detailed knowledge of techniques associated with the GROW model, motivational interviewing, cognitive behavioural coaching or solution-focused work, and we suspect we are going to need this knowledge. As a result we often ignore the skills we already have – like the ability to develop and nurture relationships. In my early days of training I was hugely, often unhelpfully aware of the technical process of running a session and of controlling my contribution to it. I was obsessed with my decisions and actions, and constantly listening to a voice in my head (Should I ask this question next? Or that one? Am I being too directive? Would this be a good moment to use that particular technique? How is my posture? How is the client's posture? What does it say about them? Do they appear nervous, anxious, irritated? Do they always look like that? Should I ask? Oops, I wasn't listening to what they said...). It was like learning to ride a bicycle again. How could I stay on this thing with a semblance of grace and purpose – especially when someone else was doing most of the steering?

I tried to redress some of this fumbling by focusing on the relationship – which I initially thought of mostly in terms of building rapport. By 'rapport-building' I meant creating a friendly environment where the client would like me enough to open up and engage in a confidential conversation with me. I believed that if we had a rapport my clients would 'get on with me'. We would be on the same wavelength. And, I think I was implying, we would agree with each other. I was to learn that this is a crude notion of rapport and only part of what it means to create, maintain and nurture a valuable coaching relationship.

I learnt more about this when working with 'Saul' – a senior manager in a public sector organisation who was struggling with aspects of his professional identity, particularly a feeling that he didn't 'fit' into the culture of his workplace. He wanted to use coaching to help him decide how to react to this feeling, and also to decide about his future plans. Saul chose me as his coach from a pool of 20 and was adamant that I was the one who could help him best. I remember being surprised by the clarity of his choice – which was based on the fact that we had once worked for the same organisation. I learnt later that finding myself surprised in this way can indicate that there is some form of transference going on – making assumptions about someone else based on their apparent similarity to another significant figure in the past. And I was a bit uncomfortable, too, as I didn't feel an immediate rapport for Saul.

Our early sessions were tense. Saul wanted me to advise him. I said that coaching was more about helping him to develop and explore his own thoughts and plans. He asked me to give him feedback on what he was like to work with. I resisted because I was reluctant to tell him the truth – that I found him friendly, but socially clumsy; intelligent, but also rather arrogant; intriguing, but also repetitive and even boring. I discussed this lack of honesty in a supervision session, where I realised that my lack of candour was protecting my feelings more than Saul's. In a later coaching session I was to get closer to a more-honest, and more-useful, exchange with Saul which explored our different ways of seeing the world. With hindsight, I wish I had found the courage to refer more directly to this friction – this opposite of rapport – much earlier on.

RELATIONSHIPS ARE MORE THAN ROLES – BUT ROLES ARE A USEFUL INDICATOR OF WHAT IS GOING ON

I have finished work with two different clients this week. And as I look back at our work together, I can see that in each one we established different types of role for me. With 'Peter', I always felt like a spectator – he held me at a distance and, while he was honest, open and thoughtful as we discussed his professional development, I'm not sure that I ever really got to know him. There were times early on, when he talked about his hobbies and family, but as we concentrated more on his professional world it all felt more distant. He wanted to use our sessions to discuss issues and relationships at work, and (towards the end) to prepare for a possible promotion. But when he didn't get that job and didn't show any emotional reaction to this, I again felt uninvolved. I was a useful sounding board, but little more.

I compare this with the relationship I have had over a similar period of time with 'Carrie'. She came to coaching to understand and move on from a diffi-cult period at work – one which had upset her greatly. She invited me into an exploration of that time, and of the echoes it was having in her current work. I felt engaged, interested, closer... welcome, I suppose. I was not just a spectator but an active part of the way she chose to confront, attend to, and address key aspects of her leadership style.

(Reflective Journal)

My experience of sociology had encouraged me to notice the different roles that I took with these two clients – one as a spectator, invited to notice and comment; and one as an engaged and empathic companion, invited to care about the future and to help Carrie start to shape it. But a sociological explanation (based on roles) does not quite feel adequate. In reaching for it, as I had in this journal entry, I realised I was missing the power of some of the other frameworks – particularly the psychological and the humanistic. Looking back, I think that what was missing from my relationship with Peter was my reflecting back to him the simple observation that I felt like a spec-tator, and that I was surprised to find myself taking that role. I wonder what would have happened had I raised this with him at the time.

RELATIONSHIPS TAKE TIME TO DEVELOP, BUT SOMETIMES WE DON'T HAVE MUCH TIME

My working relationship with Carrie was briefer than that with Peter – four sessions over six months – but became quite potent. Carrie was encouraged to have coaching after some setbacks at work and a difficult time with a direct report who had taken out a grievance procedure against her. From the start I explained to the HR Department that I don't see coaching as a remedial process which can somehow 'fix' managers. I said that, as long as coaching could be offered to Carrie as a possible way forward, allowing her to develop new approaches and to use her existing strengths to do so, I would meet her and see if she felt it would be useful. That first meeting assumed no commitment from either of us. We drank tea and talked about the situation she found herself in, how she was reacting to it, her anxieties about the future, and her keen desire to learn from this experience and to move on. I explained how I work and said that I didn't expect an answer from her straight away about coaching. Within a few days she contacted me and said that she would like to work with me. Our first two sessions were quite fraught.

> *Carrie seemed nervous and distant – wanting to explore all aspects of her situation but tending to concentrate on a few difficult relationships at work. She emailed me afterwards to say that she had found this (first) session useful and that she left feeling positive but very tired. For myself, I thought the session was a bit vague, and (while I feel she is being honest with me) I wonder if we were really getting to the bottom of what needs to be said.*

> (Reflective journal)

The second session concentrated on a tough week she had had, announcing redundancies in her team and managing another difficult colleague. She had tried to discuss this with her manager who had said, "Well, you're seeing your coach next week, why don't you sort it out with him?" When Carrie told me this, I noticed that I was a bit annoyed, and said that I felt as if I was being drawn into the office, given jobs to do, and that I didn't feel comfortable with this. Carrie said that this happened a lot at her work – people passing the difficult decisions round until they were dealt with – and as we explored this in more depth I offered her the drama triangle (Karpman 1968) as one way of exploring the process. It clicked with her straight away, and she used the triangle skilfully and flexibly to explain what was going on in the office, and the rescuing role she habitually took for herself – a role which was sometimes being re-interpreted by others as a form of persecution. It was, she said, partly what had happened to her when the grievance was taken out.

In the third session Carrie focussed on her relationships with her managers, and her plans to extend her work in the department. There was a new project she wanted to take responsibility for. I felt much more relaxed in her company and told her that I was enjoying seeing her being more positive and in control. She said that the space we had created for coaching was proving really important for her. It was somewhere she could think through her plans and build her confidence.

By the time of our final session, three months after the third, Carrie had completed that project and received significant praise for it. She described how she was handling relationships much better at work, contributing more, taking a short pause before intervening and using that moment to get things in perspective. These pauses were like miniature versions of our coaching sessions, allowing her the space to reflect and plan. We had been together for a little over seven hours in total, spaced over six months and I can see that our relationship was much more versatile and mature by the end than at the beginning.

I think about this even more at the moment, as I coach mostly in the public sector at a time when funds are tight, plans are fluid, strategies are loose (even chaotic) and coaching contracts appear to be getting shorter. Where I was originally used to a coaching relationship being over six-to-eight sessions, they are now for four-to-six sessions – or even shorter. I am about to take on some work for a public-sector client consisting of one 360-degree feedback session and one coaching session. Part of me is concerned about this – it sounds doomed to superficiality. Part of me is excited – I know that good coaching interventions can be sharp as well as protracted. I am intending to approach these with the brilliant question once asked of me by a fellow Ashridge student when I said we didn't have time to explore my issue in a short practice session. "What if we did have time?" she asked. I immediately knew the most important aspect to concentrate on and she helped me make significant progress in just a few minutes.

EMOTIONAL INSIGHTS INTO RELATIONSHIPS CAN BE AS VALID AS INTELLECTUAL INSIGHTS

In the course of my development as a coach I have learned to supress my tendency to offer cognitive insights – mainly because I have little reason to believe that my theories about my clients and their issues are likely to be more accurate than theirs. This hasn't always been easy for someone trained as an academic researcher. I have tried, in addition, to develop my capacity to notice and discuss emotional insights with my clients. As I came to the end of the final session with Carrie I wanted to ask her two questions: what could she draw on to sustain the positive experiences she was having at work? and how did she think she would react to a future crisis? The first of these questions was easy, but I noticed that I felt hesitant to raise the second. I mentioned this hesitancy to her and said that I wouldn't normally feel reluctant to ask such a question. She asked me to say more. Might it be, I wondered, if I (and perhaps others) still saw her as fragile? She thought about this, but was unworried. She felt that she was re-establishing herself in her own mind, and in others', as capable, flexible and resilient. She realised that she would face crises in future, but felt strong enough to manage them. She even felt able to discuss the original disciplinary action with others, and would be happy to say what she had learnt from the experience itself and the way she had benefited from a supportive coaching relationship. My perception of her as still potentially fragile just didn't have any useful purpose for her. Like some of my intellectual insights about Carrie's issues it was less useful than her own. But it was still valuable for me to identify and express it, since it reinforced her confidence to act and position herself well in the organisation.

RELATIONSHIPS ARE ALWAYS WORTH REFLECTING ON

[On the train.] I am on my way to a coaching session with 'Anna' (an executive in a large organisation). This will be our fifth session of eight, and I notice that I am a bit confused about our work together. I feel stuck, or is it frustrated? It's as if there is something that is preventing us from getting down to the things that really matter for her. She talks a lot – about her circumstances, about her own frustrations at work, about the way she feels undervalued and overlooked. But the sessions are all beginning to feel the same to me: we will meet, exchange pleasantries, catch up on her progress since last time, and she will tell me how she has done whatever we agreed in our previous session and that it worked well – but that she still feels unhappy and unsettled.

*I want this, our next session, to be different. It is the start of the second half of the process and this seems somehow significant to me. The half-way point. It might be a good idea to check (quite explicitly) how far she thinks we have got – where we are; where we are going with this; what she has got out of the relationship so far; what else she would like. (And for me to do the same, but to take less of this explicitly into the session, leaving the rest for my own reflection and possibly for s*upervision.)

Now seemed a good opportunity to do some of this reflecting, so I carried on writing:

I've re-read the notes from the first four sessions and looked (first) at what she has discussed; what she has concentrated on; what she has thought about; how she has been feeling; what she has said she is taking away from the sessions;

and how she tells me things have changed (or stayed the same). I've noticed some parallels between those issues and our own working relationship. She seems to behave with me in ways which are similar to the way she behaves at work. Just as she is fun, engaging and a bit confusing to coach, she may well be fun, engaging and a bit confusing to work with. She is self-deprecating, but also confident of her skills and her contribution to work. She is inclined to complain (blaming others for most things) but also very loyal about her employer. She trusts me with confidential information and opinions, but says she is totally discreet. She is ready to leave the organisation, but anxious to stay. She wants more reward, but will not ask for it.

And the way I react to her – warmly, empathically, and curious about what she has to say about herself and her work – is tempered by not knowing what she wants from the coaching relationship. I wonder if this might be the same for others she works with and, if so, what she might want to do about it. Certainly it would be helpful to me (and I believe to her) if she could be clearer about what she wants.

(Reflective Journal)

So I entered the session planning to say some of this. To draw her attention to it. To wonder why I might be thinking and feeling these things. But it didn't go that smoothly or straightforwardly. The established patterns repeated themselves and the session started like so many others – the rapport, the joking, the not-quite-getting-down-to-it, the feeling that we were stuck. After the session, I wrote:

It was really good to have done my own reflection on the relationship and its patterns before this session. And it did make me feel more engaged. But how come we have got stuck again?

In discussing this relationship with my supervisor, I mentioned that what I really wanted to tell Anna was my hunch that her refusal to take herself seriously was the greatest obstacle to her being taken seriously by anyone else. And, crucially, this is an impression that has been generated in the sessions themselves, not in the spaces between (like the times I am on the train). I was subsequently able to offer this observation to Anna, who recognised that she was prone to use humour as a form of defence and accepted that there were times when she could be less self-effacing. It continues to be a focus of our work together.

RELATIONSHIPS ARE ALSO WORTH REFLECTING IN

It was the end of the session and I was getting ready to leave. 'Jason' asked me to read a side of A4 he had produced for his Action Learning set. He said he

51

wanted my reaction to it. I was reluctant to read it – there was something about being asked to do so at the last minute, and in any case I wasn't sure what I could usefully say in such a short space of time. I didn't want to upset him by just saying no. And part of me felt flattered. I sensed myself summoning up the skills I had developed as a university lecturer – to read something very quickly and offer a useful guiding comment. But this didn't feel right either. So, instead, I said I was wondering why he wanted my reaction.

Jason said nothing. I could see in his face that my question was turning something round for him. We had recently talked about some of the theories of Transactional Analysis and he had said in the session that he wanted to develop more adult-to-adult engagements with his manager (having noticed that he was often falling, or being encouraged, into adult-to-child or parent-to-child relationships). I said that I wasn't sure what sort of reaction he wanted from me if I were to read his paper now. Was it to be proud of what he had written, to offer an opinion on it, to suggest ways of making it better? He thought about this for a moment. "No," he said, "I just want you to notice that I am capable of being passionate about my work. You have said a couple of times in this session that I seem flat today. This written piece will show you that I can be passionate". "I already know that you can be passionate," I told him. "I don't need to see it written down." We discussed his desire to impress me and agreed that he was seeking a parent-like reaction from me in this transaction rather than an adult–adult response. He took the paper back and went off to a meeting with his manager. I was pleased with myself for not having read it and, hopefully, for having done something more helpful than comment on its contents.

(Reflective Journal)

While I have learnt (or rather re-learnt) that relationships are always worth reflecting *on*, I am now placing more emphasis on the fact that they are also worth reflecting *in* (as I was doing here with Jason). This distinction, to which I constantly return, was originally made by Donald Schön (1983) between practitioners' undeniably useful ability to look back critically and reflectively on our actions *after the event*, and our even more-useful ability to do so *during the event*. Reflection *on* action gives us the benefits of hindsight. Practitioners who can also build the capacity for reflection *in* action open themselves to surprises, to fresh insights, and the opportunity to question the assumptions that form the basis of their practice. Relational coaching encourages us to reflect on relationships while we are relating to someone. It turns relationships into the context, the focus and the instrument of our work together. This can be hard and it involves a degree of risk. I am learning that it is a risk worth taking.

PART II

RADICAL PERSPECTIVES ON RELATIONAL COACHING

This section of the book contains the following chapters:

Chapter 4 – Kathleen King – The challenge of mutuality

Chapter 5 – Billy Desmond – Spirituality in the coaching relationship

Chapter 6 – Max Visser – Learning in executive coaching relationships: a behavioural systems perspective

The presence of this new relationship-focussed space gives an opportunity to explore the *connections* between the client and others, between the client and his or her organisation, and between the client and the coach. As we will see in this part of the book, this same space has also invited more radical thinking into the burgeoning field of relationship and relatedness. Here are three practitioners writing from their own highly personal perspective, offering radical interpretations of relational coaching.

Kathleen King introduces a mutuality perspective on the coaching relationship, a connection between coach and client where more can be shared. Billy Desmond, writing about spirituality in relational coaching, demonstrates how deep connectedness between client and coach could reach into spiritual domains of meaning making, a connection between coach and client where meaning is intuited on a deeper level. Max Visser argues that relational coaching can bring a revival of classical behaviourism where dyadic relationships are studied in their own right. He demonstrates that a focus on the relationship does not just bring practitioners from humanistic and psychoanalytic schools together, but also the third great school of psychotherapy and coaching, that of cognitive and behavioural change.

In the unfolding journey of this book, this part represents the 'ah' moments that mark the expansion into new territory that the relational turn has opened up, with a reappraisal of our human mutuality in coaching, of Bateson's and Skinner's contributions to psychology, and of spirituality as a cradle of meaning making.

CHAPTER 4

THE CHALLENGE OF MUTUALITY

KATHLEEN KING

In their guest editorial 'The relationship in executive coaching' (2010), de Haan and Sills argue that the bias in the field of coaching has shifted in recent years, from an emphasis on tools and models and on the coach to making the client, and especially the relationship between coach and client, more figural. Where other authors in this volume have traced the emergence of the relational turn to fields such as neuroscience, social constructionism and psychoanalysis, I want to examine a particular perspective on relationality, drawing on the considerable contribution of relational psychologists such as Carol Gilligan, Jean Baker Miller and Joyce Fletcher, because their work, which raises issues of power, authority and voice, deeply challenges existing assumptions about human growth and development.

I will argue that the way we think about organisations and our work within them is but an indication of our worldview, which includes, amongst others, issues of power and authority. The relational turn, in my view, represents a profound shift in our worldview, which we need to take into account in our coaching practice.

The editors of this book raise questions that remain to be addressed in this emerging field of relational coaching, one of which concerns the issue of 'radical' mutuality, which they see as involving a substantial focus on self and self-disclosure by the coach. Relational psychology offers a particular perspective on mutuality, which has significant implications for the way we think about the nature of coaching, our role and our relationship with our clients and for the meaning of 'mutuality' in that relationship.

I will discuss the contribution of relational psychologists and the context in which their work developed, before exploring the implications for mutuality in coaching as I see them.

REDRAWING THE MAP OF THE TERRITORY – RELATIONAL PSYCHOLOGY, A SEISMIC SHIFT IN OUR UNDERSTANDING OF HUMAN DEVELOPMENT

In *This Changes Everything*, the journalist Christina Robb (2006) traces the origins of relational psychology back to the women's movement and other human rights movements of the 1960s. She tells the compelling story of how a number of women, independently of one another, came to question what had they had learned in their training as psychologists and psychoanalysts by taking their experience seriously. In the process they discovered the political use of dissociation and disconnection to widen power disparities as well as the political and psychological power of relationship. I will discuss only a few of the many significant contributors here.

Carol Gilligan was an assistant professor of developmental psychology at Harvard. Gilligan taught with Erickson and Kohlberg, who, like Freud and Piaget, theorised that the crux of maturity was separation and individuation. She chose to study in depth the moral development of women, a project frowned upon, or ignored as irrelevant, by her peers. "Women and blacks should be left out of psychological research samples", a professor who had taught Kohlberg famously told his research students. This was standard practice at a time when subjects of developmental psychology were white, middle-class boys.

Gilligan published the outcome of her research in her seminal work *In a Different Voice* (Gilligan 1993) in which she demonstrates how developmental psychology, from Freud through Piaget, Kohlberg and Erikson, is built on the examination of the experiences of the *male* child. According to Gilligan, the dynamics of identity formation are different for boys and girls because the primary care giver for both sexes in the first three years is typically female. Female identity formation takes place in a context of on-going relationships, and girls consequently – experiencing themselves as like their mothers – fuse the experience of attachment with the process of identity formation. In contrast, boys, in defining themselves as masculine, separate themselves from their mothers, curtailing their sense of empathic ties. Male development therefore entails a more emphatic individuation and a more defensive firming of experienced ego boundaries. Difference is often interpreted in terms of 'better' or 'worse' and, according to Gilligan, this difference in development has been interpreted traditionally as 'women having weaker ego boundaries than men' rather than as 'girls having a basis of empathy built into their primary definition of self in a way that boys do not'. Consequently, the conception of adulthood favours separation, autonomy and individuation. The difference in the process of identity formation has implications for men and women's development.

Women's insistence on care is at first self-critical rather than self-protective, while men initially conceive obligation to others negatively in terms of non-interference. Development for both sexes would therefore seem to entail an integration of rights and responsibilities through the discovery of the complementarity of these disparate views...

(Gilligan 1993, p. 100)

Meanwhile, the psychiatrist and psychoanalyst Jean Baker Miller was writing about the politics of dominance and of relationship. In her ground breaking book *Toward a New Psychology of Women* of 1976, Miller, like Gilligan, argues that "our understanding of all of life has been underdeveloped and distorted because our past explanations have been created by only one half of the human species." (Miller 1986)

While it is obvious, according to Miller, that all of living and development takes place in relationships – a notion congruent with a social constructionist paradigm – our theories of development seem to be based on a notion of development as a process of separation from others. Psychologists use terms such as 'fusion' and 'dependency' to characterise a child's early relationship with its mother and terms such as 'independence', 'separation' and 'autonomy' to describe the end point of development, maturity. In our Western culture men, but not women, have been encouraged to pursue this ideal of autonomy and separation. The work of tending to relationships, especially relationships that foster development, has been assigned to women. Hence, it is from the study of women's lives, listening to women's stories and taking them seriously, that she seeks to develop a new comprehensive psychological theory to better describe all human experience.

Miller further argues that because of women's subordination, relational work has been relegated to the *private* sphere and consistently been devalued by both men and women. She views emphasis on 'male qualities' in the public sphere, such as autonomy, domination and competition, as oppressive to both men and women: "All social structures that male society has built so far have included within them the suppression of other men. In other ways, too, all of our society's advances are still a very mixed blessing. ...Technologically advanced society has led to vast improvements for a small group of men and some improvements for a somewhat larger group – at the expense of misery for many and the destruction of whole cultures for others" (ibid. pp. 77–8).

Joyce Fletcher, building on the work of her colleagues, (1994; 1998; 1999) examined the implications of the male bias in mainstream developmental psychology for organisations and challenged the prevailing organisational discourse from a relational perspective. She started from the premise that current, 'common sense' definitions of work implicitly valued certain (masculine) aspects of work and the people (mostly men) who tended to work this way, while making invisible other, arguably equally important (feminine) aspects of work and devaluing the people (mostly women) who tended to work this way. In her study of working practices of female engineers, she sought to surface those unacknowledged aspects of work by detailing a way of working that is rooted in a relational value system, which she calls 'relational practice'.

Rather than focussing on autonomy, separation, individuation and independence as central to personal growth and identity, Fletcher emphasises the role of relational interactions in the development process and calls it 'growth in connection'. She states that it is the pre-eminence of connection and mutuality over individuation that marks relational theory as feminine and that gives it the potential to challenge the existing organisational discourse (Fletcher 1998). She conceptualises growth-fostering interactions as "characterized by mutual empathy and mutual empowerment, where both parties recognize vulnerability as part of the human condition, approach the interaction expecting to grow from it, and feel a responsibility to contribute to the growth of the other. The ability to develop relationally requires certain strengths: empathy, vulnerability, the ability to experience and express emotion, the ability to participate in the development of another, and an expectation that relational interactions can yield mutual growth" (ibid., p. 31).

As an organisational consultant and coach, manager and leader I have long been puzzled by our apparent inability in organisations to live values of interdependence and mutual support. Although my clients and I espouse those values we continue to behave in individualistic, controlling and competitive ways. As I steeped myself in the work of relational psychologists, I began to make sense of this paradox. Especially enlightening to me was Fletcher's argument that we devalue, and even 'disappear', relational work, because it lacks kudos in the public arena.

If we take the relational turn seriously, we will need to examine the implications of taking a radically different approach to our work. Using relational skills to relate, to engage in 'growth in connection', rather than to achieve instrumental goals, not only alters the engagement process, it offers the possibility of outcomes that were previously unknowable (Fletcher 1999). If both partners exit an interaction having been changed by it in some way, the context in which future decisions are made is also changed. The possibility of unpredictable outcomes is a powerful challenge to our familiar discourse and to any illusion of control we may have.

In the next section I examine the implications, as I see them, of Fletcher's concept of mutuality for coaching relationships.

THE CHALLENGE OF GROWTH-FOSTERING COACHING INTERACTIONS

Although the editors of this book characterise the 'relational turn' as a move away from the focus on the coach towards the client, and especially towards the relationship between coach and client, their concept of 'radical mutuality' as involving substantial focus on self and self-disclosure seems to bring the focus right back to the coach.

I think self-disclosure and focus on self are important, but in my view mutuality (as mutual empowerment and empathy) also presents a particular challenge for clients and the way they engage with their coach. I will explore the latter first.

Many of my clients are senior and successful leaders, often holding a position which entails responsibility for a large number of people. They hold significantly responsible roles that require a considerable amount of emotional maturity and wisdom. However, many of them have been promoted into their roles because of their proven technical expertise and intellectual capability, or their extensive impression-management skills, rather than because of their maturity or relational skills. In fact, their ability to move swiftly up the career ladder can be inversely related to their capacity for empathy, vulnerability, the ability to experience and express emotion, or their ability and willingness to participate in the development of others, the very characteristics that Fletcher associates with relational working.

I believe that Tony Robbins' (1994) view on basic human needs sheds light on that conundrum. It helped me to understand why the lack of relational skills can be so prevalent in higher echelons of organisations. Like Bowlby (1988), Robbins views the need for connection as the most basic human need. He further argues that if for some reason this basic need is not met early in our development, we will try to compensate by pursuing alternative basic needs such as significance, certainty and uncertainty. Significance manifests itself as an achievement drive, certainty as the need to be in control, and uncertainty as the need for risk and challenge.

These are all basic human needs, common to all of us; however, when individuals pursue them as a compensatory mechanism to a felt inability to connect, they can lead to extreme behaviour: for example, a ruthless and tireless pursuit of career achievements, despotic behaviour, or the reckless pursuit of extreme risk or dangerous sports. If it is true that seeking significance is a way to compensate for a felt lack of deep connection, it is not surprising that some of the very senior people, who have made it their life's work to become hugely important, may have some trouble 'connecting' at a deeper than the most basic 'networking' level and show little capacity for relational work. I offer an example. One of my clients, a high-achieving, seemingly gregarious but deeply troubled person, told me the story of being left by himself over Christmas in a B&B, with only a Harrods hamper for company. He was seven years old.

Seeking to establish a mutually emphatic and empowering relationship with such clients presents a coach with significant challenges. I offer an example from my coaching practice, having changed some of the details to safeguard the anonymity of my client.

I am off to meet Jane, the HR manager of a large telecoms corporation and a steely woman, who seems singularly incapable of showing any emotion other than irritation and impatience. This is our third meeting and I have decided that something will have to change in the dynamic between us. I don't believe Jane is getting any value from our coaching relationship and I am ready to admit defeat. Moreover, I sense that Jane is out to prove to herself and to me that she really has no need for any help, from anyone, and that she has merely conceded to having a coach because it's company policy and she, as head of HR, needs to comply with it.

When I get to the space-ship-like headquarters I am kept waiting a long half hour. Jane eventually breezes in, iPhone in hand, which she puts demonstratively in front of her. "How are you?" I ask, somewhat feebly. "Exceedingly busy, as you can see" is the curt reply. The conversation once more evolves around a change project and Jane's frustration with the amount of resistance she continues to encounter from one of her senior colleagues. She wants me to advise her on "how she can get that man to see sense". I notice my growing anger and the extent to which I empathise, not with my client, but with her 'stubborn' colleague. I gather all the courage I can muster and, looking straight at her, I tell her how I feel. A shadow crosses her face. I can't read it very well, but I sense she's taken aback, no longer in charge as our conversation is taking an unexpected turn. My anger immediately subsides, giving way to concern and a sense of helplessness. I tell her about those feelings too. More silence. My voice quavers as I gently try to explain to her my need to connect with my client as a person, not as a 'holder of a role' and my inability to do so with her. I explain my experience of meeting her, of the meaning I make of being kept waiting, and I ask her what she thinks she is seeking to tell me below her executive front. "You don't understand the pressure I'm under" she says eventually. "Do you want to tell me about that?" I ask. We take our first baby steps to talking about what it is like to be Jane.

We met for a further three sessions in which I concentrated on helping Jane to 'think about how she was feeling' and to reflect on why it might be important to recognise feelings and be able to name them. Loneliness featured regularly. On one occasion she protested that "this is not therapy, you know". "No", I say, "It isn't. This is not the right environment for therapy, but I can recommend a few people if you are interested". Sadly, she wasn't.

My coaching relationship with Jane raises a number of issues which I would like to explore further.

GENDER IS PERFORMANCE

It is not by accident that I chose a woman as the subject of this case study. I imagine some readers (at least) will have bristled at the feminist constructions about identity formation and the ensuing behavioural patterns. Most of us can think of any number of people that challenge the notion that women are more relational, more caring and men more competitive or self-seeking. I certainly did, when I first engaged with the work of Gilligan. What held my attention however was the realisation that I had studied and admired the work of Piaget, Erikson and Kohlberg as an undergraduate, blissfully unaware of the gender bias in their work. I felt naïve for having not even having entertained the question. Stephen Linstead (2000, cited in Linstead & Pullen 2008) argues that "mainstream organisation theory, too, is typically presented as genderless, despite the fact that... management and organisational life is an inescapably *embodied* and therefore also gendered experience, an experience that is different for men and women" (Linstead & Pullen 2008, italics in the original).

The fact that organisations as well as the institutions that theorise about organisational life have traditionally been populated by men and focused on men's experience has led to a prominence and acceptance of masculine attitudes and thinking (Hopfl 2008). This brings with it a subtle pressure to conform to implicit masculine norms for both men and women. Steyaert & Van Looy (2010) argue that gender is not something that one *has* a priori, in other words, it is not the result of our sex, but something that one *does* on an on-going basis. We behave in ways that express and form a masculine or feminine effect, as we act into socially constructed expectations. As Simone De Beauvoir said: "One is not born, but rather becomes, a woman" (1949/1973, p. 301). I view the extent to which men and women behave in a more masculine or feminine way as a result of their ability and willingness to conform to or challenge those norms in the pursuit of their values and ambitions.

Having outlined the implications I believe the relational turn has for the way we think about the very nature of our work, I will turn my attention to some of the practical implications and to my work with Jane.

THE CRAFT OF COACHING FROM A RELATIONAL STANCE

Jane, it seemed to me, had worked very hard at being successful in a competitive, individualistic and autocratic environment, at considerable personal cost (and from some of her stories I was under the distinct impression that that was true for at least some of her male colleagues also). Inviting her to reflect on the stress of being as tough as any of her all-male board colleagues amounted to nothing less than shaking the very foundations upon which she had built her career. Jane had not entered into our coaching relationship expecting to acknowledge her vulnerability. In Fletcher's words, she was not seeking a growth-fostering interaction. Despite my frustration and anger on occasions, I could empathise with her. What would be left if the edifice of her career came tumbling down? On the other hand, colluding with her careful defensiveness would not engender any real personal growth for her. Fletcher's notion that 'growth in connection' can lead to outcomes that were previously unknowable was staring me straight in the face. I felt on shaky ground. It was not only my coaching relationship and my reputation that were at risk. Some of my colleagues were coaching other board members and Jane had the power to terminate the contract between her and my organisation. Taking a relational approach to coaching is risky business... More than once I felt my courage would desert me as I tried to calibrate carefully what both Jane and I could handle. Maybe we made only a little progress, but we both became increasingly brave in our later encounters.

I next want to turn my attention to the delicate balance between persisting and desisting when taking a client into risky, but genuinely developmental, territory.

WORKING AT OUR GROWING EDGE

Deciding that I was prepared to walk away from my client, whatever the consequences (with the blessing of my MD: I didn't take this risk carelessly), was an important first step in establishing a different quality in our relationship. The turning point was brought about by disclosing how I had felt in the faithful meeting I described above. In that moment I was not making a carefully measured decision. I took a leap of faith. With hindsight I mirrored Jane's exasperation and her willingness to express it. Only on this occasion the subject of exasperation was in the room and I was demonstrating that 'expressing frustration' could be done respectfully and with compassion. Only in the process did I become fully aware of the challenge I was presenting to Jane's construction of what our relationship was about, and more generally of how one behaves at work.

Which brings me to the issue of self-disclosure. I believe that, if we take mutuality seriously, we need to be prepared to disclose of ourselves at the same level or depth that we are inviting from our clients. It does not mean that we *have* to do so, only that we would be willing to do so if we believed it to be in service of our client. It sends the message, at an unconscious level in the first instance, that to be flawed is an integral part of the human condition and that is just fine. Living true to this conviction in itself presents a growing edge for most coaches, I imagine. It certainly does for me. In any case it certainly presents a departure from tacitly held masculine norms of behaviour.

At the same time, I doubt the feasibility and even desirability of 'being authentic' at all times. In my experience, the expression of feelings with clients and colleagues is contingent upon many variables. Will it help my client if I express how I feel? (For example, would I tell a depressed client that our conversation is dragging me down too?) Is my feeling related to what is going on in my relationship with this client, or does it originate in a different sphere of my life? Do I share my feelings in their felt intensity, or do I modify my language so that my client can hear the message? There are no recipes, I believe; only being truly present in the moment can tell me where to draw the boundary.

THE POLITICS OF FEELINGS

The organisational discourse about the significance of feelings moved on considerably in the 1990s. From viewing emotions as getting in the way of making sound decisions, and advocating restraint on emotional expressions at work, we have come to accept that they are an integral part of organisational life. Notably, Goleman's (1996; 1999) work on emotional intelligence has found its way into mainstream thinking. However, Fineman (2000) argues that it commodifies emotions and that the purveyors of emotional intelligence use it as "a bait for performance-hungry, competitively anxious, managers and executives" (p. 105). In *The Managed Heart. Commercialization of Human Feeling*, Hochschild (1983) suggests that we do indeed skilfully learn, without being aware of it, what kind of emotional display is expected. Feeling rules, a cultural prescription of how one ought to feel in a particular circumstance, set out what is owed in gestures of exchange between people. We recognise a feeling rule "by inspecting how we assess our feelings, how other people assess our emotional display, and by sanctions from ourselves and from them" (ibid., p. 57). The range of acceptable emotional displays in organisations is severely limited to 'masculine' feelings. I have often been surprised at our tolerance in organisations for unbridled expressions of aggression, anger and competitiveness, and I find myself wondering on occasions what other feelings, such as insecurity, fear and vulnerability, they might be covering up.

Relational psychologists warn against using feelings instrumentally and argue that our social world would be profoundly different if human emotions were honoured as a legitimate part of professional experience (Meyerson 2000). This is a challenging notion for relational consultants. How do I know whether my invitation to my client to discuss or express feelings is merely colluding with Fineman's notion of commodification of emotions or a genuine invitation to growth? Surely my encounter with my client is in service of their success at work? I have come to realise that it is *not* in the first instance. Instead, I seek it to be in service of their well-being, which may in some occasions mean that we work towards a termination of their current employment.

Jane certainly displayed a range of 'masculine' feelings without much restraint in our first encounters, although she resolutely refused to discuss them, insisting instead that we 'concentrate on solving the problem'. For her, talking about feelings was stressful, not least because she had very few feeling labels and difficulty recognising how she felt in the moment. Part of our work together then was to extend her vocabulary. Sharing how I felt with her, or had felt in similar situations to the one she was describing, and to do it with humour (for instance by using hugely exaggerated labels!) helped her in that process. Learning to recognise that she sometimes felt anxious, helpless or lonely was part of our work together. Seemingly paradoxically it helped her to develop a sense of confidence, however tentative, that had not been there at the start.

TO PARAPHRASE TONY CURTIS AND MARYLIN MONROE IN *SOME LIKE IT HOT*: "IT'S NOT JUST WHO YOU MEET, IT'S WHERE YOU'RE MEETING THEM"

To say that mutuality is a quality of the coaching relationship is stating the obvious. What is perhaps less obvious is the impact of seemingly peripheral factors, such as the context in which coach and client meet, which is where I turn my attention next.

Jane had been adamant that we meet in her office because it was the only way she could squeeze out the time. From our first meeting I had felt uncomfortable and constrained in the high-tech, slick offices, with their chrome, leather and glass furniture and their arctic air conditioning. I was aware of and distracted by Jane's PA on the other side of the wall, and by the hubbub outside her office. As our conversations became more personal, the anonymity of our surroundings became more intrusive and oppressive to me. I did not feel able to challenge her choice of location, but at our last-but-one meeting I brought a small bunch of daffodils. Stuck in a glass on the corner of her desk they looked oddly fragile and alive, almost comically so. They became the focus of Jane's glance when she talked about her loneliness, and in a particularly poignant moment she gently touched one of the petals as she made a fleeting reference to the garden in her parents' home, the only glimpse into her private life I was ever allowed. As winter turned to spring, and we were meeting for the last time, I asked her whether we could go for a walk. "Why would I want to do that?" she wanted to know. "Because it is such a lovely day and I don't expect you'll get much of a chance to enjoy it otherwise", I replied. Reluctantly she agreed. Once outdoors I explained how walking alongside one another, looking in the same direction, can free us up and open up a space for a different conversation. "That was nice, indeed", she said warmly as we shook hands in front of the reception desk. She was right. It was good. It was the best conversation we had.

The physical locations in which we meet our clients can greatly affect our chances of engaging in a person-to-person encounter. Physical spaces tend to 'set the scene' quite literally, with their symbols of power, hierarchy, detachment or, conversely, of closeness, informality, openness.

A particular challenge, not one most of us would encounter, was presented to speech therapist Lionel Logue. Tom Cooper's film, *The King's Speech*, tells the story of King George VI of Britain, his impromptu ascension to the throne and his relationnship with Lionel. The therapist insists that they meet in his consulting room rather than in the palace and that they address one another by first names. Although 'George' is reluctant to divulge any personal information, Lionel gently persists and we discover some of the traumas the king was subjected to as a child, which most probably contributed to his profound stammer. As the story unfolds we witness the loving irreverence of the therapist and his dedicated pursuit of a relationship between equals. He does get given his marching orders after a particularly heated interaction, but is re-engaged when the king's fear of a life of public speaking becomes stronger than his pride. They remain friends for life.

It is a beautiful example, in my view, of the value of insisting that our clients, whatever their status or reputation, are *persons* in the first instance. I work hard with my clients to reduce any sense of hierarchy, whether they ascribe a higher status to themselves or to me. Reducing power differentials is an integral part of mutuality (Fletcher 1999), not in the least because it can begin to un-stick the notion my clients may have carried that the pursuit of significance (status, career, power) is what earns them a rightful place in the human race.

WHEN RELATIONAL COACHING MAKES OUR HEARTS SING

I may have given the impression that relational coaching is hard, perilous work. It certainly can be. It is also joyous, exhilarating even, and utterly fulfilling. I found the work with Jane taxing but I learned and grew in the process. The moments in which we really connected were precious and rewarding.

Many of my clients treasure the opportunities that relational coaching offers them. They can let their habitual guard down, relax into talking about what really matters to them, let go of the need to be seen to be on top of everything. They appreciate being met as a person who is worthy of another's undivided attention and care because of who they are, rather than because of the significance of their position. It also often painfully reminds them of the difference between conditional and unconditional regard (Rogers 1951). Clients often comment that they feel refreshed and reinvigorated as a result of our encounters, even if at least part of it was challenging or even distressing. I usually leave a coaching meeting feeling the blissful tiredness that follows a good day's work.

My favourite example of mutual engagement is Clive. His organisation was going through a particularly turbulent time when we first met in Ashridge's London offices. Clive was a pleasant and articulate person. Although our encounters were friendly, he remained somewhat guarded, as if not quite able to shake off his boardroom persona. As the heat in the organisation mounted and Clive became more stressed, I insisted that, despite the pressure on this diary, we meet in Ashridge and start with lunch. Clive arrived looking relaxed in his casual outfit and enchanted by the surroundings. During that first lunch we talked about our families, lives and interests outside work. We continued our meandering conversation during a walk in the beautiful gardens, and then spent the rest of the afternoon holed up in a coaching room, working hard and with purposeful concentration.

Our coaching relationship is on-going and we now meet regularly at Ashridge, despite the tremendous pressure of Clive's new role. An Ashridge meeting always starts with lunch and, weather permitting, a walk. We inquire into each other's life and work and I am often touched to realise quite how closely Clive has followed my interests. Even when we meet in the formal London office we make time for re-connecting. We have discussed the impact of the quality of our relationship on our work together and have been surprised by its significance. We also continue to conclude our meetings by sharing what we have each learned. It is a small but important acknowledgement of its reciprocal quality.

CHAPTER 5

SPIRITUALITY IN THE COACHING RELATIONSHIP

BILLY DESMOND

There has been sustained interest in spirituality in the workplace and in management studies since the mid 1990s (Oswick 2009). Some of the purported benefits associated with workplace spirituality include personal fulfilment (Mitroff & Denton 1999), empowerment (Neck & Milliman 1994) and enhanced team performance (Daniel 2010). Also, there are some suggested links between workplace spirituality and increased honesty and trust in organisations (Wagner-Marsh & Conley 1999), improved decision making (Biberman & Whitty 1997) and a greater commitment to organisational goals (Leigh 1997). However, spirituality within executive-coaching relationships seems to be relatively unexplored. To bring spirituality in coaching to life I will start by introducing work with a client whose details have been changed to ensure anonymity.

> *In the middle of a coaching session, Jennifer, a senior commercial director in a global retailer, was telling me the details of an ethical crisis she was struggling with. Jennifer was pondering if their current supplier-expansion strategy in emerging markets was going to be detrimental to the incumbent local communities. I noticed a fluttering in my heart, a tightening in my stomach. A metaphor came to mind and appeared to persist, yet did not seem related to the current issue being explored. A recurring image emerged of three people walking through lush woodland, coming upon an open clearing with a running stream. It did not seem in any way connected to the issue being discussed, yet it prevailed and called for my attention. I chose not to discard this but continued to hold it, considering it as an aspect of the co-created relational field of our work.*

In my coaching session with Jennifer, I recognised my bodily sensations as feelings of anxiety and fear in relation to the ethical issue being explored. I was noticing my increasing concern that if she handled this poorly it would have significant repercussions on her role and potentially the organisational brand. I noticed her breathing was shallow and she was talking quickly as if desiring to run away from this thorny issue. The image prevailed and became more vibrant. Rather than dismiss it, I chose to trust this as an aspect of our work together.

I decided to share my image with Jennifer. I put my assumptions and hypothesis to one side. I did not interpret or subscribe meaning to the image. Instead, I invited Jennifer to describe what resonated, if anything, for her. Her immediate, strong association was with a metaphor that echoed a historical event, which had occurred over six years previously, one that she had pushed out of her awareness. She recognised the three people in the image as herself, her colleague the technical director, and the supplier. For her, the trees represented the business opportunity they developed as a product offering that generated significant economic benefits for all parties and the local community. However, when she started describing the clearing and stream she went pale. She became tearful and looked in pain. She was recognising that the ethical issue she was now addressing was a result of not attending more carefully to the wider ecological and environmental implications of this unique product, something they had briefly discussed but decided was not an issue. However, they had never reviewed this perspective in light of rapidly changing social and ecological needs. Jennifer realised that while she often had recurring dreams where she was seeking a place of solace and peace (surprisingly often, in a vast mountain forest) she had interpreted this as a symptom of being overworked and stressed. She now realised that the duration of her dreams coincided with the time she was director for the part of the business that was now being affected. Jennifer felt a deep sense of relief and sitting back in her chair she realised what she now needed to do. I felt a sense of hope – a lightness in my chest and sense of freshness loomed around us as if new air, light and space had entered the room.

It seemed in that moment, without saying a word, that we both knew what course of action would be required. Jennifer in her vulnerability was open to sensing deeply the wider world around her. She later took a courageous decision congruent for her and which reflected the responsibility of her role in the organisation but also to the environment within which they operated.

I consider this helpfulness of a subjective experience and multiple ways of knowing that emerge within a relationship to be spirituality in coaching. Spirituality is intrinsic to being human and is an embodied experience – this is my perspective. I will now illustrate how we can weave spirituality into the fabric of our coaching relationships, grounded in an epistemology that is congruent with a relational coaching perspective.

Spirituality – An Abyss in Our Relational World

People need to make meaning of their lives not in an abstract way, but by inquiring into their own lives and taking responsibility for the choices they make (Frankl 1959/1992; Perls, Hefferline & Goodman 1951; Yalom 1980). Victor Frankl (1992; 1978) argues that meaning- making and spirituality are intimately connected as people need to make sense of their lives. He suggests spirituality is a genuine human need that cannot be explained by a reductionist model, and warns us of problems that may ensue if we choose to ignore this aspect of humanity. Abbs (2003) argues that a challenge in discussing spirituality is "due to the powerful, pervasive, yet quite erroneous assumption that fundamentally our world can be explained through science or through the methods of science" (p. 33). In our industrialised countries, rapid scientific advancements, alongside our emphasis on materialistic perspectives has often resulted in a spiritual side of life being denied (Neal 2005). For example, it seems such advancements in neuroscience, genetics and cosmology make us believe that we are more rational beings.

In our Western economy, I wonder whether our pursuit of growth and profit – often with little regard to our human community of people and our planet – has given rise to some of the challenges we are experiencing. Has our emphasis on logical reasoning, acquisition of knowledge and material for self-advancement merely replaced the role of traditional establishments, such as the churches, family, employers and life-long employment? The world of capitalism involves us paying homage and reverence to consumer brands as they offer us a lifestyle which we ought to aspire to (Klein 2000), a way of being in the world previously offered by institutionalised religions, perhaps. It seems to me that both paradigms – the world of religion and the world of business – hold a prevailing assumption that the nature of human desire and solace is to be found outside oneself. In the former, it is found in an omnipotent God. In the latter, it is the acquisition of a lifestyle that involves acquiring more knowledge or material goods. Both seem to be orientated towards one's own self-interest, whether seeking salvation, or a tendency to accumulate to better oneself, often without much awareness of the impact this has on the wider world. Sometimes, for me and my clients, aspects of such orientations are evident, as they are familiar and soothe a sense of anxiety that is an integral part of human existence.

I am aware that this is a simplification of a complex argument that is outside the domain of this chapter, but it begins to outline the context from which both clients and coaches meet each other in the coaching relationship. It would be naïve to imagine that such factors do not exhibit considerable influence in how we arrive and configure ourselves in relationship to each other in our coaching practice. Denham-Vaughan (2010) says that in our Western society growth is socially valued, as evidenced in our capitalistic culture with its emphasis on expansion. She points out "how strongly this context configures our action" (p. 36). Likewise, most of our cultures in the West are informed and shaped by religions which propagate the concept of transcendent truth and knowledge being sought outside oneself. In our organisational worlds this is often manifest as an emphasis on the rational where the embodiment of spirituality as part of our human experience is rare and, most often, absent. It tends to be left to the private sphere, as are our bodies, and to a lesser degree our emotions. In organisations it seems that the Cartesian split between mind and body, body and spirit is under-pinned by the concept of self as something deeply internal, private and separate. In my mind, this leads to the disowning of parts of ourselves, where many coaching clients arrive with a deeply internalised belief that 'knowing' is a cognitive process that occurs either within or outside one's self – rarely emerging from relationship to others.

It is now fifty years since Victor Frankl's insight. In 2011 we are living in a Western world where confidence in institutions that include some of our major world religions, government bodies, financial regulators, formerly trusted brands and organisations is fragmenting. Rational, scientific, mate-rial and growth-orientated sense-making processes within organisations appear generally to be embraced at the expense of the more spiritually orien-tated. While this way of operating business seems to grow our economies, it also leaves people struggling to make sense of their lives and work in the society they inhabit.

So I wonder, is this in part due to the fact that we have ignored an aspect of human living, namely spirituality? The spirituality I refer to in this context is what Marques (2006) defines as an "experience of interconnectedness and trust among those involved in a work process... epitomised by reciprocity and solidarity" (p. 285). It seems that Frankl (1992; 1969) sees a person's desire for making meaning of his or her life as being the primary motivation for living and fulfilment, and it is in this quest that spirituality emerges. He argues that this process of meaning-making happens in relationship, where "the true meaning of life is to be discovered in the world rather than within man or his own psyche" (Frankl 1992, p. 115). Buber (1947/1965, p. 80) suggests knowing another requires us to go "beyond what is obvious and focus on the *'soul'* of the person, to truly understand and be in awe of the whole of the person, as they long to be deeply understood by another human being". Clearly, Marques, Frankl and Buber see spirituality as being about people connecting and in relationship with each other. However, it appears that the current cult of individualism, encouraged through the preponderance of rationalism and expressed in argumentative discourse, has left little space for 'the other' in our relationships. We tend to be bound by rationalist traditions of understanding where "what we cannot speak about we must pass over in silence" (Wittgenstein 1961, p. 74). It is as if we have objectified the face of 'the other' – that other being people, our communities and our planet, whose needs may be divergent from ours with our preoccupation and emphasis on growth.

DEFINING SPIRITUALITY

Parlett (1991, p. 73) states that "no part of the total field can be excluded in advance as inherently irrelevant, however mundane, ubiquitous, or apparently tangential it may appear to be". Hence, it calls upon us to attend to the aspect of the coaching relationship that is spirituality. Defining spirituality is a challenge. However, I believe it necessary to offer a way of understanding spirituality so it is not "excluded in advance as inherently irrelevant" in our coaching relationships.

Spirituality connotes the whole of life, including bodily, psychological, emotional, social and political dimensions of a person (Tacey 2004). Spirituality is experienced as a "sense of connectivity, a relationship" (Burke 2006, p. 15) and includes "the possibility of relation with all otherness" (Buber, 1947/1965, p. 65). Spirituality refers to the "wisdom and experiences that a variety of spiritual traditions represent; experiencing peacefulness, calmness, stillness, strength, direction, or meaning" (Williams & Plagens 2009, p. 179). It can be seen as encompassing the wisdom of cultural traditions over several millennia that are both immanent and transcendent in our here-and-now co-created relationships (ibid.). The immanent includes the human spirit as experienced in the person-to-person encounter, an experience that is sometimes inexplicable "with our language of nouns and pronouns" (Gergen 2009, p. 373), yet resonant and confirming of a person and their potential. The transcendent may be what emerges from spiritual practices (such as meditation, prayer and reflection, as opposed to dogmatic teachings) that include Christian and Muslim mysticism, Buddhism, Judaism and Hinduism.

As nothing fundamentally "exists for us outside our immersion in relational processes" (Gergen 2009, p. 372), then spirituality is an aspect of our coaching relationships. Spirituality is part of the intersubjective relationship – the 'between', where both coach and client are open to what is emerging and what each is, in the mutuality of their dynamic encounter. This also requires us to be open to the possibility that we are constantly in process, always in "the act of becoming" in our multiple and varied co-created relationships. We may experience this as a continual striving, not towards a pre-determined outcome, but as a way to live "one's life as constantly in process of becoming" in relation to the infinite (Weston 1994, p. 31). For me, the infinite is that which emerges from the 'between' so it can become known to both persons in the dialogical relationship. A scary thought perhaps, particularly for those of us who have a desire to be in control and who have been rewarded for knowing and leading with certainty.

Kennedy (1998) identifies factors, such as being present, noting we are all equal in our humanity, and co-creative dialogue, which facilitate spirituality. From a relational perspective, we believe in the mutuality of relationship, interpenetrating each other's worlds (Wheeler 2000; 2009) where both clients and we are open to being changed in the encounter. Beisser (1970) suggests that change and development for our clients is most likely to occur when the coach is also open to being changed. This requires us with awareness to adjust creatively how we make contact with our clients in a way that is supportive of the emerging figures in the here-and-now relationship. According to Wheeler (2003), creativity in the co-created relationship occurs in the "space between", an experimental zone where each person in the relationship is mutually informing the other and their worlds interpenetrate. In my experience this place of creativity is characterised by a willingness to let go of anything familiar, combined with openness to what is emerging and unfolding. It requires both coach and client to come face to face with each other in a process of discerning in the dialogical relationship. I believe that this place of creativity is the source of our spirituality. Spirituality can be "embodied, shared and developed non-discursively" (Abbs 2003, p. 37) through creative expression. It requires us to trust multiple ways of knowing over and beyond the rational and emotional. Such creativity is embodied and may manifest as metaphor, imagining, dreams, creative expression and somatic experiences.

A RELATIONAL PERSPECTIVE IN COACHING, INCLUSIVE OF SPIRITUALITY

Humans are inherently relational (Hycner 1993); we are 'wired' for relationship (Gerhardt 2004; Wheeler 2000). A relational turn in our coaching practice invites us to include 'the other' (our client), as co-inquirer in the here and now of the relationship. It requires moving from a stance of primarily I–It relating to one which encompasses both I–It and I–Thou modes of relating (Buber 1923/1958), a dialogical relationship. This means that in our co-created dialogical relationships with each other we "focus both on the data (I–It mode) to make sense of our world, and at the same time we are open to meeting another in a way that deeply understands their experience as if it were our very own (I–Thou mode)" (Desmond 2011, p. 29). Adopting an I–Thou attitude, we are open to the mystery of being and we are genuinely curious about any new awareness, creation or event that may emerge 'between' one person and another (Mackewn 1997). Growth and learning occurs not in the coach or client but in what emerges between them (ibid.).

As a Gestalt-orientated executive coach and organisation-development consultant, I seek to nurture spirituality through this focus on the 'between'. However, I often struggle. I wonder if we as coaches are also influenced by the contemporary rationalist and scientific culture in our hesitation to acknowledge spirituality as an aspect of the person and the context within which we live, work and play? In my experience, the complexity of dwelling with not-knowing in a world that values the rational, instant gratification and success may feel threatening to some leaders when they come for coaching. For example, when my client Jennifer first arrived for coaching she was feeling nervous and seeking answers from me. I felt the 'pull' to be clever and insightful, and felt anxious as I didn't have the expertise she sought! However, noticing my responses I chose not to offer these and instead checked if she was interested in exploring the here and now of our relationship. She agreed. *Together*, we inquired into what she was experiencing in the present with me and what both our parts were in this co-created event. She developed awareness of how she construed relationships where the face of 'the other' (the other being me in this instance) was "an instrument and resource to be utilised". This seemed to heighten her anxiety and fear of not knowing.

We know from recent neuroscience research that the interpersonal is intra-personal (Philippson 2009). We co-create each other's inner world. We are all interconnected, "the 'individual' and the social, 'inner' and 'outer' worlds interpenetrate" (Wheeler 2009, p. 346). Spirituality is the feeling of "being connected with one's *complete* self, others and the entire universe" (Mitroff & Denton 1999, p. 83, italics added). I suggest that our co-created coaching relationships require us to remain open to the novel, the unknown, and alert to the numinous and its manifestations that emerge in the 'between' with our clients, and the wider world. In my experience it is a place of vulnerability, knowing that I, as a coach, am engaging in the co-creating of a relationship where I too am open to being changed in this meeting with my client. This vulnerability, while at times scary, is also a gift of courage. It keeps us attuned to the other and "more open and receptive to the surprise of the new" (Ó Murchú 2010, p. 47). Perhaps, trusting the novel and mystery of the human-to-human encounter in a dialogical relationship is a way of acknowledging and integrating spirituality in our coaching work.

ALLOWING SPIRITUALITY TO EMERGE IN THE COACHING RELATIONSHIP

As relational coaches, we can foster the conditions that support spirituality emerging in our co-created relationships. I will describe how this can be facilitated by referring back to my earlier coaching vignette with my client Jennifer.

In Gestalt we are encouraged to trust and apply what we know and understand deep within us, where:

> every part of the field is a part of each of us... and in our belongingness, to each other and to the field we share, lies our full humanity, and our fullest individual development of self...

> (Wheeler 2002, p. 78)

My and my client's 'belongingness' arises from our on-going process of relating that includes, for example, gender, sexuality, ethnicity, personal and professional histories, the organisational context and socio-cultural environment. If we are unable to interact fully with the world then we have less sense of self, including our 'space between', and the environment in which we live. It is the deepening dialogue with others that bring us beyond ourselves (Hycner 1993), where we invite our clients to become aware of their inner aliveness and embody it. Gestalt, phenomenological in its meaning-making, enables us to inquire into the nature of our clients' and our own unique existence while remaining creatively indifferent to any outcome. Gestalt therapy supports knowing through direct experience. Gestaltists adopt a phenomenological method of inquiry which involves three elements – bracketing, description and horizontalism (Spinelli 1989, pp. 17–19) – as a way of understanding the subjective nature of our clients, their way of being in the world and the genesis of their unique self. It is a method that supports re-owning aspects of ourselves that heighten awareness and further enliven us. Bracketing involves putting our assumptions to one side; description involves inviting the client to describe their immediate experience; and horizontalism requires that all phenomena are given equal value and significance at the outset.

In my work with Jennifer, the phenomenological method offered the necessary support that enabled us to co-inquire and discern the immanent aspects of spirituality in the here and now relationship. For example, I invited Jennifer to *"describe what resonated [in the metaphor] if anything, for her"*. The aim is to understand the *"meanings the client gives* to the people and events" (Crocker and Philippson 2005, p. 68, italics in original), where support for spirituality can "lead to enhanced creativity, honesty and trust" (Krishnakumar & Neck 2002, p. 161) in our co-created relationships. Attending to Jennifer's subjective experience in the creative 'space between' of our interdependent coaching relationship, she connected with issues and made meaning that had wider ecological and environmental implications. Thich Nhat Hanh (2008) says "when you touch one thing with deep awareness, you touch everything... when you touch one moment with deep awareness, you touch all moments... the one contains the all" (p. 91). In a dialogical coaching relationship, this quality of contact requires the coach to have presence – which involves "bringing the fullness of oneself to the interaction" (Jacobs 1995, p. 220). With Jennifer, presence required me to show myself as I truly am in the here and now, not who I'd like to be. I attended to my own embodied experience and selectively shared my responses that I believed were in the service of our work. I believe it is in those moments when a coach and client deeply resonate with each other's experience, a new awareness may emerge from 'between' that belongs not only to one or the other but to *both* the relationship *and* wider relational field, and is embodied. In my coaching relationship with Jennifer, this was manifest in the persistent metaphor.

This image of "three people walking through lush woodland, coming upon an open clearing with a running stream" was significant. Heron and Reason (1997) describe this as presentational knowing – an intuitive grasp of the significance of our resonance with and imaging of our world given life in the realm of metaphors. O'Neill & Gaffney (2008) describe such metaphors as the "emergent creation", where the image does not come from one person or the co-created relationship but from the generative and creative nature of our wider context, which includes the interaction of all aspects of the unspoken, forgotten and unresolved past. With Jennifer, we can understand the emerging metaphor as an aspect of the unresolved 'there and then' historical context of her previous role, which calls for attention in the 'here and now' of our dialogical relationship. Our coaching relationship is embedded and interpenetrated within the wider and historical context that is always present, yet ever-changing and often unknown. It is within the dialogical relationship, the 'space between' that the unknown becomes embodied and known. It then becomes a resource and support for purposeful meaning making where decisions are made with greater awareness.

Such a moment happened when "Jennifer felt a deep sense of relief and sitting back in her chair she realised what she now needed to do. I felt a sense of hope". In the work that ensued, Jennifer and I were able to meet one another with a heightened awareness of the intricately connected co-created relationship and the wider context. In our dialogical relationship we remained open to an I–Thou meeting, where 'Thou' extended beyond our co-created relationship. In the instances in which this occurred, it was first experienced at an embodied level. Language was difficult to access. Yet, a felt knowing that is characteristic of what we may call spirituality – trusting different ways of knowing beyond the rational, a solitude yet connectedness in knowing through direct experience was present. It was the moment when a "sense of freshness loomed around us as if new air, light and space had entered the room".

This knowing is messy, full of doubt, as it was in the moments where I seemed to be learning as much as my client, Jennifer. Yet, I appeared to have 'wisdom' (in trusting the metaphor) that surprised me and perhaps even my client in those moments! Embodied knowing was considerately given expression with clarity of words that deeply resonated with my client. In such instances I have often felt humbled. Knowing through direct experience – the presence of a hunch, the image within, our creative source, seemed inclusive but more than the co-created relationship between me and the other. I suggest that trusting spirituality as capacities of a person, the co-created relationship, the wider environment and the creative 'space between', where we are intricately connected with each other, may enrich the quality of our coaching practice. The purpose of trusting the creative 'space between' is to engender a sense of deepening inquiry into what is not yet know, while remaining aware that what is discovered is provisional, and is always in the 'process of becoming'.

TRUSTING OUR CREATIVITY IN THE 'SPACE BETWEEN'

In this chapter, the epistemological bases of relational Gestalt I've referred to in reclaiming spirituality are: dialogical relationship where we include the 'other' and remain genuinely curious and open to the mystery of what emerges 'between' one person and another; interconnectedness where clients' and coaches' inner and outer experiences are a source of creativity in the 'space between'; and a phenomenological method where subjective experience is trusted. I hope adopting these in our coaching practice will foster a richness of meaning and clarity of direction that supports sustainable growth both for individuals and their organisations.

In our relational turn within coaching, spirituality as part of the person is of and from the coach–client relationship and the wider context. Spirituality is perhaps the search for connectedness between the many parts of a person, the desire for meaningful contact with others, within and between organisations, and ultimately between the human community and the earth we inhabit. Perhaps now is the time for discernment and integration of spirituality in the coaching relationship. I invite all relational-orientated coaching practitioners to embrace our vulnerability and courage, discerning through direct experience the embodied knowing of spirituality, an aspect of our self and the co-created relational field of our dialogical coaching relationships. It is then and perhaps only then, that the creative source of spirituality as a human need may have the potential to enhance the quality of our relationships as it extends beyond coaching, into the wider world in which we live, work and play.

CHAPTER 6

LEARNING IN EXECUTIVE COACHING RELATIONSHIPS: A BEHAVIOURAL SYSTEMS PERSPECTIVE

MAX VISSER

ABSTRACT

In recent research the strength and nature of the relationship between coaches and executives appears as a critical success factor in successful coaching outcomes. However, little theory has as yet been devoted to an analysis of how relationships are used in executive coaching. Such an analysis requires going from the monadic, individual level of analysis to the dyadic, relational level. The purpose of this chapter is to analyse learning in executive coaching relationships at this dyadic level of analysis. Conceptually, this analysis draws on a combination of the behavioural (Skinner) and systems (Bateson) perspectives. A verbatim of a coaching conversation serves as an illustration. It is found that the behavioural and systems perspectives may be fruitfully combined in one behavioural systems perspective. This perspective and its outcomes add to and can be clearly distinguished from the more common humanistic, psychodynamic and cognitive perspectives to executive coaching.

INTRODUCTION

Executive coaching has become a blossoming field of activity in the past decade. With the advent of post-industrial forms of organisation and increasing levels of employee work competence and demands, CEOs and senior managers have become aware of the importance of their "people skills" and networking capabilities to maintain their positions and to prosper in their careers. Increasingly they engage executive coaches to help them develop these skills and capabilities, increase their organisational effectiveness and consider appropriate career steps (De Haan 2008a and b; Hall et al. 1999; Thach & Heinselman 1999).

The growing dependence of executives on coaching poses challenges to the practice and scientific study of executive coaching. Regarding practice, the profession of executive coach is not (yet) protected by law or subject to norms and regulation by a strong professional community. This means that anybody can decide to become an executive coach, regulated only by market conditions and the spread of good or bad rumours regarding one's coaching achievements. Given the coaches' positions of relative influence *vis-à-vis* executives, there are some "very real dangers" involved in current executive coaching practices (Berglas 2002; Hall et al. 1999; Thach & Heinselman 1999).

Partly to alleviate these dangers, the scientific study of executive coaching has sought to establish empirical relations between executive coaching efforts and coaching outcomes. Similarly as in medicine and psychotherapy, researchers strive to identify evidence-based coaching practices and attempt to translate these into programs for continuing professional development of coaches (De Haan 2008b; Feldman & Lankau 2005).

In these studies the relationship between coach and executive increasingly has received attention. Forming and maintaining a strong and productive relationship with clients has been identified as a critical success factor in successful coaching outcomes, slightly more than professional attitude and working methods of the executive coach (Bluckert 2005b; Kilburg 1996; Wasylyshyn 2003). The relationship is considered as the prime vehicle of the influence executive coaches may have on their clients (De Haan 2008a; Hall et al. 1999).

Important as the relationship is considered to be, little theory and research has as yet been devoted to the analysis of how relationships are used in executive coaching. Most students of executive coaching inquire into the ways coaches and executives as individuals perceive and experience the coaching relationship, into what they individually learn, and into the qualities of coaches and executives that influence these perceptions and experiences (e.g. Berg & Karlsen 2007; De Haan 2008a and b; Feldman & Lankau 2005; Hall et al. 1999).

This individualist orientation is reinforced by most of the theoretical perspectives in the field, i.e. humanistic, psychodynamic, cognitive, behavioural and systems (De Haan & Burger 2005). Of these, the humanistic and psychodynamic perspectives appear to be favoured by most researchers and practitioners (e.g. Bluckert 2005b; Hall et al. 1999; Kets de Vries 2006). Some propose an eclectic perspective (Berg & Karlsen 2007), while others appear to follow a combination of psychodynamic and systems perspectives (De

Haan 2008a and b; Kilburg 1996). The humanistic, cognitive and psychodynamic perspectives centre on the individual as object of analysis, inquiring into individual needs, attitudes and cognitions. However, if we want to analyse how relationships are used as relationships in executive coaching, we need to go from the monadic, individual level of analysis to the dyadic, relational level. In this chapter I propose an analysis of learning in executive coaching at this dyadic level of analysis, drawing on a combined behavioural systems perspective.

Throughout this chapter I will define executive coaching as a professional relationship, in which the coach helps the executive in becoming more effective in work-related situations. As such, executive coaching is distinguished from consulting to the extent that executive coaching constitutes a more personal, in-depth involvement with executive development and effectiveness instead of a more general, superficial involvement with organisational development and effectiveness (Berman & Bradt 2006). Further, executive coaching is distinguished from psychotherapy, to the extent that executive coaching is more oriented towards improving personal work effectiveness and less towards addressing non-work issues, painful experiences or severe psychopathology (Bluckert 2005a; Gray 2006).

Further, throughout the chapter a verbatim, 'the coaching conversation', is used to illustrate the analysis from the behavioural systems perspective.* The sequences are numbered for reference in this chapter. The text in square brackets outlines the thoughts of the coach and author of the verbatim, here called Caroline, at the time of the exchange.

VERBATIM: 'THE COACHING CONVERSATION'

Ellen is a young, recently graduated account manager in an agency. Ellen has called on a coach, Caroline, because she is experiencing difficulties in her communication with colleagues and superiors which may jeopardise her career in the agency. In the current second session, Ellen expresses distress around an interaction she had the previous day with the managing director of the agency, Robert. Caroline tries to help Ellen to see herself from his perspective by inviting her to take part in the 'two chair exercise', where she tries to speak as Robert. The following exchange unfolds:

1. *Caroline: Shall we move you out of Robert and get you back to the coachee seat and see what you learnt from him...*

---

* The content of the verbatim was made available by courtesy of the Ashridge Centre for Coaching, with permission of the coach and coachee. Names were changed to safeguard privacy and anonymity. The interpretation of the events in the verbatim is the sole responsibility of the author of this chapter.

2. *Ellen: That's quite good. [Both laugh]*

3. *Caroline: ...or about him?*

4. *Ellen: Hmmm.*

5. *Caroline: ...or you can tell me how you felt first if you want, whatever comes to your mind.*

6. *Ellen: Hmmm. How it felt? It felt, hmmm, it's unusual; it's different because I am not in that position, I am never in that position. I don't get to speak to him so it's quite useful to have an insight of how it might be.*

7. *Caroline:* [senses that the exercise has not engaged Ellen as it should and therefore explains her intention] *Yes, because we never think of doing that, you know, of putting ourselves in somebody else's shoes and we've done a lot of that and that seems to be something that helps. So what else did you... did you get anything else from that, anything that you thought: "I've never looked at it from quite that perspective" perhaps... or not?*

8. *Ellen: Not really, I mean everything there, I kind of, I knew really [laughs] so... it's not new information, but it's helpful to see him from his point of view. Especially, I've been thinking that maybe he was only harsh with me because he was in a bad mood. I did think that but... I can't see any other reason for it really. Why would he want to do that...*

9. *Caroline:* [feels as if she is getting some progress as Ellen is starting to reflect on the incident] *And the way he arrived in your office, or in your area, saying "Come on, let's do this". It didn't sound like it was emotionally neutral to start with. You see what I mean. He was arriving... It started very emotionally charged.*

10. *Ellen: Does that mean that you think he was wound up?*

11. *Caroline:* [feels she's being trapped into a logic she does not want to be trapped into. She has let himself state an opinion that seems to be transformed into letting Ellen off the hook without responsibility for the incident] *Yeah, I think so, it sounded...*

12. *Ellen: That it had nothing to do with me.*

13. *Caroline:* [consciously tries to return to a more middle ground where Ellen might continue exploring what she contributed to the incident] *It doesn't sound like it, no. [Silence.] However, you know, if that happens a lot...*

14. *Ellen: It does. He does get wound up quite a lot. What it is, I don't know how to judge him or read him, I suspect so I can't really protect myself.*

15. *Caroline:* [starts mirroring what she sees, but then notices herself saying things that are too harsh and wondering why she is saying them] *I think, I think that's something I've heard several times from you, which is why I am getting you to see it from other people's perspectives. It seems you are not... you are unaware of how people see you or what they need... either you don't see it or you don't... or you see it but you don't pay attention to what it means... It's like you were deaf and dumb and you were just doing... deaf and blind sorry, yes, not hearing, not seeing and therefore your actions might hurt somebody or miss the, miss the target because you don't know where they are.*

16. *Ellen: I think that's also true on his part.*

17. *Caroline: Oh, yes.*

18. *Ellen: He doesn't... He is...*

19. *Caroline: He doesn't care.*

20. *Ellen: Yes, that's the truth.*

21. *Caroline: Although, do you not care as well? That could be the same reason...*

22. *Ellen: About how he...*

23. *Caroline: How other people are.*

24. *Ellen: No, I do. I do. That's the difference. I want to make a good impression so I do. [laugh]*

25. *Caroline:* [continues being challenging for no good reason except that Ellen seems to be slipping away from every exploration she tries to invite] *Not the same. Do you care about how people ARE? You may care about what people THINK of you, that's COMPLETELY different!*

26. *Ellen: What do you mean by how they are?*

27. *Caroline:* [feels Ellen has 'caught her' and now she has to explain her challenge to her] *Hmmm. For example with him, Robert. You could see he was upset, or annoyed and really wound up so therefore not the right time to even engage, if he says "Let's look at it."*

28. *Ellen: HE, He came to see ME!*

29. *Caroline:* [notices the emotion in Ellen's tone of voice, and interprets it as the beginnings of anger in the light of unfairness. She returns to her guiding intention as a way to re-establish the relationship] *No, I know, I know. He came to see you and possibly saying "As you're in a rush, I can see it it's not the right time" or just this sort of... noticing he's in a certain mood. That's a... Yeah... [Pause] What's... I am trying to find a reason for why you don't notice what people have as moods...*

30. *Ellen: OK.*

This chapter proceeds as follows. In the next section the behavioural systems perspective is outlined and its concepts are applied to an analysis of learning in executive coaching, using the verbatim as an example. Finally, the chapter ends with discussion and conclusions.

A BEHAVIOURAL SYSTEMS PERSPECTIVE ON LEARNING

The behavioural systems perspective is largely based on the work of the British anthropologist and cybernetician Gregory Bateson and the American psychologist B.F. Skinner (De Haan & Burger 2005). Although not often considered together, their work shares several characteristics (Cullari & Redmon 1982; Visser 2003; 2010). Skinner (1957; 1974) developed an overall framework for the description, explanation and control of behaviour, in which he posited a radical environmentalism and firmly rejected mentalist explanations of behaviour. Bateson and the so-called Palo Alto group he assembled in the 1950s worked in a comparable non-mentalist framework, be it without adopting or explicitly referring to radical behaviourism. However, they considered their pragmatic theory of communication, with its strong emphasis on relationship and function, to be closer to mathematical logic than to mainstream psychology, with its strong emphasis on individuals and their mental states (Bavelas 2007; Sluzki & Ransom 1976; Watzlawick et al. 1967).

In his thinking on learning, Bateson (1972) adopted the ground rule that all biological systems (organisms and their social or ecological organisations) are capable of adaptive change. Such change depends upon feedback loops, provided by natural selection and by individual reinforcement. Inherent in these loops is always trial-and-error and a mechanism of comparison. Trial necessarily involves some error, which is biologically and psychologically expensive. It follows that adaptive change always must be hierarchical. Since such change involves learning, it also follows that learning must be hierarchical. Learning processes then can be ordered at different levels, of which Bateson distinguished four. For the purpose of this article, two levels are especially relevant: proto-learning and deutero-learning.

PROTO-LEARNING

Proto-learning (also referred to by Bateson as learning I, simple learning, or operational learning) refers to the adaptation of behaviour in response to contingencies of reinforcement. This learning occurs in all classic and instrumental conditioning experiments inside and outside the psychological laboratories. Fundamental in proto-learning is Skinner's (1957; 1974) distinction between two forms of behaviour: respondent and operant. Respondent behaviour is reflexive in nature. It occurs as a direct response to a stimulus, such as when the sight of meat powder makes Pavlov's dog salivate automatically. Operant behaviour is non-reflexive in nature. It does not occur as a direct response to a stimulus but is spontaneously emitted by the organism from time to time. Operant behaviour has an effect on the organism's environment, to the extent that there are consequences attached to that behaviour. These consequences in their turn determine the likelihood of reoccurrence of the previously emitted behaviour. When this behaviour increases in frequency, the consequence is called reinforcement. When the behaviour decreases in frequency, the consequence is called punishment.

The relation between the consequences, the stimulus upon which a response occurs and the response itself is regarded as probabilistic or contingent and generally referred to as the contingencies of reinforcement. In this scheme, stimuli do not elicit responses. Instead they control responses by signalling to the organism that a certain response-reinforcement contingency is in effect which in the past has led to reinforcing consequences. Since these stimuli enable the organism to distinguish (or discriminate) a reinforcing situation from a non-reinforcing one, they are called discriminative stimuli. Further, the relation between response and reinforcement is also contingent, depending upon various schedules of reinforcement (Holland & Skinner 1961; Skinner 1974).

Skinner applied his radical behaviourism to animal and to human behaviour without modification. His most important application pertained to the interpretation of language, or verbal behaviour (Skinner 1957). In Skinner's analysis this form of behaviour is, like all behaviour, under the control of environmental contingencies that are now social in nature, i.e. controlled by the verbal community to which the speaker belongs. Speaking words may have the function of operant response (with all possible positive or negative consequences attached to it) and of discriminative stimulus (setting the occasion for verbal responses of the listener). Thus in the verbatim, Caroline and Ellen, engaged in a coaching dialogue, each in turn serve as a reinforcer of speech or as a discriminative stimulus to the other, according to Skinner.

For such proto-learning to occur, it must be assumed that the context of learning can be repeated at different points in time. Without this assumption, all learning would be necessarily of the zero-order kind, i.e. fully genetically determined. To account for contextual change, Bateson (1972) introduced the term 'context marker'. It denotes a signal that informs an organism that context [A] of stimulus [a] is different from context [B] of stimulus [a] and therefore elicits a different response, even though the stimulus remains the same. For example, the question "How was your work today?" is responded to differently in the context of family evening dinner than in the context of a coaching conversation.

From the assumption of repeatable contexts it also follows that for every organism the sequence of life events is in some way segmented or punctuated into contexts, which may be differentiated or equated by the organism. The distinction between stimulus, response and reinforcement in an experimental setup here attains the status of a hypothesis about how the experimental subject punctuates that sequence: "in Learning I, every item of... behaviour may be stimulus, response or reinforcement according to how the total sequence of interaction is punctuated" (Bateson 1972, p. 292; Bateson & Jackson 1968).

DEUTERO-LEARNING
Deutero-learning (also referred to by Bateson as learning II, learning to learn, or Gestalt learning) refers to changes in proto-learning as a result of insight in the structure (or class) of the situation in which proto-learning takes place. Such learning acquires particular importance in the field of human relations. Bateson emphasises that relations have no 'thing' quality in themselves, but are immanent in the exchange of messages: "the messages constitute the relationship" (Bateson 1972, p. 275). Here deutero-learning implies the learning of characteristic patterns of contingency (or contexts of conditioning) in a relationship.

Context in a relation is introduced in two ways. First, a message, sent by one person, sets the context for a certain class of response by the other person. Second, insofar as such messages are verbal, the non-verbal signs in interaction function as a context marker of the verbal message, therefore as a context of context for the other person. This setting of contexts is inevitable in interpersonal exchange, since in interaction the categories stimulus, response and reinforcement are never 'empty'. All behaviours (verbal and non-verbal) occurring between persons who are conscious of each other's presence have (reinforcing or punishing) effects, whether intended or not. Such effects have interpersonal message value and thus are communicative in nature. It follows that in interaction it is impossible not to behave, and therefore impossible not to communicate (Bavelas 1990; Critchley 2010; Visser 2007a; Watzlawick et al. 1967). In the verbatim, in sequence 24–25, Ellen's laughing appears to convey a non-verbal message to Caroline that she is not taking her perspective very seriously, to which Caroline non-verbally responds by raising her voice. Similarly, in sequence 28–29 Ellen's emotional outburst appears to convey a powerful non-verbal message to Caroline that her prodding transcends the limits of the definition of their relationship as complementary and co-operative, which is fairly common in coaching.

Similar to Skinner, Bateson noted that all references to mental states can be redefined in terms of transactions (or relations) between persons and their social and physical environment. In such transactions one can readily discover contexts of proto-learning that bring about that deutero-learning to which the mental state refers. In relationships, stimuli, responses and reinforcements acquire meaning in contingency patterns of interaction. These patterns are defined by the participants as certain characteristics of the relation, depending upon their subjective punctuation of events (Bateson 1963; 1972; Bateson & Jackson 1968). In the verbatim the relationship is characterised by attempts by Caroline to make Ellen explore her own responsibility in communicating to Robert and by attempts by Ellen to evade this exploration. The harder Caroline pushes, the more Ellen evades, for example by seizing the opportunity to blame Robert for being "wound up" (sequences 9–10, 10–11), by laughing (sequence 24–25), and finally by apparently becoming angry (sequence 27–28). When Caroline backs down, she appears to return to a less emotional state (sequence 29–30). From Ellen's subjective punctuation, this may lead to an initial interpretation of Caroline's behaviour as 'concerned', but later on as 'pushy' or even 'intrusive'. From Caroline's subjective punctuation, we are able to discern her interpretation of Ellen's behaviour as 'evasive' and 'slippery'.

Patterns in interaction may develop into rules or stabilised definitions of the relationship between coach and executive (Haley 1963; Watzlawick et al. 1967). In the verbatim, Caroline and Ellen have defined their relationship as complementary and co-operative. The issues that Ellen proposes are leading and Caroline adopts a helping and encouraging stance towards these issues (e.g. sequences 5–6, 8–9, 12–13). However, feeling justified by the particular context of the session, Caroline increasingly adopts a more probing, almost inquisitive position (e.g. sequences 14–15, 24–25). At the end this appears to alter their definition of the relationship from complementary and co-operative into symmetrical and competitive (sequence 28–29), after which Caroline backs down (sequence 29–30).

Deutero-learning in human relations implies that subjects improve their ability to adapt to contexts of conditioning. For example, a person who is subject to a prolonged situation of classic conditioning will increasingly expect a world (context) in which signs of future reinforcements can be detected, but nothing can be done to influence the occurrence of reinforcement. In mental terms this person is likely to adopt an attitude of fatalism. Such experience with earlier contingency patterns in its turn leads to a habit of acting as if all new contexts exhibit the same pattern. This habit of expecting a certain punctuation of events tends to become self-validating (and hence self-fulfilling) by promoting certain behaviours and by discouraging others. Behaviours are thus not regarded as discrete events, with causation flowing in one direction only, but as interconnected events that are both cause and effect and, ultimately, their own cause (Bateson 1972; Visser 2007b; Watzlawick et al. 1967). In the verbatim, the particular behaviours that Caroline and Ellen display are interlocking and only fully intelligible with the knowledge of what went before and after those particular behaviours. For example, in sequence 27–28 Ellen's emotional outburst becomes intelligible from Caroline's insistent attempts to make her explore her own responsibility in communicating with Robert (sequences 6–7, 14–15, 24–25, 26–27) and Ellen's equally persistent attempts to evade this exploration (sequences 9–10, 13–14, 23–24).

Finally, deutero-learning in coaching relationships does not always lead to personal growth and development of the participants. Coach and executive improve their ability to adapt to contexts of conditioning as they are presented to them, but such adaptation may range from more to less healthy. Executives may become overly dependent upon their coach, which may give the coach direct influence on the executive's business decisions (Berglas 2002; Visser 2007a and b). In the verbatim, such a situation does not seem to occur. It is only the second coaching session between Caroline and Ellen, and Ellen does not appear to be particularly dependent upon Caroline. Whenever Caroline pushes Ellen and attempts to influence her more directly, either she manages to evade Caroline's attempts or Caroline retreats somewhat, sensing that she is jeopardising their relationship. There are no signs that withdrawal from this coaching relationship is difficult for Ellen (or Caroline).

DISCUSSION AND CONCLUSIONS

Analysing learning in executive coaching from a behavioural systems perspective provides coaches with three important lessons that appear to be less covered by the other perspectives to executive coaching and related fields.

A first lesson is: interactions may shape mental states. The humanistic, psychodynamic and cognitive perspectives tend to emphasise the important causal role of individual needs, attitudes and cognitions in steering behaviour. The behavioural systems perspective to coaching argues that these mental states can often fruitfully be redefined as collateral products of specific interaction patterns between coach and executive. While these patterns give rise to subjective mental interpretations, these should not be reified as immutable mental states or traits. Often interpretations constitute a form of retrospective sense-making: we emit a certain behaviour and afterwards we attribute mental meaning to it (Bem 1967; Skinner 1974; Weick 1979). For example, in the verbatim we see how the attitudes and cognitions of Caroline are shaped by the specific interactional dynamics of her exchange with Ellen. Sometimes her intentions appear to follow her behaviour, sometimes her behaviour appears to follow her intentions.

A second lesson is: concentrate on the here and now of behaviour don't always look for past causes. The psychodynamic and (to some extent) humanistic perspectives tend to emphasise the role of past unresolved psychic conflicts, repressed drive tendencies and thwarted growth needs in current behavioural problems. The behavioural systems perspective argues that coaches should concentrate more on the here and now of behavioural problems. They should deal with them in real time in the current setting of the relationship between coach and executive. Often psychodynamic mechanisms like defence, transference and repression directly translate into interpersonal patterns and experiences (Thomas et al. 2007; Westerman 1998). For example, in the verbatim, Ellen's 'defensiveness' may directly manifest itself in response to Caroline's particular approach to this coaching conversation, pushing hard to learn Ellen to assume responsibility.

A third lesson is: it is impossible not to manipulate in coaching, so use this as a beneficent tool. The humanistic, psychodynamic and cognitive perspectives have often objected to the behavioural systems perspective as being overtly manipulative and thus detrimental to humanistic values like free will and voluntary choice, sometimes invoking literary examples like Burgess' *A Clockwork Orange* or Huxley's *Brave New World* (e.g. Huczynski & Buchanan 2010, p. 164; Kreitner et al. 2002, pp. 273–4; Locke 1977). The behavioural systems perspective has countered these objections by pointing out the impossibility of not communicating in relationships. Reciprocal influencing is inevitable whenever people meet in a coaching or other social context. Further, the behavioural systems perspective does not question free will and voluntary choice on philosophical grounds, but argues that, empirically speaking, individual choices often are more influenced by contextual factors than most people are willing to realise (Gray 1979; Haley 1963; Skinner 1974; Watzlawick et al. 1967). For example, in the verbatim all verbal and non-verbal behaviours displayed by Caroline and Ellen can be regarded as forms of conscious or subconscious manipulation of one other.

Coaches using the behavioural systems perspective will accept this impossibility not to manipulate and use it for improving the coaching relationship and helping the coachee. By providing and focusing on contextual influences these coaches increase the awareness of coachees of their current behaviour and its impact on and from the context. This makes it possible to influence their behaviour in more positive directions and to provide enduring relief in a relatively brief period of time.

ACKNOWLEDGMENTS

I thank Erik de Haan, Charlotte Sills, Marijke Spanjersberg, Paul Tosey and Marius Rietdijk for their stimulating and critical remarks on earlier drafts of this chapter.

PART III

CONTRACTING AND MONITORING THE COACHING RELATIONSHIP

This section of the book contains the following chapters:

Chapter 7 – Charlotte Sills – The coaching contract: a mutual commitment

Chapter 8 – David Skinner – Outside forces in the coaching room: how to work with multiparty contracts

Chapter 9 – Michael Carroll and Robert Moore – The supervisory relationship in executive coaching

This part of the book explores the establishment of a relationship in which the client can learn and develop, from the point of view of contracting and monitoring the development of that relationship. Charlotte Sills offers an introduction to the many levels of written and unwritten contracts, and demonstrates how contracts help to contain and to focus on the objectives, content and emotions that will emerge in a coaching relationship. With a wider lens, David Skinner takes a pragmatic view of the vicissitudes of multi-party contracting in a corporate or organisational environment, showing how the boundaries of the relationship need to be established and monitored carefully in political environments. Michael Carroll and Bobby Moore carry relational principles through to relational supervision as a helpful frame outside of the strict coaching contract that serves to monitor the quality and development of what goes on within it.

In the unfolding journey of this book, this part represents the need to make a map of the routes, abysses and swamps that the travellers will need to negotiate together – as well as the coaching inns that will be vital to them. This part is a reminder of the concern and care that relationships need in those 'container' moments.

CHAPTER 7

THE COACHING CONTRACT: A MUTUAL COMMITMENT

CHARLOTTE SILLS

Pete was running out of the house – half into his jacket and with his toast clenched between his teeth, when the phone rang. It was Colin, HR director for Chemwell, an international chemicals firm with whom he had done business several times. He liked Colin and the work he had got from him had always been interesting and rewarding – coaching, project development, consulting to the leadership team. As he drove to his meeting, he listened to Colin through the earpiece. A situation had arisen – Henry, one of his senior managers was up for promotion to the board. Their only concern – and it was a major one – was that his leadership skills were hopeless and that was holding him back. Getting the promotion depended on his developing in that area. Meanwhile, another senior manager who had been taking care of the Far East office was coming home – and he was expecting that place on the board. Tricky. Pete listened – half an ear on Colin, half his mind on the meeting he was going to – he simply must do well at this presentation; getting the contract to do all the leadership development for a large government office would look great on his CV. And with the new baby on the way he could do with the money. Colin was getting to the point. Would Pete coach Henry to see if he can be got ready for board level work? Intensive stuff – got to be done by the year end – otherwise the post would go to the other guy. The usual rates and agreements. Pete was happy to agree and told Colin to ask Henry to give him a ring so they could talk about the possibilities.

Three days later, Henry rang and Pete arranged a meeting with him. Pete was slightly disconcerted when Henry introduced himself as "taking over the director position in January". That didn't seem to fit with what Colin had said. But perhaps something had changed. Cautiously, Pete asked Henry what he hoped to get from coaching. Henry laughed cheerfully. "Oh, we all get coaches when we're heading for stardom," he said "I think it would be a good place to just take some time to reflect on my life". Pete began to wish that he had engaged earlier in the dynamic activity of making the contract – or setting the frame.

SOME THOUGHTS AND THEORIES

A contract is an agreement between two or more people concerning the type of activity or relationship they will have with each other. In coaching, it is the agreement between coach and client about their work together; the mutual undertaking to enter into a coaching relationship. However, as all coaches know, things are not as simple as that: a coaching engagement involves a wide variety of contracts and contexts – from the initial contact with the purchaser to the subtle negotiation of an on-going and evolving coaching commitment.

Human society is founded on explicit and implicit agreements about how we can live in relationship with one another. They are one of the ways that we use to try to put order into a world that is essentially unpredictable and potentially dangerous. Despite the obvious argument that human relationships cannot be controlled by contracts, it remains the case that they are an indispensable part of the functioning of any political, legal and social system. They are therefore an essential feature of any 'safe' coaching agreement (and by 'safe', I mean safety as much for the coach as for the coachee).

And there is something else that is highlighted by the contract, something unconscious and unspoken. That is the fact that if we need a contract, we are acknowledging a 'me' and a 'you' – two subjectivities in relationship. In making contracts, we are facing the existential reality that we are separate and different and we may have different desires – and yet we are also connected and can join in mutual commitment. At best, coaching engages with that challenge of existential encounter, resisting the pull of familiar patterns.

Depending on their theoretical orientation, their personal preferences and their experience, coaches vary enormously in the amount and type of contracts that they make. At one extreme, for example, for an internal coach, there may be a simple offer of a space and an opportunity to talk without any other expectations or agreements about time frame or process. It may seem to some that it would be hard to take sufficient distance to be facilitative in this relatively structureless context. Yet many internal coaches find that they can offer very real support and guidance this way 'in real time'. People can be useful to each other simply through engaging in a conversation, without making formal agreements about it.

Despite the beneficial effect of simple human contact, most coaches would agree that further contracting is essential. Whether they work as internal coaches, independent consultants or for a coaching organisation, there will be, at the very least, a need for agreements about such administrative details as time, place, fees (if any) and duration as well as a broad agreement about goals. What is more, a significant body of research (see the Introduction for an overview) indicates that a clear agreement about the aims of coaching and also how the participants will work together is vital for a strong 'working alliance' and an important element of effective coaching. As long ago as 1977, Goldberg cited seven research studies addressing the vital importance of contracting and concluded that the *contractual relationship* is "an arrangement between equals that, when explicitly formulated, rejects coercion and fosters personal freedom" (p. 32). The implication for coaching seems clear. The contract is not simply a business case, a prediction about effect on ROI, a way of reassuring purchasers of coaching that it is 'worth the money': it is a vital and subtle part of the coaching relationship and its effectiveness.

However, as we come to understand the reasons for this importance, we also become aware that there is a significant factor which is a consistent influence on our contract-making and needs to be mentioned here. This is the inevitable tension between structure and emergence – order and chaos – which is a vital part of creative relational coaching.

Earlier, I commented that humans have an essential tendency to attempt to impose order in a chaotic world. We have a strong need to make sense of the world, to provide it with structure and make it more predictable. It can be argued that the coaching relationship, with its inevitable risk of exposure and its capacity to arouse emotional and disturbing issues, is in particular need of structure to contain it. The contract helps to provide this structure.

However, as Einstein reminded us, a problem cannot be solved with the same thinking that created it. In order truly to make transformative changes, we have to work in the area of "bounded instability" (Stacey 1992) between certainty and uncertainty in a sort of temporary beneficial disorder that allows for something new to emerge. Here lies the coach's dilemma. The contract needs to accommodate the tension between the certainty of structure and the need for creative uncertainty. This creates a real *caveat* in relation to those contracts which identify specific goals for change – and which coach has not been persuaded by the outcome-driven attitudes of purchasers? It points to the need for subtle flexibility in contracting and for it to be an evolving process. This chapter hopes to guide the reader through some of the complexities and subtleties of the process of contracting so that coach and client can co-create the right path.

LEVELS OF CONTRACT

The model here is based on five 'levels' of contracting process (Sills 2006). It continues the idea of the contract being the container or the 'frame' for the work. The five levels of contracting start with the largest contextual container and then work down the levels to the micro-moment. When colleague Brigid Proctor talks about them, she uses a set of Russian dolls. Each one nestles safely inside the container of the previous one – each separate but contributing to a whole. The dolls capture the idea that the contract, at best, acts as a safe container for the creative work in the area of bounded instability and that it can do this best if it itself is 'contained' by the clarity and safety of the previous level of contract.

LEVEL 1: THE CONTRACT WITH THE WORLD – SOCIETY, THE PLANET

This first level of contract is not one that is negotiated by or with the organisation. It is a personal contract or commitment that an individual holds with the wider world. Between coaches, the details may be different. The essential thing is that there are some principles and values that we will not transgress. They may be to do with harming human beings or degrading the planet. They may concern working within the law or respecting diversity. Many coaches make clear to the client the professional organisations to which they belong and the ethical codes to which they adhere. An interesting reflection here is to ask yourself the question: what work would I need to refuse or give up? What would I be willing to lose my job over?

> In Pete's case, his particular contract with himself and the world concerned his own integrity and respect for people. He had worked for Chemwell before and knew that in the past he had liked the way they conducted their work and how they treated their employees. He had also experienced liking and respect from them. He had not, therefore, felt the need to question Colin, the HR Director, about what was happening to the people involved.

LEVEL 2: THE CONTRACT WITH THE ORGANISATION AND ITS PARTS

In 1975, Fanita English wrote a two page article called 'The Three-Cornered Contract'. Her simple model was a triangle that looked like this:

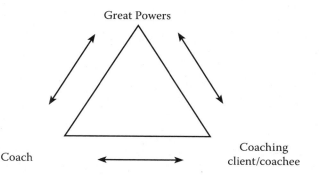

Figure 7.1

The 'Great Powers' are the organisation, or the HR department or whoever is purchasing the coach's skills and has the power to dictate whether and how the work will go forward. The other two points on the triangle are coach and client. The simple message of this important article is that there are certain things that must be transparently agreed, on all three vectors of the triangle, in order for any coaching engagement to be safe and effective. English's work was developed by Micholt (1992) who drew triangles with sides of unequal lengths to indicate allegiance or distance between the parties. The triangular scheme can be developed to map multiple stake-holders and lines of authority (see Skinner in this volume).

Eric Berne (the founder of transactional analysis) identifies three forms of contract: the *administrative*, the *professional* (which we will call the *learning and development contract*) and the *psychological* (Berne 1966). The first two are relevant here. The psychological contract will be discussed later.

THE ADMINISTRATIVE CONTRACT

Sometimes also referred to as the business contract, this deals with all the practical arrangements such as time, place, duration, fees (if any), agreements with referring bodies or agencies, confidentiality and its limits. Normally it also includes a broad agreement about the purpose of coaching. These are all apparently straightforward but it is surprising how often coaches, with their eyes firmly fixed on the coaching work to come, can be unclear about them or overlook their fundamental importance. Not only is clarity about administrative agreements essential to the world of business, the creation of this structure creates a safe space within which to allow what is not known to emerge.

The administrative contract covers the following areas:

- *The venue, the time, the frequency, and the duration of the coaching sessions and changes to the agreements*

- *Fees* including the possibility of fee increase over the course of a long coaching commitment; also perhaps a policy for cancellations

- *The context of the coaching*

- *Confidentiality* and any imposed or inevitable limits, agreements to report back and so on; obligations in law and in ethics; coach's supervision arrangements

- *Record keeping arrangements* (for more information on coaching contracts and the law (in the UK) see Jenkins 2007)

- *How the coaching will be evaluated* for example informally by the participants or with the manager, or against KPIs etc.

- *What sort of coaching?* There are many types of coach – from the expert who hopes to pass on his skills and expertise, to the facilitator who sees his role as simply to help the coachee take space for his own thoughts. It is important to be able to articulate one's coaching proposition – even to guide the client as to what might be most suitable. Turning down work because it is not the type of coaching we offer is likely to make a better impression on potential future purchasers than trying to be a 'one coach fits all'. It may be especially important to give a detailed explanation of the approach when proposing to work cross-culturally.

THE 'PROFESSIONAL' OR LEARNING AND DEVELOPMENT CONTRACT

This contract defines the purpose and focus of the coaching and how it will proceed. It is mainly the concern of coach and coachee. However, often it needs also to be part of the three-cornered contract with the organisation. For example, a coach may be engaged specifically to develop future leaders, to facilitate a transition or to build particular skills. This purpose is thus one of the transparent details that is known by all. It can also be part of planning for the evaluation process.

On a more sinister note, organisations – sometimes knowingly, sometimes unconsciously – may use a coach or even an entire team of consultants as part of a plan to achieve a hidden end. We discuss this later under 'psychological contracts'.

In our example involving Pete, it is easy to see that here is a place where there was serious slippage.

Because Pete was in a hurry – and preoccupied – and because he knew and liked Colin, it hadn't occurred to him that there might be anything problematic in the air. Normally, he would have suggested a three-way conversation between himself, Colin and Henry so that he could ensure that Colin had given all the information to Henry that had gone to Pete. As it was, he was left feeling somewhat compromised. Colin had told him that Henry's future was seriously at risk, but it seemed that Henry was unaware. Neither did he appear to know about the hero returning from the Far East with his eye on the board reward. Belatedly, Pete suggested the three-way meeting but Henry didn't feel it was necessary. Pete felt anxious and didn't know what to do.

LEVEL 3: THE CONTRACT WITH THE COACHING CLIENT

When all this measurable detail is clarified, the coach and coachee are free to move into the coaching work itself, which starts with a deeper exploration of the *learning and development contract* – the goal of the work and the tasks involved for the coach and the coachee; in other words, an agreement not only about direction but also about how they will work together.

Coaches vary as to how much they explain their role as coach and there is no special rule about what needs to be said. However, it is worth remembering that there is considerable evidence to suggest that failed or discontinued work is largely caused by an unaddressed difference in expectations between practitioner and client (Goldberg 1977). Clear contracting about how the client sees the problem and what he needs, as well as how the coach normally works and how together they will address inevitable misunderstandings, helps to avoid later problems de-railing the coaching or, worse, going underground.

The core of this conversation will, of course, be the discussion about the goal of the coaching. Until the last few years, coaching was somewhat hamstrung by the image of either being a remedial activity or for improving performance. This, as well as the inevitable focus on measurable ROI, led to contracts being automatically framed as behavioural and testable. Of course, there is a place for such contracts, but to think that this is the only kind of contract is to do an injury to the contracting process. Contracting is a rich, flexible activity that is constantly responsive to the situation and the changing needs of the client, that acknowledges the mutuality (see King in this volume) of the relationship and the importance of emergence. Negotiations about the potential scope of the coaching, its boundaries and its changing and emerging goals are a vital part of the work (sometimes they *are* the work).

There are two parameters that are useful in thinking about contracts. The first is the continuum from 'hard' to 'soft' contracts. In a hard contract the goal is clearly defined in measurable terms: for example, "to find myself a new job within six months", "to implement this new system with my team" or "to delegate the operations and concentrate on networking". Soft contracts are more subjective and less specific, for example "to develop as a team player" or "to get to know myself as a leader".

There are some powerful advantages to making 'hard' change contracts:

- Clients are encouraged by the contract-making process to believe and feel that they have options and that the power for change is in their own hands. This can instil hope in the process of coaching, along with the sense of personal power, both of which are identified as being factors involved in successful therapy outcome (Asay and Lambert 1999; Duncan and Miller 2000).

- They provide a useful yardstick for assessing the effectiveness of the work, which is essential if coaches are to demonstrate their efficacy! If contracts are not being achieved this should be explored: perhaps something significant has been missed; perhaps the wrong contract has been chosen, in which case it should be renegotiated. Possibly coach and client are not suited or the issues are outside the coach's competence.

- They provide clarity of focus, which gives both coach and client something to aim for and leads to economy of time and expense in the long run.

- They use the power of envisaged potential so that the client not only works consciously towards the goal but, at a deeper level, has already accepted the possibility of the outcome in his mind.

- They help to avoid misunderstandings and unrealistic expectations on the part of both client and coach, for instance that the coach actually has a magic wand! Contracts help to reinforce the notion that we make change happen, even if we cannot always predict all the consequences.

However, there are some significant disadvantages and caveats to the concept of 'hard' contracts for change and the thoughtful coach will bear them in mind:

- Inevitably, a behavioural goal often implies that there is something unsatisfactory in the present moment. In other words, the work immediately becomes problem focused, while so many studies are pointing to the importance of enquiring into the positive.

- Some clients have a personality type which strives for achievement. They may turn their contract into yet another performance hurdle to overcome.

- A softer contract allows for more of an exploration into what 'is', what works and what could emerge. Remember also the paradoxical theory of change, which states that "change occurs when one becomes what he is, not when he tries to become what he is not" (Beisser 1970, p. 88).

- A very precisely defined behavioural goal runs the risk of restricting the scope of the conversation so that clients feel that they cannot talk about deeper feelings and thoughts which might emerge in the coaching process. Only when the contract is specifically for short-term, outcome-focused work is it appropriate to limit the content of the sessions to the defined and agreed area – an approach which is summed up rather deftly by a colleague, Angus Igwe, who (adopting the words of philosopher Ziggy Zigler) says "The main thing... is to let the main thing... be the main thing!"

- Finally, there is another caveat about hard contracts which was mentioned earlier. If a client is capable of imagining an outcome, it must come from his current frame of reference. It is therefore not going to be truly transformational. A fundamental shift will be made only when clients have risked entering that area of "bounded insta-bility" (Stacey 1992) between the known and the unknown with willingness to be open to new ideas. It is essential that the contract be non-restrictive, renegotiable and flexible, so that the client is available to his creativity.

INTO THE UNKNOWN

The question of 'hard' versus 'soft' becomes further moderated by the issue of whether the coachee (and also the coach) has a clear understanding of where he is and what he wants. While many clients come to coaching with full understanding of what their difficulty is or their goal may be, many others do not. Clients who genuinely don't know what they need may feel inadequate if a hard contract is asked of them. They are simply aware of a generalised malaise: "I have been feeling miserable in my new role for months and I don't know why" or "I want to know who I am as a leader." Or they may be offered two sessions of coaching as part of a training programme and have no idea what is 'on offer'. An appropriate initial (soft) contract might be simply "to explore myself in my role".

Clients who have been 'sent' to coaching (like Henry, whose job is on the line if he does not develop leadership skills) or who have unrealistic goals (like the highflier who is competing against an internal candidate who is also the Chairman's son-in-law) may hurry to make contracts which are doomed to failure.

Even those clients who do know what they want may not know the full significance of the change they are seeking. We human beings do not remain stuck in our difficulties for no reason and the patterns we develop have served us well at some time (for example in our previous organisation or even in our childhood). We may need to understand fully the meaning of our choice before we can carry it through. Consequently many coaches, as a matter of course, agree an initial contract to explore the client's situation, or to make a small behavioural change. Then at a later stage, after the relationship is established and the client knows herself more fully, a contract for greater change is negotiated.

THE CONTRACTING MATRIX

The Contracting Matrix (see Figure 7.2) is a way of organising some of these parameters into four types of agreement for the work's direction, each of which has implications for what might be required from the practitioner in terms of relationship and approach. The model seeks to address the limitations of goal-led coaching, while retaining the benefits of clear contracts.

Types of Contracts

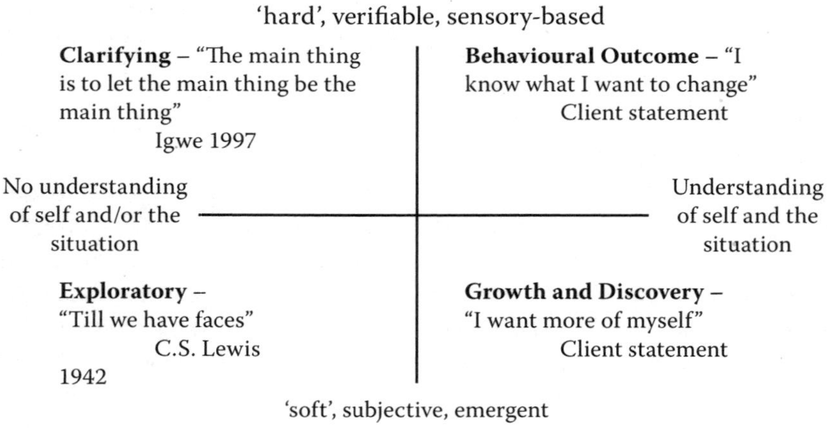

'hard', verifiable, sensory-based

Clarifying – "The main thing is to let the main thing be the main thing" Igwe 1997	**Behavioural Outcome** – "I know what I want to change" Client statement

No understanding of self and/or the situation ———————————— Understanding of self and the situation

Exploratory – "Till we have faces" C.S. Lewis 1942	**Growth and Discovery** – "I want more of myself" Client statement

'soft', subjective, emergent

Figure 7.2

The vertical axis describes the continuum between the 'hard' contract, which is observable, verifiable, sensory-based – and the 'soft' contract, which allows the unknown to emerge, is subjective and intangible. The horizontal axis reflects the degree to which the client has a clear idea of what changes he needs or wants to make. The resulting matrix offers four types of contract that allow the coach to respond to the client where he is – according to his perceived and experienced needs and wants, his personality style and level of self-awareness – and the time frame in which they are working. As the work unfolds and the coaching couple explores the issues together, the contract will be reviewed, adapted and updated as new goals emerge.

The *behavioural contract* (top right) requires of the client a high level of clarity about his problem and desired goals as well as an ability to describe those goals in behavioural terms. Clients who come to coaching with a clear aim – and perhaps a time-limited frame – may find these contracts most useful. A newly appointed manager realised that her job involved making presentations to clients. She saw a coach to help her overcome her shyness and learn some communication skills. Her work focussed on building her confidence and working though her anxieties. She decided also to enrol on a public-speaking course. This sort of contract is often associated with mentoring or 'expert' coaching where the coach is presumed to have some experience and knowledge in the area of the desired learning.

The *clarifying contract* (top left) is one offered to the client when he knows broadly what he wants, or at least that he wants clearly definable change, but he does not understand what the obstacles are and what he needs to do. Here the contract may be to identify the key issues and then review the direction. An example is the man who referred himself to a coach in despair about being overlooked once again for promotion. His experience was that although his managers appeared at first to support him, and his psychometric capability assessment was high, when he actually applied for promotion the support melted away. He very much wanted the next promotion and this was his stated contract. First he needed to find out what he was doing to sabotage his possibilities and what skills and competence he needed to develop.

At the bottom of the matrix lie two types of contract which do not articulate a measurable outcome. They are for clients whose need is for a subjective internal change or development, not an externally defined one. The *exploratory contract* may be suitable for someone who can identify dissatisfaction with their work, or someone who is new in post and wants support as they discover what the challenges are and 'who' they will be in their new role. These clients don't yet understand themselves and therefore are certainly not capable of identifying a behavioural goal. The contract is represented by words from C.S. Lewis: "Till we have faces". The full quotation is "How can we come face to face with the gods until we have faces?" (Lewis 1978) In other words, how can we come face to face with our potential self until we know the face of our present self? How can we face the challenges of our lives and decide who and how we want to be until we know who we are now? The completion of this contract may be followed by a behavioural contract, or it may not.

Finally, there is what might be called a *discovery contract* or perhaps an *engagement contract*. The signature phrase for this type of contract is "I want more of myself". This was said by a successful client who had been in an action-learning set with the coach in the past. She returned saying that she had discovered all sorts of new aspects of herself during her time in the set. She had come back, not because she was in difficulty but because she wanted to discover more about herself. It would have been completely inappropriate to pin her down to a contract for change.

The process of agreeing a contract should be a relational and on-going affair. Clarifying the details and renegotiating the direction can prove to be the meat of the coaching.

> As Pete sat with Henry, his mind raced. There appeared to be a distinct disso-
> nance between Henry's understanding of the coaching and what Colin had
> seemed to be saying. Henry clearly was leaning towards a 'discovery contract'.
> Pete decided to offer an exploratory one, and made a note to himself to talk
> with Colin as soon as possible, and insist that he sit down honestly with Henry.
> He suggested to Henry that they take a session to explore the ground and
> review the contract at that point. Henry agreed.

LEVEL 4: THE SESSIONAL CONTRACT

Most coaches will want to make some kind of contract for the individual session. Some coaches, whose style is more business focused or performance related, will have a structured beginning to the session, checking on any actions that the coachee undertook after the last session and negotiating the day's goal. One colleague always starts his sessions "So what do you want to change today?"

Other coaches are more relational in their approach, waiting to see where the coachee is and what is in the forefront of his mind. Another colleague begins "So what is important today?" or "What is figural?" from the Gestalt idea of 'figure and ground' – the figure stands out from the background of our perception, taking our energy and attention.

> When Pete spoke to Colin about the misunderstanding over the purpose of
> coaching, he was in part relieved and in part disturbed to hear Colin say that
> Henry had been told on numerous occasions that in order to secure the board

job, he needed to raise the level of his leadership skills. At the next session, Pete wondered how to address this. He started the session by asking what Henry would like to focus on. Henry identified his work–life balance as the issue. Biding his time, Pete listened as Henry talked about the stresses of work and home. From time to time he made comments or observations that Henry appeared not to hear. He barely paused when Pete spoke, and simply went on with his monologue.

Level 5: Moment-by-moment contracts

There are also here and now 'instant' contracts, which clarify something or find a way forward in a session. They might involve the coachee asking for some feedback and the coach agreeing, or the coach making a suggestion which the client accepts. Examples from the coach are:

"I have a suggestion for you, do you want to hear it?"

"Do you want some information about that?"

It is important to listen to the client's answer and make sure there is agreement before continuing. It is not necessary to make this sort of contract every time an intervention is made that changes the direction of the work. Permission to do this is normally implicit within a good working alliance. However, it can be useful in helping the coach find his way in the process, or in ensuring that a client does not feel pushed. This sort of contract is also valuable for heightening here-and-now awareness and self-responsibility.

Pete noticed that he felt rather irritated at being ignored and he began to wonder if others in Henry's life experienced the same. It seemed that Colin did! Even if he had been less than absolutely clear with Henry (and in Pete's experience, HR directors sometimes pulled their punches), he had obviously had the conversation several times about Henry's development need.

When there was a pause, Pete apologised for interrupting the flow and asked if Henry would be willing to hear some feedback about Pete's experience of him. Looking surprised, Henry agreed. Pete told him that his impression was of being unheard. Immediately Henry apologised and admitted that he was so inside his own thoughts that he hadn't really taken in the fact that Pete had spoken. Pete wondered aloud if Henry was like that at work. Henry thought it was possible. The two discussed the implications of this – as a result of which, Pete was able to suggest to Henry that it may be useful for him to go and talk to his colleagues – including Colin – to find out what feedback they had for him about his upcoming career. Henry agreed to do this and to make notes for their next meeting.

At the following session, after checking that Henry had carried out his plan, Pete asked if Henry would be willing to make the feedback the subject of the session. Shooting him a wary glance, Henry agreed.

BREACHES OF CONTRACT

Whatever the coach's approach, the learning and development contract is made, along with the administrative contract, as a formal offer and acceptance of a coaching commitment. The coach needs to think about how to respond if the contract is broken – by either party. It is important that she be clear from the outset which agreements are immutable and which negotiable. A breach of contract on either side is likely to be symbolic of psychological processes that must be addressed – what might be called 'disturbances to the frame'. The exploration of such breaches can often yield valuable and powerful learning opportunities as tacit knowledge emerges into the realm of conscious understanding.

In theory, either side has recourse to the courts if a legal contract is broken, but in practice it is very unlikely that a coach would take a client to court, even for such clear breaches as non-payment of fees. Indeed, Hans Cohn (personal communication), in somewhat humorous vein, said that the reason that practitioners use the word 'contract' at all is "because it gives them the feeling that they are in charge". What is important is that any broken contract be sensitively explored for its implications and significance. An overemphasis on contracts may point to an excessive desire for control – a denial of human changeability. However, impatience with, or abhorrence of, contracts may imply avoidance of boundaries, of commitment and of the responsibility of choice.

THE PSYCHOLOGICAL CONTRACT

The psychological contract consists of the unspoken, and often unconscious, expectations that are brought to the coaching session by both coach and client, resulting in a sort of implicit agreement which can have positive or negative consequences. Berne's choice of words reminds us powerfully of the strength of such unspoken and unchosen pacts.

Psychological contracts are, at best, empathic and respectful connections – the core of the essential working alliance, in which the client feels trusting enough to share his concerns. If the administrative and professional contracts are made carefully and appropriately, coach and client are ready to embark on whatever journey they have agreed. At the psychological level, the client may already be feeling hopeful and optimistic about what he can achieve. If the coach feels similarly confident, if they have effectively explored the client's needs and agreed the focus, and she believes that she is able to offer help, a bond is developed which is likely to affect the positive outcome of the coaching. This is also the realm of "right brain–right brain" connection (Schore 2003) or "limbic resonance" (Lewis, Amini & Lannon 2000) which is key in the development of healthy relating.

however, there are other, and inevitable, unspoken expectations that both coach and coachee bring to their encounter, which will not be in their conscious awareness and will be based on past experience of life and relationships. For example, a coachee who has, through bitter experience, concluded that nobody will help him and that to show vulnerability is weakness brings a rather distant, dismissive attitude to the coaching session. The coach feels anxious and slightly humiliated. If she responds to the 'invitation' by trying ineffectually to please the client, from a one-down position, the coaching can then be founded on this destructive bond, repeating what Wachtel (1977) calls the "cyclical dynamics". This sort of transferential relating, if not recognised, can influence the coaching in an adverse way, becoming an enactment of the client's (and almost certainly also the coach's) negative beliefs about themselves in the world. As relational coaches we see it as our task to help our client become aware of how they bring their old patterns into the here-and-now relationship and how those patterns may be contributing to difficulties in their work life. We will also notice how we do the same. The coaching relationship can then become a fertile ground for learning, for experimenting with new relational patterns and for vital feedback.

Another way that the psychological contract can create a destructive outcome is through the unvoiced fears, fantasies or even manipulations that find their way into the coaching, creating what Kapur (1987) called the "bargain agreement". One coachee is 'sent' to coaching in order that the organisation can show 'how hard they tried' to help him, before they reluctantly let him go. Another may come to coaching with the unexpressed goal that it will get his manager off his back. Another client appears to have come voluntarily but has actually been threatened by his team. And so on. It is not unusual for coaches to complain that they are being used as the deliverers of difficult messages, or gentle axe men. All these scenarios are potentially within the conscious awareness of all parties. The simple questions "why me, why now?" "do I really believe I can help?" that the coach asks both himself and the purchaser, can help to avoid such unwelcome situations.

Sometimes the coach and client collude to avoid some fact of reality which is part of their mutual field. The unspoken 'bargain' is "I don't confront you by pointing out this unpalatable fact about your skills or organisation or future, and in return, you will continue to keep me in lucrative work". Surprisingly frequently, a hidden agenda on both sides of the relationship concerns unrealistic expectations of what the coach could and should do. If the professional contract has not been clarified with sufficient care, this hidden agenda becomes built into the coaching dyad, and both parties end up disappointed.

> *Pete and Henry were at risk of getting into a negative psychological contract from the start of their relationship. The lack of clarity about the contract and the feeling that he was holding a secret, made Pete feel very uncomfortable. Henry's bluff and cheerful manner made him seem miles away. At their third session, when Pete suggested the contract to look at the feedback, Henry quickly put two and two together. He looked straight at Pete and said "Colin told me that I might not be up for that promotion to the board. Did you already know?" Pete felt as if he had been caught out by the headmaster. Briefly, he noticed with interest the intensity of his feelings, but he bravely met Henry's gaze. "Yes", he said simply. Henry looked thoughtfully at him. "Why didn't you tell me straight?" he asked. Pete nodded his understanding of this excellent question. He took a moment to reflect. Was it simply that he had felt loyalty to Colin? Or was there something else?*
>
> *"I wanted to check – perhaps I had made a mistake... But there was something else... I think it was because you were so happy", he said at last "I didn't want to spoil it". He smiled ruefully, but Henry was looking very serious. "Yes, I know what you mean" he said slowly. "I was always like that with my father. He was so happy and jolly but if we did something to upset him, he plunged into a depression. We spent our lives tip-toeing around him." He paused, then "I wonder if I am being my father at the office."*
>
> *For some time they discussed Henry's withdrawal behind the bluff cheerfulness that he had learned from his father. Only after the session was over did Pete remember Colin's cheery manner at their first phone call. Was this happy façade an organisational face? Suddenly he had an image of the string quartet playing while the Titanic went down. He resolved to enquire more closely into the organisational culture at their next session.*

CONCLUSION

The aim of this chapter has been to explore some of the range of contractual agreements that coaches and their clients can make together. Whether we, as coaches, opt for making only *administrative contracts* or whether we make explicit contracts for behavioural change, there is a common factor in our contracting. Both explicitly and implicitly, coach and client make a mutual commitment to a relationship which will be in the service of the coachee's growth and development. We aim to create a container that structures and guides some of the many dynamics and expectations of the relationship, without imprisoning and impeding the creativity. The contract is an essential part of the effective working alliance that is the heart of successful coaching.

CHAPTER 8

OUTSIDE FORCES IN THE COACHING ROOM: HOW TO WORK WITH MULTIPARTY CONTRACTS

DAVID SKINNER

ABSTRACT

Coaches choosing to work with executives in large commercial organisations must recognise and accept that they face many dilemmas arising from the influence of relationships *outside* the coaching room. The purpose of this chapter is to explore the potential impact on coaching relationships of organisational politics and interpersonal influences that executive coaches and their coachees might experience during their work together. In the concluding part of this chapter, I draw on field experience to propose pragmatic ways executive coaches might manage the dilemmas they face for the benefit of their coachees, their organisational clients and themselves.

The focus of the exploration is on coaching relationships between executive coachees and those coaches in particular who adopt a relational approach to their clients. Through this relational approach, coaches make an active effort to empathise and understand the subject matter contributed to the here-and-now coaching relationship by the coachee's past and present relationships (De Haan 2008).

In addition, business realities can mean that coaches and coachees will find themselves sharing relationships with the same multiparty stakeholders within the organisation. So, coaches can also bring into the coaching room, unknowingly as well as consciously, their own emotional aspirations, fears and fantasies related to these stakeholders in the organisation. Whether recognised or not, the ebb and flow of complex and messy tensions will surely continue to affect the nature of the relationship between coach and coachee throughout the period of the contract.

In the event that executive coaches successfully demonstrate personal credibility and effectiveness within their targeted client organisations, over time they are likely to win a continuing flow of contracts, and possibly even a range of different types of developmental interventions, from within those same clients – because they become known and trusted by the wider community of line executives involved. In such commercial organisations, particularly multi-national ones, decisions about investment in coaching, funding sign-off and coach selection usually involve a number of people. As a result, each of these individuals will become external stakeholders in coaching relationships, albeit perhaps with differing levels of interest in the conduct and outcome of the coaching process.

In the previous chapter, Charlotte Sills describes the way in which unrecognised psychological contracts and implicit expectations can lead to hidden agendas, both within the coaching room and with the wider stakeholder group. In the back of their minds, some coachees might hope their coach will contribute to their positive-impression management within their employer organisation. Line executives signing off the funding might hope coachees will be persuaded to behave in a way that they think will drive business growth. And some coaches might feel tempted to 'put on a good show' for the people they see as external stakeholders so they win the next piece of work from the client organisation.

CONTEXT – ORGANISATIONAL POLITICS

Regardless of whether they choose to acknowledge it or not, coaches funded by large organisations to work with executive coachees will find themselves operating in a political environment with many powerful stakeholders. At the point of initial administrative contracting some of these stakeholders might not be visible to the coach, or even to the commissioning manager. However, in highly competitive commercial circumstances these stakeholders will, in some way, show an interest and bring their influence to bear on coach and coachee alike before, during and after the administrative contract is enacted.

The political forces from outside the coaching room can have many drivers. For example:

- Line executives are likely enthusiastically to support the growth of their chosen coachee(s). They will be hoping for increased contribution to business performance from them as a direct result of the coaching and their own performance contract will probably include a 'people development' component.

- Corporate policies usually require at least one third party to sign off the financial investment for the coaching. That individual signatory is likely to be in a position of power within the organisational hierarchy. However, once they take the decision to sign off the administrative contract they will carry some sense of accountability and even personal risk related to the success of the coaching work.

- Most line executives will not have had either the time, or perhaps even a reason, to become knowledgeable in detail about the standards and practices that accredited executive coaches typically adopt as a result of their specialised professional education. This can lead to widely differing and unspoken expectations on the part of coachee, coach and external stakeholders about the intended outcomes, boundaries and relationship-management processes involved.

- Others in the organisation might perceive that they might be impacted, either positively or negatively, by any behavioural changes the coachee chooses to make.

- Executives are usually highly competitive and their peers, even though not directly involved in the coaching, might consider it as aiding the chosen coachee to increase their personal power, status or chances of advancement to secure scarce promotion opportunities.

- Continuously turbulent economic conditions might, during the period of the coaching contract, lead to rapidly changing perceptions of the coachee's business performance, even though many of the factors involved are outside the control of the individual.

VIGNETTE 1

"Hi, I'm Laura – new secretary to Rolf, the general manager. He noticed you working in the conference room with Alex earlier and he would like a quick chat with you before you leave.

"[Light-hearted tone] Don't worry, I think he just wants to make sure he is spending his development budget wisely – especially as Alex's business unit is having such a tough time. If you could possibly come up to the top floor right now I could get you 10 minutes or so with Rolf..."

Human nature being what it is, the stakeholders carrying the sense of accountability, personal risk or aspiration for beneficial outcome from the coaching work are likely to try to influence every stage of the process. As a general rule, the higher the level of the coachee in the organisation, the stronger will be the external political forces impacting the relationship between coach and coachee.

THE CORPORATE DECISION-MAKING ENVIRONMENT – BUSINESS REALITIES

For line executives who might commission coaching, particularly in large, sophisticated organisations, the need to achieve ever-increasing productivity while reducing costs is usually a key goal. At the same time they will feel driven to promote and protect their personal brand in the eyes of all the stakeholders whom they perceive as having some influence on their own career advancement.

Due to the typical scale and geographic reach of their organisations, plus the relentless demand for their hour-by-hour attention to operational matters, line executives will be left with much less time than they would want to concentrate on the development of their people. These continuous performance pressures lead to high stress levels and under these conditions people-development decisions are understandably made more frequently on the basis of expediency than deep objective analysis. As a result, while the theory regularly espoused (Argyris 1991) by line executives acknowledges the importance of investment of appropriate resources in people development such as coaching, the theory more realistically in use is – *do what is possible in the short time available, and work if you can with suppliers whom you already know and trust.*

These time and logistical pressures, in addition to the political forces described earlier, can lead line executives to sponsor or initiate coaching activities for their direct reports for any of the following reasons:

- To help the coachee to develop in line with business performance and career development plans

- To demonstrate that as senior leaders they are acting as good corporate citizens in following the company's learning and development strategy

- To reward their direct reports (where the organisational culture views having a coach as a signal of being a high-potential person)

- To absolve themselves of the responsibility of confronting poor performance or non-compliance with expectations or requirements

- To invite external help to resolve relationship tension or conflict with the coachee

- To convey a warning signal that performance is not meeting expectations (where the organisational culture views having a coach as a sign of a remedial need)

- To signal performance values and expectations to the wider team

- To change a communication- or leadership-style approach where the need for change is based on differing cultural expectations

- To build the willingness and/or capability of their team members to share the responsibility of taking on a new challenge with which the senior executive has been tasked by the board.

Regardless of background, the taken-for-granted assumption that senior executives often bring is that coaching will quickly *persuade* their direct report to behave and perform in a way that better meets, or exceeds, their performance expectations. Having made the decision that coaching will produce the desired developmental result, they will usually initiate the coach selection procedure by involving the person within the HR team with whom they feel it is quickest, easiest and most productive for them to interact.

In mature organisations, corporate procedures usually require 'Learning and Development' departments to take responsibility for the design and arrangement of executive coaching programmes. L&D directors, or in some cases human resource vice presidents will be involved in gaining line-executive approval for coaching budgets. They do this by demonstrating – or more accurately, by promising – that hurdle rates of commercial return can be achieved through strategically aligned investment in development programmes of which coaching frequently forms a part. It is at this point that these HR executives become stakeholders in the successful outcome of the coaching.

Without any negative intent on the part of the individuals involved, personality types and interpersonal styles can also start to impact the communication between the line executives and HR leaders involved in the contracting process (Sills & Wide 2006). For example, imagine that the line executive initiating the request for coaching has personality factors leading them to a personal preference for a high degree of affiliation with their peers and superiors. This will probably cause them to work collaboratively with the HR personnel, putting effort into understanding and following agreed corporate procedures for the commissioning of coaches. If they had previously built a trust-based relationship with an external coach or an organisational consultant, then they might use their collaborative approach with HR personnel to influence the selection of that trusted person to provide coaching services for their direct reports.

Alternatively, a line executive with a strong need for personal recognition might, for example, respond to the combination of intense time pressure and corporate politics by operating from a 'rebellious child' ego state (Berne 1966). They might use their position power to push through a coaching strategy, or even choice of individual coach, without sufficient consultation with others who actually carry functional responsibility for coaching policy, budgeting or coach selection.

With the added complexity of differing interpersonal styles and different psychological contracts, implicit expectations and tensions can be established between stakeholders even before coaches are selected or briefed.

ILLUSTRATION

Although not representative of all coach selection and administrative contracting approaches the quote below is intended to illustrate some of the dilemmas and complexity an executive coach might face as they set up and manage coaching contracts. This statement was delivered hurriedly by a Vice President of a multi-national company in a corridor of the corporate headquarters. He was widely respected in the company for his passionate commitment to the success of the business and to the employees whom he supported...

VIGNETTE 2

"Hey David, didn't know you were in – give me a call soon because we need to talk about one of our high-potential guys. You worked with him once in a team session and you seemed to get on alright together. I think he's great but the Chief isn't so sure. Could be a bit of a culture clash really, but you need to sort him out for me – I have a lot riding on his success.

"Oh, and by the way, the Regional Leadership Conference is coming up and you and I need to talk about a design. I've left it late to get started on that but you always pull something out of the hat for us. Must dash, talk to Candice about a date for us to get together..."

It would be interesting to speculate about this particular client's intent based on the nature or content of this quote. However, it is essential for coaches operating in such circumstances to be sensitive to the potential implications for the eventual coaching relationship emanating from the spoken and unspoken messages in communication like this.

RELATIONSHIP BETWEEN COACHEES AND THEIR EXTERNAL STAKEHOLDERS

Potential coachees in large organisations generally perceive the news that they will be given a coach as a signal of their status (Rock 2009) in the eyes of their line executives. If the prevailing norms and beliefs in the organisational culture position coaching as a positive signal, then the coachee will usually become enthusiastically involved in the coach selection process. He or she will work either through official or unofficial channels to influence the choice of coach that they believe will be most beneficial to them.

Despite the best efforts of coaches to maintain client confidentiality, gossip within the organisation will usually imbue them with a personal brand and projected position within the corporate hierarchy. Typically, the unwritten rules of the game (Scott-Morgan 1994) imply that coachees have higher status if they are seen to be coached by individuals who are already known to be well established in coaching senior executives within their organisations.

If they secure a coach that they believe sends the right signals about their personal status, coachees will then often use subtle means to share within the organisation any detail regarding their coaching relationship about which they feel positive. In no time this largely invisible communication process can conspire to create a positive reputation for the coach which is not necessarily based on the efficacy of the service they actually provide.

Conversely, in organisational circumstances where the engagement of a coach is taken as a signal suggesting that line executives see coachees as having a remedial need, those nominated to be coached can attempt to undermine the coach selection process. Some might even encourage selection of a coach whom they construct as most likely to collude with them to show their line executives that coaching was not necessary for them in the first place.

PERSPECTIVE OF THE COACH

Executive coaches wanting to build their practices in large client organisations will soon find that their personal success results as much from selling themselves effectively as it does from delivering their coaching service effectively and ethically. The successful coach is likely to be comfortable taking the initiative to network within their target organisations to prospect for fee-paying work. He or she will probably consider that deep knowledge of the organisation's culture, decision-making processes, internal political forces, unwritten values and rules, business aims and challenges, as well as trust-based relationships at all levels will be a key advantage to help them be frequently contracted into the coaching room.

Providing they use this knowledge of the organisation in a mutually beneficial way they are likely to be trusted by key executives. As a result, given the time pressures impacting executive decision-making processes, such coaches are likely to be selected as vendors of choice from the wider range of possibly unknown and untried alternatives available. Contracts can continue to be awarded over many years on this basis and so the coach will naturally come to see the organisation as an 'important customer'.

Tenbrunsel et al. (2010) describe the existence of a cognitive bias they call "bounded ethicality". They show that where circumstances are uncertain or stressful, for example, because of the potential for large gains or losses from important customers, then individuals are likely to predict that they will behave more ethically than they in fact do. And when reflecting on their behaviour after the event, they are likely to assess that they behaved more ethically than they did.

VIGNETTE 3

Maxine prides herself on her very strong commitment to maintain confidentially and boundaries with all the clients she has coached over the years within MultiCo Inc. She knows she is trusted because the CEO and other members of his team tell her so quite regularly.

One day the HR VP sees Maxine in the car park and asks, "How's your work going with our problem-child finance guy in Spain then?" Maxine looks slightly skywards, rolls her eyes and replies, "Oh please, just don't ask"... Then she grins cheekily and walks away. The following day Maxine emphasises to her supervisor how hard she works to maintain boundaries in the organisations she works in.

IMPLICATIONS FOR THE COACHING RELATIONSHIP

The external factors described here will act strongly on both the coachee and the coach as their relationship develops and grows. Despite their best intentions, any coach would be naive to believe that they can simply establish some kind of "three-way contract" (English,1975) once and for all at the beginning of a relationship with an executive in a large organisation – and then be left alone to manage it without external interference. Especially when they are working to win new contracts within a client organisation, executive coaches need to be mindful of stakeholder expectations that might develop as a result of their personal interactions or reputational influences. These stakeholder expectations are almost certain to come back to haunt their relationships when they start to work with coachees.

VIGNETTE 4

"Oh hello, so you're the coach working with one of my team in the marketing department. I signed off the budget for the coaching because I'd heard you always produced results really fast. Not heard about much change in the marketing guy yet, and we are already a couple of months in... let's talk about it shall we?"

Line executives accountable for the funding and commissioning managers who originally conduct the coach selection and administrative contracting might behave in a way that has a positive effect once the coaching is underway. They might conspicuously demonstrate their efforts to respect the procedural and behavioural standards and boundaries agreed with the coach and the coachee during the initial contracting discussions. This behaviour should hopefully have an encouraging effect on the quality of one-to-one learning that goes on in the coaching room.

Alternatively, external stakeholders might be driven either unknowingly or deliberately to behave in response to personal goals, fears or aspirations regarding the coaching relationship. Overly enthusiastic line executives can, for example, show excessive interest in the progress of the coaching and this can be perceived within the coaching room as pressure to meet certain growth expectations that might never have been contracted with the coachee in the first place.

Coachees will probably notice this intense external stakeholder interest and their willingness to open up in the coaching room might be affected, even if they have an underlying level of trust in the integrity of the coach and their commitment to confidentiality.

Influences with potentially positive or negative effects on the coaching relationship can be targeted by stakeholders towards the coachee or the coach driven by motivations of which those stakeholders are not consciously aware. For example, if any of the commissioning managers is operating from the psychological role of 'persecutor' (Karpman 1971) then they are likely to apply more negative pressures to the coaching dyad itself, or to attempt to undermine the perception of the coaching relationship within the wider stakeholder group.

VIGNETTE 5

"Even though people say she is a high performer this girl really needs to change her ways – I'm tired of hearing everyone complaining about her arrogance. Her line manager won't do anything so I'm going to confront her, for her own good of course – and you need to help me with that."

On the other hand, commissioning managers operating unknowingly with a 'rescuer' tendency (Karpman 1971) will possibly try to offer uninvited help to support the coaching process – or engage in positive impression management about it within the wider organisational context.

VIGNETTE 6

"Ahmed is a really great guy. He has always put his heart and soul into the business and he's built up teams for us over the years in some of the toughest emerging markets. Because of his promotion he has to operate in the head-office environment now and I'm watching his back while he smoothes off some of his rough edges. I know you coach his boss too, so perhaps you could put in a good word for him... but only when it seems appropriate... don't make it too obvious. I usually find a way to do it for him myself during exec meetings, but people listen to you more sometimes because you are an outsider..."

External stakeholders will sometimes create their own psychological contract that the coach is going to persuade the coachee to change their behaviour in a way that will quickly show up in measurably improved business results. This can lead to a sense of disappointment quite soon in the life of the relationship. Powerful stakeholders with this perception can view the coach as 'letting them down' and will sometimes make ulterior references to the potential for future work for the coach within the organisation if persuasion of the coachee is not soon evident.

As described earlier, perceptions and evaluations of them by the external stakeholder group are usually of central importance to the executive coachee. As a result they will surely bring their own mental construct of the organisational forces acting on them into the coaching room. The degree to which they construct their key stakeholders as being positively supportive, or potentially threatening towards them, will in turn influence the way they react to their external influences on the coaching relationship.

Executive coachees will almost certainly want their coach to help them with some degree of impression management with their stakeholder group – even if they do not overtly include this wish in the contract. This could be anywhere along a spectrum from an un-healthy attitude expressed as "I don't really want to change, I just want to make my bosses like me" through to "The way I will prosper in the company is to demonstrate my capacity to learn and grow in line with a carefully aligned personal development plan".

Coachees with a negative assessment of their stakeholders might take longer to build trust with their coach and so might require an extended time before they are prepared to talk openly – in case anything inadvertently leaks from the coaching room to their stakeholders, despite assurances of confidentiality from the coach.

Coachees with a positive perception of their stakeholders might be keen to share their thoughts and experiences and will, on occasions, even invite some of those stakeholders into their discussions in the coaching room

– possibly to 'show how well they are doing'. Interestingly, this positivity can lead to scope-creep* from the original focus of the coaching contract. Invitations from the coachee such as "Why don't you come and talk to my team about this because they can benefit too" can potentially be seductive for the coach, but can at the same time lead to loss of focus and unintended boundary crossing.

PRAGMATIC APPROACHES TO MANAGING THE DILEMMAS

As we have seen from the exploration so far, political influences, organisational time and performance pressures, complex decision-making processes, interpersonal style differences, psychological contracting and cognitive biases are among the many possible factors that can lead to differing implicit expectations and resulting stakeholder influences on coaching relationships.

External interest in the coaching work will not come to a stop when the administrative contract is signed. In different ways this interest will continue throughout the life of the work and, given the perceptions or sensitivities of the coach or the coachee, at any point the impact can be either positive or negative.

For reasons already described, organisational clients generally want to commission coaches they feel they can trust and so they prefer to commit to suppliers who already know their organisation and have established personal credibility with key stakeholders. Coaches who establish themselves as favoured suppliers within a client organisation might find that they are in a highly lucrative position with significant potential for future growth in their income as well as professional fulfilment from the work. In these circumstances their own cognitive biases will surely bring temptations and have some effect on their judgement that reference to boundaries and codes of conduct alone might not be able fully to mitigate.

So, coaches choosing to work with executives in large commercial organisations do well to recognise and accept that they face many dilemmas arising from the influence of relationships outside the coaching room.

The experience-based guidance that follows is intended as a pragmatic approach to meeting the needs, and sometimes competing expectations, of the various multi-party stakeholders outside the coaching room – with the sole intent of maximising the value and ethical maturity of the work that goes on within it.

---

* 'Scope creep' is a term originating in the project management function. It refers to a phenomenon where uncontrolled additions to a project's objectives evolve without approved additions to budgets or time deadlines.

Executive coaches should find it beneficial to themselves, their organisational clients and their individual coachees if they:

- Accept that they have a professional duty to the organisational client providing the funding as well as to the individual coachee

- Approach multi-party contracting not as a one-time event at the beginning of the contract, but rather as a continuing and evolving process requiring vigilance and regular re-negotiation with interested parties to maintain alignment in the turbulent commercial environment (see Vignette 1 as a practical example of where this approach would be key for continuing mutual benefit of all parties involved)

- Build their self-awareness so they can recognise and better manage their own perceptual, emotional and behavioural patterns as well as the impact of their communication in response to the stresses and temptations they might experience when dealing with complex, politically charged dilemmas (see Vignettes 2 and 3 as examples of situations emphasising the importance of deep reflection by the coach, taking account of regular client feedback, to ensure their sensitivity to the potential impact of communications – their own, as well as those of their stakeholders)

- Work diligently during the phase before administrative contracting to identify the external stakeholders and understand as much as possible about their business as well as personal interests that relate to the conduct and outcome of the coaching

- Take account of the personal style and behavioural preferences of stakeholders where possible – thereby better enabling them to assess the probable intent as well the impact of those stakeholders on their coaching relationships

- Recognise and surface for productive discussion at an early stage any implicit expectation by external stakeholders that the coaching will be used to persuade the coachee; note that the coach should not take personal responsibility to protect the coachee from this attempted persuasion – experience shows that coachees might well choose to be persuaded to perform in a certain way if they feel this is in line with legitimate corporate expectations, and it might aid their chances of advancement in the organisation (see Vignette 4 as a practical example of how stakeholder expectations might be communicated to the coach in a potentially unsettling way)

- Remain mindful that their focus should be first on adding value through support for learning and growth in the client organisation avoiding any fixation on what might be their own process preferences or future business-development opportunities

- Pay attention, notice and raise through discussion first with the coachee any perception of external interference that either party assesses as having a negative impact on the progress of the coaching relationship (see Vignettes 5 and 6 illustrating examples of very different causes of such interference)

- Use supervision to be watchful for any boundary crossings or violations they may feel coerced or tempted into committing through application of external influence; remember that, by its very nature as a cognitive bias, their own tendency for bounded ethicality is difficult for any professional to identify without the involvement of a trusted third party.

CONCLUSION

Executive coaches need to realise that in coaching an executive while being funded by their organisation they are making an intervention in a complex adaptive system – even though they might not feel comfortable seeing it that way. As a result of their entry into a multi-party system, forces will be applied continuously from outside the coaching room on both the coachee and the coach.

The coach does not serve his or her various client stakeholders well by simply adhering with positive intent to boundaries or codes of conduct. Business realities frequently drive those stakeholders to behave in unexpected ways and not necessarily the way the coach feels that they 'should'.

One way for the coach to address the dilemmas they might face in any intervention is to refuse to engage in relationships outside the coaching room once initial administrative contracting is complete. A coach taking this approach might feel they are respecting and protecting their own professional standards. However, in the event they will probably discover that they do not actually serve any of their stakeholders interests well – and as a result they are unlikely to win continuing work from the commercial organisation.

On the other hand, coaches who do choose to engage widely with the client organisation must notice and have the courage to respond effectively to any influences from outside the coaching room that negatively impact their ability to support productive learning and personal growth for coachees – balancing the best interests of that organisational client as well.

CHAPTER 9

THE SUPERVISORY RELATIONSHIP IN EXECUTIVE COACHING

MICHAEL CARROLL AND ROBERT MOORE

INTRODUCTION

Sarah has been coaching John for several months now and notices that she always comes away from the coaching sessions with a depressed feeling. With her other clients she regularly experiences a great deal of hope as they structure a way forward in the areas of their lives they want to transform. John too envisages a great future returning to each session with reports of what he has achieved. Yet Sarah continues to have overwhelming feelings of lethargy after the sessions. She notices also that she is beginning to question her career choice as an executive coach.

In coaching supervision two things happen. First of all, Sarah's supervisor, Suzanne, also experiences tiredness during their supervision session and a feeling of inadequacy to meet Sarah's needs. She is alert enough to monitor and articulate this in the session as an open enquiry and without making Sarah feel she is causing these reactions within Suzanne. As part of this openness to what is happening, Sarah is introduced to the idea of empathic resonance – perhaps she is experiencing something of an unspoken sense of hopelessness that John does not speak about yet communicates emotionally. Perhaps Sarah's questioning of herself was similar to internal questions John carried about his own choice, as was Suzanne's questioning of herself. Sarah and Suzanne trace a theme running through the whole system and initiated by John. Each of the participants is infected with the mood and the inner world of the others and in each co-created space (the coaching relationship, the coaching supervision relationship) a similar dynamic is played out – the dynamic of depression and inadequacy.

As a result of supervision, Sarah focuses more on building her relationship with John who gradually admits that the change he reports is not entirely true. He speaks of a series of shaming experiences he had in school that left him with a profound sense of sadness that his dreams could not be realised. What facilitates change for John is Sarah's openness to the relationship that she explores in supervision to unfold emotional insight and her openness to what is happening between her and her coaching supervisor. She has Suzanne access a series of tools for managing emotions and relationships that help John to let go of the old convictions and begin opening to new possibilities.

The vignette above captures some of the dynamics we want to focus on in this chapter. Our central tenet is that the relationship between coach and supervisor provides the emotional containment that sets off the reflective process which in turn leads to learning from what has happened in the coaching arrangement. We will look at several arenas that interweave throughout the relationship in coaching supervision: the relationship between coach and supervisor reflects and parallels the relationship between coach and coachee; the emotions engendered in the coach, in the supervisor and between them become sources of vital information about what is happening 'out there' in the coaching relationship.

We link the supervision relationship with empathic resonance and provide coaching supervisors with a process framework for making the most of the supervisory relationship. The focus will then change to the increasing role and importance of supervision in executive coaching and will define what coaching supervision means. Finally the article will concentrate on the supervisory relationship in executive coaching, what it means and how it becomes the foundation stone of learning for supervisees. Using insights from the doctoral research of Robert Moore (2008), the article will suggest that the initial point of learning in coaching supervision is the actual supervisory relationship itself as expressed through emotional resonance.

What is meant by 'supervision'?

At its simplest, supervision is a forum where supervisees (in this case executive coaches) review and reflect on their work in order to do it better. Coaches bring their practice to another person (individual supervision) or to a group (small group or team supervision) and with their help review what happened in their practice in order to learn from that experience. Ultimately, supervision is for better coaching work. In a relationship of trust and transparency, supervisees talk about their work and through reflection and thoughtfulness learn from it and return to do it differently. Supervision is based on the assumption that reflecting on work provides the basis for learning from that work and doing it more creatively (Bolton 2001; King & Strohm-Kitchener 1994; Moon 1999).

Ryan (2004) puts it well:

> Supervision is an inquiry into practice. It is a compassionate appreciative inquiry.... In supervision we re-write the stories of our own practice... supervision interrupts practice. It wakes us up to what we are doing. When we are alive to what we are doing we wake up to what is, instead of falling asleep in the comfort stories of our clinical routines.
>
> (p. 44)

Executive coaching supervision is a form of experiential learning. Supervision is reflection-on-action or indeed, reflection-in-action to result in reflection-for-action.

Hawkins and Smith (2006) emphasise the systemic view of coaching supervision when they write:

> Coaching supervision is the process by which a Coach with the help of a Supervisor, who is not working directly with the Client, can attend to understanding better both the Client System and themselves as part of the Client–Coach system, and by so doing transform their work. It also allows the coach to discover where he or she is not currently creating the shift for the benefit of the client and client organisation.

SUPERVISION IN EXECUTIVE COACHING

Recently, supervision is being applied to the various fields of coaching and in particular executive coaching (Hawkins & Smith 2006). However, quite rightly, coaching psychology is wary of transferring models of supervision pertinent to other professions into the coaching arena. Pampallis-Paisley (2006) asks a key question here: "whether the existing models of supervision are sufficient for the demands of coaching" and answers it with a "both... and...". Coaching supervision can borrow elements and models from supervision as applied to other professions and there is room to look at coaching as "a distinctive enough discipline to require a particular frame of supervision and a particular theory to support this". What is the added value supervision can give to executive coaching keeping in mind "the need for multiple layers and levels of complexity that the executive coach finds him or herself in when working in organisations" (Pampallis-Paisley 2006)?

THE RELATIONSHIP IN SUPERVISION (AN OVERVIEW)

Donovan (private paper) summarises the research involved in the triadic relationship of supervisor, supervisee and client:

Relationships have been demonstrated to contribute significantly to the success or difficulties of the triadic system involved in client treatment. There is evidence of the importance of relationship in: the relationship between supervisor and supervisee (e.g. Mueller & Kell 1972; Holloway 1995; Worthen & McNeill 1996); the therapeutic relationship between supervisee/therapist and client (e.g. Horvath & Symonds 1991; Orlinsky, Grawe & Parks 1994; Martin, Garske & Davis 2000); and the link between supervisory and therapeutic relationships (Patton & Kivlighan 1997).

Despite the positive tone of Donovan's stance, Milne (2009) points out, quite rightly, that "evidence to support the assumption (the importance of the supervisory alliance) is surprisingly wanting... it is embarrassing that there is such a deficiency in the research sphere" (p. 93). So while this chapter cannot build on a strong evidence-based bedrock of research into the importance and relevance of the supervisory relationship within executive coaching, it can certainly continue conversations already begun.

Relationships entail a large number of factors, which at different times have been emphasised within the general field of supervision (although not all have been tested or applied in the supervision of coaching and executive coaching):

Emotional engagement
- ∞ The relationship is a container for emotions (Moore 2008; Dixon 2009)

- ∞ Relationships involve emotional engagement (Holloway 1995)

- ∞ The relationship is one where the supervisor provides empathy and acceptance (Moore 2008; Carroll & Gilbert 2005; Rogers 1995)

Power and boundaries
- ∞ Power is an essential aspect of supervisory relationships and needs careful attention especially when evaluation and assessment is part of the relationship (Holloway 1995)

- ∞ Professional relationships need clear boundaries

- ∞ Relationships involve a number of roles and responsibilities which need to be clarified (Carroll 1996; Holloway 1995)

Developmental stages and contexts

∞ Supervisory relationships go through a number of stages (Holloway 1995; Pelling & Agostinelle 2009)

∞ Relationships take place in contexts that impact on them and differences between the various partners need consideration and accommodation (e.g. race, culture, sexual orientation etc.) (Authur & Collins 2009)

∞ Parallel process is a systemic part of relationships in supervision and takes place when one system (the coaching one) is replicated in another system (the supervision one). Supervisees re-enact in supervision what happened in the coaching relationship often without being aware of it (Dixon 2009)

Challenge and growth through healthy relationship

∞ Relationships involve trust and reciprocity (Safran & Muran 2000)

∞ Ruptures and interruptions to supervisory and coaching relationships are not uncommon and if handled well can strengthen the relationship (De Haan 2008c)

∞ Relationships can be detrimental and harmful to supervisees as well as being helpful and supportive of professional development (Nelson & Friedlander 2001)

∞ Support and challenge are the twin skills offered by the supervisor (Carroll & Gilbert 2005)

From the above it is easy to see how complicated relationships are: hence the difficulty in studying and researching them. In this chapter we want to focus on the role of emotions in coaching supervision. Like all other relationships, coaching is an emotional experience and supervision is emerging as a crucial factor in facilitating learning for coaching practitioners as they reflect on this emotional encounter with their clients. Supervision too is fundamentally an emotional experience. In fact, if it isn't an emotional experience then it can easily degenerate into a monologue with one person attempting to manipulate another.

Moore's doctoral research (2008) has built a bridge between the emotional connections within work or practice and the experience of supervision providing a solid foundation for exploring emotions and relationship in coaching supervision.

THE PROCESS MODEL FOR MANAGING EMOTION IN THE SUPERVISORY RELATIONSHIP

This process model, as a boundaried yet flexible container, offers a tool for reflexive learning that can be used to explore in greater depth some aspect of the supervisory process to which other models draw our attention (Page & Wosket 1994; Holloway 1995).

THE PROCESS FRAMEWORK – AN OVERVIEW

By way of example we will draw on an experience of coaching supervision with a female supervisee (Eileen) who, as an executive coach, presented her work with a male departmental director in a large bank (Ousep). For ease of reading we will refer throughout to the departmental director, Ousep, as the 'coachee'; the executive coach, Eileen, as the 'supervisee'; and the coaching supervisor, Esme, as the 'supervisor'. However, some background is needed to help the reader (and indeed the supervisor). Ousep has recently been promoted to departmental head within a large bank where his new role entails him managing a large international team (there are offices in London, New York and Tokyo). His boss (Vivienne) suggested he use their appointed executive-coaching company to help him in the first three months of engaging with his new role. He interviewed three coaches and opted to work with Eileen. Eileen is not quite sure why he chose her but she imagines it's because she combines a warm style with firm feedback. She had mentioned the cultural difference between them (she comes from Britain and Ousep was raised and educated in Pakistan) and wondered how gender and race difference might impact their relationship and work together. Ousep felt strongly that neither would be a negative influence.

In their initial meeting, Ousep talked firstly about his fears for the future (the bank has been part of the downturn and credit crunch fallout) and there is some talk of redundancies. Secondly, he expressed his anger at not getting his bonus – while the bank has done poorly overall, his department has done quite well. Thirdly, he shared his frustrations working with the present team he has inherited and also his frustrations in working with his boss (Vivienne) whom he feels doesn't give him enough responsibility. Vivienne has been giving him feedback about his poor delegation and communication skills (one of the reasons she suggested coaching).

After the first meeting, Eileen received no contact from Ousep. She was expecting 'homework' from him: some surveys, a psychometric test. There was no response to her emails and their subsequent arranged meeting was cancelled the day before due to his heavy schedule. She is beginning to feel 'messed about' and wonders about Ousep's commitment and investment in coaching.

We focus here on the importance of the learning relationship between the supervisor and the supervisee. Within this learning agreement the supervisee continues to think in terms of her coaching practice and the supervisor (while a practising coach herself) thinks primarily as a facilitator of learning. Figure 1 portrays the process framework as incorporating a cycle of reflection occurring between cycles of experience within an emotionally containing relationship. The grey boxes trace the coachee's journey into and between professional encounters, the clear boxes trace the reflexive journey of the supervisee while the two-tone boxes represent where the two paths meet.

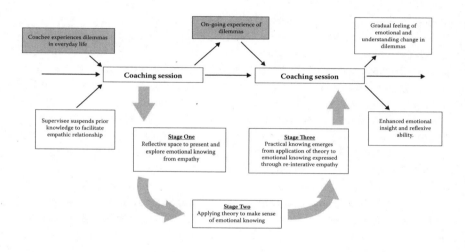

Figure 1. Process framework for learning in supervision

The coachee (Ousep) brought dilemmas from his practice along with the emotions that these challenges stirred in him (frustration, anger and fear) to the first coaching session. The supervisee (Eileen) initially adopted a stance of empathic openness to the encounter with Ousep. This first phase of the work was predominantly experiential and consequently Eileen experienced some of her coachee's frustration, anger and fear noticing how her own levels of stress and anxiety similarly increased. So too does the supervisor (Esme). In the first supervision session when Eileen presents Ousep, Esme also picks up and begins to feel frustration, anger, confusion and fear. Not having entered the supervisory session with these feelings, she knows they come from the relational space between herself and Eileen. She guesses that they are neither hers nor Eileen's and presumes they belong with Ousep. In

131

articulating and beginning to look at where and how these feelings have invaded the supervisory room, both participants realise that they are carrying (in their relationship) similar themes to what is occurring in the relationship between Eileen and Ousep.

While these feelings are overwhelming for the coachee, supervision offers the supervisee a reflexive space to explore the empathic impact and draw meaning out of it. Supervision also provides a relationship forum to look in some detail at what is happening between supervisee and supervisor that reflects the relationship between supervisee and coachee. The supervisee requires a high degree of self-awareness to differentiate between those feelings arising from her own experiences and those 'given to her in empathy'. Since empathic feelings always belong to both participants, rather than simply one or the other, the reflective task is one of discerning which is the predominant source. It is seldom easy to acknowledge the intense emotions that supervisees can experience empathically and so the supervisee requires a safe, inquiring rather than harshly critical supervisory space. Exploring the emotional impact in depth (as it applies in both systems) and applying her theoretical understanding helps the supervisee to make sense of her own emotions and gain insight into the client's dilemmas. This second phase is principally about understanding and learning to "think feelingly" (Assagioli 1985) as experience is reflected on in the light of theory.

The meaning that emerges draws the supervisee towards the kind of interventions that might communicate emotional understanding to her coachee. Having that emotional understanding modelled by Esme has helped Eileen enormously. Esme has been able to stop, review what is happening to herself and locate the source of the feelings within the relationship with Eileen, understanding how those reactions have been brought from the coaching relationship. She also started to help herself and Eileen own what is theirs and what belongs within another system and to another individual (Ousep).

At this point it is important for Eileen to remember that Ousep has not gone through this reflexive process having meanwhile returned to the on-going experience of life as a department director. While the next coaching session is a fresh experience, it is one into which the supervisee can bring a new emotional sensitivity to her coachee. Engaging at a deeper emotional level provides containment and through reiterative empathy (Stein 1916) Ousep gradually experiences an emotional containment of his anxieties. This third phase of practical intervention is informed by the understanding that has emerged from reflection on the emotional experience. The supervisee meanwhile continues to allow the coachee's emotions to impact on her, attending carefully to the subtle differences in each coaching session. The process framework does not seek to lessen the impact of emotional connection and coaches of many years practice will continue to experience intense feelings when coachees bring their anxieties to them. Over time they will have an enhanced capacity to tolerate and work creatively with strong emotions.

In summary, the role of the supervisor is to facilitate learning environments within a containing relationship where the supervisee can develop her ways of knowing through three dynamic learning stages: a) experience (primarily through empathy), b) understanding (informed by empathic experience and coaching literature) and c) applying knowledge (enhanced through re-iterative empathy) as portrayed in Figure 2.

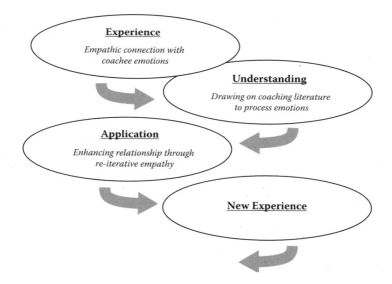

Figure 2. Three stages of process framework

Supervision provides opportunities for reflection-in-action which moves from practice (Schön 1983; 1987) to reflexivity (Alvesson & Skoldberg 2000). The term 'reflection' can also be used to indicate a reflective stance towards experiences in any of the three stages. Reflexivity draws our attention to the dynamic, interactive process of learning that unfolds across all three stages. Firstly, the crucial component of Eileen's emotional encounter with Ousep and what it communicates to her about his dilemmas. Secondly, the way in which her theories of coaching have prepared her to help Ousep make meaning out of his experiences. Thirdly, how she draws on this emotional and theoretical awareness to communicate a deeper understanding of her coachee's struggles. To achieve this, the supervisee becomes active at multiple levels of intelligence and knowledge development, as outlined in Figure 3. In this way the reflexive supervisory relationship replicates the practical working relationship that the supervisee has with her client.

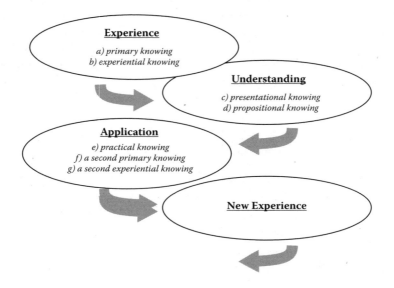

Figure 3. Reflexive deepening of supervisee knowing

The outline used is summarised below:

STAGE ONE

∞ *primary knowing* (suspension of prior knowledge) that facilitates the supervisee's openness to empathic impact (Scharmer 2007)

∞ *experiential knowing* that differentiates between feelings arising from herself and those given to her empathically by the client

STAGE TWO

∞ *presentational knowing* that allows her to present the client's emotions in the supervisory space

∞ *propositional knowing* that consists of her capacity to apply theoretical perspectives to the empathic experience

STAGE THREE

- ∞ *practical knowing* that allows her to apply the understanding in a way that is helpful for the client through reiterative empathy

- ∞ a second *primary knowing* reminds her that the client has not undertaken this reflexive journey and he needs to be open to what she brings rather than impose his potential insights and finally

- ∞ a second *experiential knowing* that is sensitive to the subtle changes in the emotional experience of the client as she receives his reiterated empathic communication.

FACILITATING LEARNING IN COACHING SUPERVISION

STAGE ONE – EXPERIENCE: AN OPEN MIND AND AN OPEN HEART FOR EMPATHIC RESONANCE

We will use the example outlined above to illustrate the stages of the supervisory relationship and how the relationship facilitates both containment and learning.

It is useful at this beginning stage for the supervisee (Eileen) to introduce her coachee (Ousep) simply by saying that he is a male departmental director whom she has seen for two sessions. She might want to state briefly the feelings she has been left with after the last coaching session. Supervisees often think that supervisors need to have all the information and life story that they have and much supervision time is taken up by details rather than substance. Suspending the need to know everything allows both supervisor and supervisee to get to the underlying emotional experience much quicker.

The supervisee is encouraged to reflect on the emotional impact that Ousep has had on her. This might be by way of a quiet reflective time at the beginning of the session in which the supervisee goes back to the point of the last coaching session and becomes aware of the feelings stirred in her at the time. Alternatively the supervisor might use guided imagery to allow an image to emerge in the mind of the supervisee from the feelings she is aware of in herself as she sits with the coachee. Emotional intelligence is important as the supervisee differentiates the range of feelings that are familiar to her and those that feel unusual and may be a communication from the coachee (Stein 1916). Alternatively the supervisee might spend some time in preparation for supervision so that what she brings into the learning space is a symbol or drawing that reflects the emotions she experiences with the coachee or a written description on the feelings.

> Eileen prepares for her coaching supervision session by spending time reflecting on what has happened within and after the first coaching session. She monitors both Ousep's feelings of fear, frustration and anger and realises that her own feelings somewhat mirror his. She too is feeling angry with him for not being more responsible in getting his work to her and in managing his time. She is feeling frustrated that he is not letting her work with him. Similarly Esme, the supervisor, reflects in preparation on what is unfolding within the supervisory relationship. She is finding Eileen very keen to develop her coaching practice yet resistant to bringing difficulties and challenges into the supervisory space. Esme is feeling kept at a distance by Eileen. As supervisor, Esme will bring a philosophy of learning to the next supervision session that can acknowledge these feelings in a non-shaming manner. This will allow Eileen to explore her experiences within the safety of the supervisory relationship.

The supervisee is engaged in primary knowing that suspends the judgements coming from her previous knowledge of Ousep in order to be open to the emotional knowing that arises from his communications in the present moment. The next task then is to bring that emotional awareness into the supervisory space and conversation with the supervisor.

STAGE TWO – UNDERSTANDING: WEAR YOUR THEORY LIGHTLY BUT DON'T GO WITHOUT IT

Presentational knowing is the supervisee's task of giving expression in supervision to her emotional knowledge. This too can be a challenge for supervisees who often want to talk about what they are thinking when with the client or what they want to do by way of practical intervention. Rothschild (2006) reminds us that neurological studies associate empathy with the motor division of the peripheral nervous system. The motor division controls movement and action so it is not surprising that supervisees in the throes of emotional experiences want to move quickly to solutions. The reflective space in supervision provides an opportunity to slow the process down and put words to the emotions.

> In the coaching supervision session, Eileen shares her thoughts and feelings about what is happening to Ousep within his system, what is happening between herself and Ousep, and what is happening to her. When Esme identifies how these feelings also resonate within the supervisory relationship, Eileen can adopt a different, reflective stance on them. The containment of the supervision relationship now allows her to see these four subsystems as intertwined and somewhat separate as well. She is able to connect her own feelings to an overall feeling of what success means for her as a coach and

how lack of contact with Ousep impacts on her feelings of rejection and isolation. She wonders if this is also how Ousep feels. This understanding eases the intensity of the feelings Eileen was struggling with and reiterative empathy describes how she communicates an emotional understanding to Ousep. Eileen's capacity to do this is a product of the non-shaming supervisory relationship in which feelings are acknowledged, explored and understood as opposed to judged or denied.

Empathic resonance can add a depth of insight to the dilemmas that the coachee brings verbally to the coaching session. We might think of the words and body language as the text of the session while the emotions form the sub-text. In the supervision space the supervisee is able to put the text and sub-text together to enrich her understanding of what the client is struggling with. At this point the supervisee is able to draw on the wider coachee material in a much more informed, focused and useful way.

Eileen sets up a phone call with Ousep and suggests they have a review. He insists he wants to continue the coaching arrangement and is committed to it but that his schedule is not allowing him to take time off. Eileen uses her empathic insights to acknowledge his feelings and shares that she too has similar feelings. This seems to unblock something in Ousep who immediately sets up another appointment and keeps it. Still no homework forthcoming, however. In their second meeting, Eileen helps Ousep see that he is actually ambivalent about coaching: on one hand he wants it and on the other hand he is quite frightened about what it might reveal to him that he would best not know. They use the image of a tightrope as a metaphor of where he is. Eileen connects this to what is happening in his life and that perhaps ambivalence is a theme he is working with and one that might be communicating itself to others in the bank.

Our understanding of empathy suggests that anyone the client meets with in his life will resonate with much the same feelings as the supervisee. The difference here is that the supervisee is a trained coach and is going to bring her propositional knowledge from the world of coaching to help the client make meaning out of his at times very troubling experiences.

Having slowed down sufficiently to engage emotionally with Ousep and his dilemma, the supervisee can now wonder how she needs to be with him in the light of the knowledge generated in the reflective process.

STAGE THREE – PRACTICAL APPLICATION: IT'S HOW YOU SAY WHAT YOU SAY THAT MATTERS

In the light of emotional knowing and theoretical understanding, the supervisee can consider how she needs to be with Ousep in the next session. Re-iterative empathy (Stein 1916) describes the way in which the feelings the supervisee has about her coachee have transformed through her reflective time. She carries a qualitatively richer emotional sensitivity to her coachee into the next coaching session. The confusing feelings of fear, frustration and anger have been modified through empathic containment and insights into their significance for Ousep. He in turn experiences this as a deeper level of acceptance and understanding that helps contain the dilemmas he struggles with. The process framework reminds us that the coachee has not gone through this reflective phase since, meanwhile, he has returned to the life experiences that he is bringing to the supervisee. It is again important for the supervisee to suspend any judgements about the learning that has emerged in order to be open to how the coachee is at the next coaching session.

> In her next coaching session, Eileen is much more relaxed about her involvement with Ousep. Rather than feeling angry and frustrated with him, she helps Ousep get in touch with and articulate several major themes in his life: his working with women, especially when that woman is his boss; his ambivalence about being involved and not being involved (with coaching); and his reluctance to give up control. He sees the implications for these in his work and indeed in his life. Eileen begins to help him devise strategies for dealing with them in a more positive way. Eileen is, of course, mirroring what happened in her supervision session with Esme. Esme helped her look at her feelings of inadequacy and frustration by articulating what was happening to her (Esme) in an open, transparent manner.

Our example above illustrates the steps and stages of the process model of coaching supervision. It goes beneath the problems and the words to the emotional impact generated within supervision and uses that impact as a conduit for articulating and dealing with the themes and problems brought by coachees. It also looks at the supervisory co-created space as a wonderful forum for reflection on how the supervisory relationship itself carries and hopefully, contains what is unconsciously communicated through the supervisee.

CONCLUSION

This article has reviewed the centrality of the relationship in coaching supervision. The relationship has been seen as primarily an emotional connection and container between supervisor and supervisee where the supervisor provides an engagement, an environment and experiences that allow the supervisee to work with the impact of her work on herself both personally and professionally. With that emotional connection and containment comes security in supervision that allows more open reflection and new awareness to enter the coaching system. Shifts within the supervisee occur in the supervision session as she allows her feelings to emerge, connects them to her relationship with her coachee and uses her knowledge and prior experience to create narratives that explain what is happening. Her work with her coachee becomes an action-inquiry research project within supervision where a safe and protected supervisory relationship allows transparency and openness to new ideas and thoughts and feelings.

Martin Buber once remarked that "all learning takes place in relationship" (1965, p. xiv). Our belief is that this applies both to coaching and to coaching supervision.

PART IV

INQUIRING INTO THE COACHING RELATIONSHIP

This section of the book contains the following chapters:

This part of the book contains three explorations of coaching relationship dynamics where a microscope is focussed onto this intimate bond. John Nuttall gives an overview of all the ways in which a relationship can be experienced as meaningful, locating this relational thinking within established concepts such as working alliance, attachment, transference and the parallel process. Simon Cavicchia looks deeply into the presence of *shame* in helping relationships, exploring how such a painful and terrifying experience can evolve into a deep understanding of this and other relationships. Jane Cox inquires into the significance of language and communication, exploring the very contemporary topic of working across the language divide, and working in second or third languages.

In the unfolding journey of the book, coach and client encounter each other in many ways. This part of the book looks at some of those moments of meeting and exposes some of the vulnerabilities involved in them.

CHAPTER 10

RELATIONAL MODALITIES IN EXECUTIVE COACHING

JOHN NUTTALL

Executive and management coaching is now a well-accepted way of improving relational dynamics and leadership style in business organisations (Peltier 2001). Many coaches "draw from the frameworks of humanistic, existential, behavioural and psychodynamic psychology... to fit the client, the situation and the need" (Kiel, Rimmer, Williams & Doyle 1996, p. 68). In this chapter, I should like to explore how a framework developed to explain relational states in psychotherapy (Clarkson 1995a) can be used to understand the relationship between management coach and client, and those within management organisations generally. One professor of management science (Sutton 2007) asks, "If you are truly tired of living in Jerk City – if you don't want every day to walk down Asshole Avenue – well, it's your job to help shape a civilised workplace. Sure, you already know that. But isn't it time to do something about it?" (p. 184) Executive and management coaching is charged with shaping a more civilised workforce and, as Goleman (1998) asserts, "The rules for work are changing. We're being judged by a new yardstick: not just by how smart we are, or by our training and expertise, but also how well we handle ourselves and each other" (p. 3) – although recent research suggests such "emotional intelligence" also has its dark side (Alexander 2011).

Existentially, we are in a state of relationship *ab initio* and are thrown into a world in which we must "learn to hone our relational capacity" (Deurzen-Smith 1997, p. 37). Management organisations constitute such a world for the individual and a range of theories have emerged to explain management practices and relational dynamics (De Board 1995; Pugh and Hickson 1996; Sexton 1970). Clarkson (1995a), an organisational psychologist and professor of psychotherapy, writes, "Relationship is the first condition of being human... It is so obvious that it is frequently taken for granted, and so mysterious that many... have made it a focal point of a lifetime's preoccupying passion" (p. 4). Contemporary relational psychotherapy now considers satisfactory relationship to be the key human motivational drive (Wachtel 2008) and the core conditions of empathy, congruence and unconditional positive regard (Rogers 1990) are universally accepted interpersonal competences for "any situation in which the development of the person is a goal" (1990, p. 135). Similar characteristics are enumerated in a new style of leadership (Spears 2002; Greenleaf & Spears 1998).

As we near the end of the twentieth century, we are beginning to see that traditional modes of leadership are slowly yielding to a newer model – one that attempts simultaneously to enhance the personal growth of workers and improve the quality and caring of our institutions... This emerging approach to leadership and service is called *servant-leadership* (Spears 1995).

Clarkson's research (1995a) distinguished five domains of discourse about the therapeutic relationship – the working alliance, the transferential, the developmentally needed, the person-to-person and the transpersonal. From this she created a framework for relationship whose strength lies "in the articulation and layering of many different theoretical angles" (Hawke 1996, p. 406), which allow for different priorities and emphasis. She argued that "these five modes (aspects, dimensions or facets) are present in all relationship" (Clarkson 2002, p. 5) and has demonstrated this in dyadic, group and organisational situations (Clarkson 1995b). I think it brings the same attributes to management theory and provides a higher-order paradigm that embraces a range of classical theories about working relationships and management tasks. It is a useful tool for management coaches, to help them understand and reflect on the coaching relationship and to identify areas for client development – individual or organisational. Each modality carries implied imperatives, admonitions and values about relationship. Clarkson (1995a) emphasises, "these are not developmental stages but states... often subtly 'overlapping', in and between which a client construes his or her unique experience" (p. xiii). All are immanent but, "it is unlikely that two or more can be operative at the same moment" (ibid. p. 7). Below, I review each of these modes and, whilst making links to classical management theories, use them to elucidate vignettes of management behaviour and the coaching relationship I have experienced as a management consultant. I hope, by this, to help identify the kinds of relational skills and insights that contribute to good management practice and also effective coaching.

THE WORKING ALLIANCE MODE OF RELATIONSHIP

Clarkson (1995a) describes this as the bond that enables a client and a therapist to work together, *"even when the patient or client experiences some desires to the contrary"* (p. 31). It usually contains the necessary contractual arrangements such as the stating of competencies and boundaries, the agreement to attend and co-operate and, occasionally, to decline destructive behaviours (Stuart 2010). In the management context it is represented by the employment contract and company procedures or, more informally, the co-operative arrangement executives might have to work together on, say, a new product or financial forecast. In the coaching contract it may involve making the conditions and expectations explicit, agreeing the nature and time frame for goals and achievements, specifying the co-operative arrangements, and the commensurate level of remuneration. It is an alliance where the parties are "joined together in a shared enterprise, each making his or her contribution to the work" (Gelso and Carter 1985, p. 163) and it should be free of ulterior motives that would jeopardise positive outcomes.

In the broader context of management theory, the working alliance is, arguably, central to the early ideas of Taylor (1911) and Gilbreth (1912) who were concerned with efficient working practices that could be measured and agreed. Their ideas were amplified by Fayol (1949) and Urwick (1947), who argued organisational tasks fall into definable categories that require planning and structure. Later theorists (Drucker 1964; Cyert & March 1963) emphasised the everyday process tasks managers undertake. The implication is that individuals perform organisational roles that become enshrined in employment contracts, which, generally, say little about personal motivation, relationships, job satisfaction or autonomy. These factors are usually part of a "psychological work contract" based on an "unwritten set of expectations" that "govern the relationships between the employees and management and among the employees" (Argyris 1970, p. 201). Such contracts are often influenced by the parties' "inner needs, what they have learned from others, traditions and norms, their own past experiences, and a host of other sources" (Schein 1988, p. 24). They are often entered without full awareness and autonomy and, although may be considered an aspect of the working alliance, often bring influences which fit more within the domain of the transferential relationship, discussed below. The most sustainable working alliances are those made "despite the neurotic transference reactions" (Greenson 1965, p. 29); between colleagues who know and trust each other's motives and abilities, or who share similar aspirations, such as those of a sales team sharing a collective target. Such a working alliance needs to be fostered between coach and client, but there are times when these fail because of prevailing psychological contracts. This is illustrated below in a company where I was coach–consultant to the group directorate, contracted to help a new management team adjust to organisational change.

The new Group, part of a conglomerate, was formed from four merged consumer products companies that were previously competitors. The new management centralised the activities of marketing, sales, human resources and finance in a new Group headquarters. All other functions operated at the original, now divisional, company sites. A Group director headed each Group activity and Operating Division. The new Group marketing director and his team, made up of executives from the 'old' companies, had the task of co-ordinating the marketing of the Group, but without having direct control.

Shortly after the merger, the need for a new Group price list required a level of co-ordination and co-operation that would test the company's new structure. The marketing director, determined to show his department's skills accepted the task of co-ordination, design and final production, whereas the divisional product managers, and the Group sales and finance directors took responsibility for the content. I felt some apprehension at this dubious alliance, which I sensed was more about protecting or asserting organisational roles than producing the new brochure. As their coach, I discussed this with the marketing director, who laughingly inquired "whose side are you on?" and assertively declared he considered it time to take control. I suggested he set clear guidelines, which he usurped by setting unrealistic deadlines. I felt he viewed my interventions as interference, and I had to remind myself of the working alliance, which was to help working through, for the whole team, and not to give advice to any one member.

The competitive history and ambiguous structure of the new Group inevitably led to mistrust, and psychological contracts based on the old companies dominated. There was discontent with the design, content arrived late and often badly written, proofs were not properly checked, and several key prices were printed incorrectly. There was a great deal of recrimination and Group marketing, as co-ordinator, took the blame and embarrassment. At a meeting with all departments, I shared with them my analysis of the alliance and, following an angry session and some reflection, it became apparent to all that ulterior motives were operating aimed at manipulating the balance of power within the new organisational structure. Only after mentoring, aimed at relinquishing omnipotence and developing trust, was there acceptance of the structural changes and the need to face evolving market conditions.

Argyris (1970) asserts that it is because the employee is "not permitted to truly realize his potentials that he makes the decision to 'sign the psychological work contract'" (p. 207). The effective working alliance keeps the work in focus despite maladaptive influences of the kind above. Nevertheless, such influences can be mitigated by interventions that raise awareness, clarify role ambiguity and conflict and, if appropriate, by written expression of the aims and conditions of the alliance.

THE TRANSFERENTIAL MODE OF RELATIONSHIP

This is the relational mode that has its theoretical origins in psychoanalysis. Freud (1905) defined transference as a process "in which a whole series of psychological experiences are revived, not as belonging to the past, but as applying to the person of the physician at the moment". And the physician may respond with attitudes related to their past or induced by the client's transference – the so-called counter-transference. Such phenomena are now considered useful in comprehending the client's unconscious relational dynamics (Clarkson and Nuttall 2000). Clarkson (1995a) states that "transference is everywhere and unavoidable" (p. 75) and this often leads to unwarranted or inappropriate interpersonal attribution detrimental to the working alliance or work group function (Bion 1961; Nuttall 2001). It is the mode of relationship usually at the base of political rivalry and inter-departmental strife and can lead to what Schwartz (1990) refers to as "the snake pit organisation" where "anxiety and stress are constant companions" (p. 78).

Transference experiences are revived, usually early and familial, relational paradigms that were unrequited and laden with anxiety and ambivalent feelings. As adults we might unconsciously construe or engineer life events to represent these early situations symbolically (Segal 1988), so that they might be resolved, or relived as familiar attitudes in highly anxious situations – a phenomenon known in psychoanalysis as the "compulsion to repeat". The objective reality of industrial organisations is often evocative of such early anxiety situations. Rather like the developing individual, a company's task is to relate, grow, compete and create wealth, to self-actualise in some way. But products can fail, inducing feelings of rejection and paranoia, as jobs could be lost. Executive language often evokes aggressive scenes with terms like 'market warfare' and 'killing the competition'; or scenes of reparation with 'building market share', 'adding value' and 'customer friendly'. And at the individual level, there are often ambivalent feelings of dependency and isolation in relation to others redolent of early familial relationship (Diamond 1991). This modality has been tacitly recognised by psycho-sociological management theorists such as Argyris (1970) and McGregor (1960). It is central to psychoanalytic management theories and has been illustrated in industrial relations (Jacques 1951), hospital care (Menzies 1960) and interdepartmental relations (Nuttall 2001). Such transferences are often active in senior managers and "clinical investigation shows that many organisational problems originate in the private, inner world of the organisation's senior executives" (Kets de Vries 1991, p. 3) – as I now describe in this continuation of the above case study:

> The new Group managing director when recruiting the new Group marketing director promised him control of a totally integrated marketing function. However, on appointment, he gave him control of only the advertising, sales promotion and market research activities; product management was retained at division level and the sales force reported to a peer group director. The marketing director felt betrayed and inadequate and described his function as "being in bits" and expressed great anxiety about co-ordinating such a fragmented activity. The managing director, an HR professional, needed his new structure to work, but after several months of missed targets he felt "at a loss and out of control".

> As coach/consultant I experienced the relational dynamics at work. One major factor was the managing director's own feelings of inadequacy as an HR professional in charge of a consumer products company. This being intolerable for him, he created an organisational structure that transferred this anxiety onto (and into) his new marketing director. The new marketing director, technically very capable, developed the creative programmes required but, nevertheless, sales targets were regularly missed. He believed the sales and divisional directors purposely foiled his department's efforts and were contemptuous of its existence and power. Frustrated, he grew angry with his team, which he perceived to be failing, and felt abandoned by the managing director. The level of personal stress in the organisation was high and there were signs of depression in some individuals. This permeated the organisation, resulting in malicious rivalry between the marketing, sales and divisional managements.

> As a marketing man myself, I strongly empathised with his difficult position and his frustration and anger, and on one occasion was drawn into acting as a marketing adviser. I quickly realised my intense counter-transferences were dragging me into acting in some procedural role instead of bringing insight to the individuals involved. In the meantime the marketing director seemed to unconsciously dispose of his feelings by inducing them in his colleagues and boss by obduracy and innuendo. Equally, I sensed in the managing director sadness and parental disappointment with the marketing director. Why had he not made this important organisational role clear? He declared unease with the marketing director's belligerence and rationalised that he wanted him to prove himself first.

148

As I got to know the managing director I realised he had, unconsciously, structured the new organisation to emulate his family paradigm. He was the middle of three brothers and, unsure of his position in the family, often found himself feeling 'out of control' and having to 'give way to others', in order to gain parental accolade. In his new position, his need to keep control, paradoxically, resulted in a lack of clear boundaries and organisational definition. He placed his marketing director in a similar ambiguous position and by transferring his own dilemma in this way was vicariously repeating his unresolved familial role. And by maintaining poor performance below, he maintained his own insecurity *vis-à-vis* his superiors – a 'parent' company that demanded improved results.

These executives consciously wanted to engage successfully but strong transferences interfered with the process. Trained coaches can often spot such dynamics operating in repetitive behaviours and expression of associated 'bad' feelings, and through awareness of their own counter-transferences. They are often resolved by interpretation and linking of behaviour patterns and attitudes, and can be brought into focus by cognitive challenge and reality checking using a variety of interventions (Gould 1991). This brings to the fore the developmentally needed mode of relationship.

THE DEVELOPMENTALLY NEEDED MODE OF RELATIONSHIP

This relational domain represents the "intentional provision... of a corrective, reparative or replenishing relationship or action" (Clarkson 1995a, p. 108). This is the core of a therapist's job, but more recently it is being understood also as part of a manager's and an executive coach's job (Peltier 2001). One of the tenets of servant leadership emphasises: "We must be silent before we can listen. We must listen before we can learn. We must learn before we can prepare. We must prepare before we can serve. We must serve before we can lead" (Ward 1999, p. 11). Such a developmental style seems to be a characteristic of excellent companies, which "give people control of their destinies; they make meaning for people. They let, even insist that, people stick out. They accentuate the positive" (Peters and Waterman 1982, p. 239). This is provided in many companies by executive development programmes and by mentoring and employee-assistance schemes, but to be effective and sustainable a conducive management style is necessary.

This is an aspect of management addressed by Mayo (1949) and concepts like McGregor's theory X and Y (1960), Argyris's model I and II behaviour (1970) and Herzberg's motivation-hygiene theory (1968). These elaborate the organisational factors and management styles that influence the level of employee motivation and job satisfaction. "Having established that it is indeed a new kind of relationship which is required... the task is to identify the nature, intensity, duration and variety of reparative relationship which is required" (Clarkson 1995a, p. 119). Skilful management coaches can engender such reparative action from the top management down, as the following example illustrates.

In a large industrial products company, the adoption of a marketing-centred structure (Nuttall 1974) caused resentment in the previously dominant production and R&D departments. Instead of the production management making what it wanted to optimise its resources, it felt suddenly controlled by the 'whims of the marketing department' and incurred negative budget variances for which it felt blameless. A malevolent finance department seemed delighted to point out that marketing were too whimsical and production too inflexible for performance to improve. Such change of ethos often evokes the kinds of transferences described earlier. The production and R&D departments felt abandoned by the managing director, previously their head. The marketing department, on the other hand, felt dependent on his support to defend against these well-established engineering departments. The finance department positioned itself as the family big brother, delighted to 'objectively' report the younger sibling's poor behaviour. As coach, I experienced the situation as a typical family squabble and felt like a 'kind aunt', who would listen and 'persuade dad to give them attention'.

Initially, the managing director was irritated by the rivalry amongst his senior executives, but by using his feelings and my counter-transferences as a guide, he realised he needed to provide a better balance of support across all his direct reports. Accordingly, he scheduled a series of meetings where key executives presented their department's work and how it interfaced with the greater organisation. He attended all the meetings, encouraged discussion of feelings, and clarified roles and boundaries (Schneider 1991), admitting occasionally how he might have misunderstood these. However, the decisive developmental act was his setting, and adhering to, a schedule of short regular weekly meetings with each of his direct reports. Alongside all the other meetings these private exchanges gave each of his managers the feeling that their concerns were being heard, valued and resolved. The confidence this engendered overcame the relational conflict as each manager began to understand his or her value and role.

This approach is like that between therapist and patient and...

leads to two results that are analogous to the outcome of normal childhood development: (1) his occasional failures, constituting optimal frustration, lead to the building up of self structure, while (2) his, on the whole, adequately maintained understanding leads to the patient's increasing realisation that, contrary to his experience in childhood, the sustaining echo of empathic resonance is indeed available in this world.

(Kohut 1984, pp. 77–8)

Peters and Waterman (1982) echo this sentiment: "We are beginning to perceive, however dimly, a central theme that in our minds makes excellent companies great... like good parents, they cared a lot – and expected a lot" (p. 96). However, it is essential that the delivery of these conditions should be genuine and real, and not seen as what they called a "lip-service disaster" or "gimmicks disaster" (ibid. p. 239). This brings me to the next dimension of relationship, the person-to-person or 'real' relationship.

THE PERSON-TO-PERSON MODE OF RELATIONSHIP

"The person to person relationship is the real relationship or core relationship" (Clarkson 1995a, p. 146), a mode best expounded by the existential school (Deurzen-Smith 1997). It is characterised by acceptance of others' subjective experience of life and the emotional here and now of relational encounter; and "the extent, level and quality of this vector can vary enormously" (Clarkson 1995a, p. 153). It raises anxiety for many managers, as it requires genuineness in their interface with colleagues, customers, investors and government. It involves being emotionally intelligent and aware but, as Greenleaf observed, "Awareness is not a giver of solace – it is just the opposite. It is a disturber and an awakener" (quoted in Spears 2002, p. 3). Working in organisations can often awaken anxieties around the existential concerns of meaning-making, isolation and relationship, freedom and responsibility, and survival and death (Yalom 1980).

In the management setting the real relationship is most likely to be experienced when individuals, regardless of hierarchy, share their anxieties, aspirations and experience in a genuine effort to achieve a mutual goal. It is characterised by "the establishment of a relationship that permits more openness, the sharing of feelings, perceptions, and assumptions, and the development of subsequent actions based on more accurate and valid information" (Schein 1988, p. 129). It involves the realisation that the boss and colleagues are similar others struggling with the same kinds of problems in life, and might not be the 'all knowing', 'brilliant' or 'back-stabbing' individuals seen through the eyes of transference. It represents a position of mutuality similar to that described by Argyris as Model II behaviour (Argyris and Schön 1978) and by Cox and Makin as interdependence (1994). This does not mean losing sight of the job or allowing our needs for affiliation to dominate our actions. As Stern (2010) asserts, "The true heroes are largely unsung and prefer to remain that way" (p. 40). In my experience, this modality comes to the fore when managers are faced with mutual existential decisions – usually of a painful sort such as those about redundancies, re-structuring or responding to extraneous market forces. The coach or consultant, with similar experience, can often connect at a personal level with such realities. The coach's capacity to bring insight and verbalise ulterior processes can also engender real rapport that instils confidence in the client to move forward. The following describes such a situation.

A consumer products company found a new product was not returning expected profits. Yet deliveries exceeded target and back orders were high. Paradoxically, profits worsened as sales increased, and capital requirements spiralled out of control. The CEO, head of three companies, wanting "more accurate and valid information", asked me to review the situation.

As I examined the accounts, read through the minutes of meetings and talked to the directors, it became apparent that internal working alliances were distorted by psychological contracts and transferences of unrealistic expectations. I sensed the dedication of the relatively inexperienced directors and their overwhelming desire to please the CEO and impress each other. Implicit challenges existed between them – the marketing department to beat budgeted sales, production to make whatever marketing wanted, and engineering to source everything in-house. Marketing did beat the sales targets but with excessive promotional costs, negative price and product variances, and extended credit. This, in turn, resulted in production bottlenecks and payroll variances. Engineering's desire to produce everything in-house brought excessive work-in-progress and component costs.

As I engaged with the issues, I felt like a 'spoiler' and a 'pessimistic clever clogs' and wondered what reparative interventions I could bring. I decided to disclose these feelings to the directors to indicate how each of them might have feared similar feelings in their collective planning. Over time, awareness grew of how each had played a part in creating optimistic expectations, and that now a major 'reality check' was needed. The perceptions of their own and each other's capacities needed revision and, at one meeting, the feelings of loss and guilt were palpable. All the vested interests and aspirations tied to the new product's success dissolved as reality was faced. A new mutual respect emerged as new fears were shared about the effect of the loss on the company's performance, its employees, individual reputations and hopes. Real relationship developed with a determination in all to resolve the situation.

These executives faced an existential situation that challenged their meaning-making, freedom, self-esteem and relationships with each other. Clarkson (1995a) asserts, "There is an intrinsic human *mutuality* in the face of such universal human experiences" (p. 158) which can bring a new level of respect for and confidence in the other. At other times, like the meeting of difficult deadlines, or the success of a new product, when things go well, a collective acknowledgement and mutual respect occurs, regardless of hierarchy, for everyone's effort. Managers in this mode, "look for contributions from others who are competent; they are able to confront their own basic assumptions and take part in testing them in public, which allows of their changing" (Pugh and Hickson 1996, p. 201).

THE TRANSPERSONAL MODE OF RELATIONSHIP

This "refers to the spiritual or inexplicable dimension of relationship" (Clarkson 1995a, p. 20). It includes the esoteric, mystical and archetypal experiences of relationship that might be couched in discourses from the overtly religious to the new sciences of chaos and complexity. Transpersonal ideas emerged from the US humanistic psychology movement and the ideas of James, Jung, Assagioli, May and the psychologist and management theorist Maslow, who, according to Sutich (1976), coined the term in a letter to Stanislav Grof:

> in the course of our conversation we thought of using the word "transpersonal" instead of the clumsier word "transhumanistic" or "transhuman". The more I think of it, the more this word says what we are trying to say, that is, beyond individuality, beyond the development of the individual person into something which is more elusive than the individual person, or which is bigger than he is.

> (Maslow quoted in Sutich 1976, p. 16)

Such views help us deal with paradox, ambiguity, contradiction and simultaneity in human interaction. Thus, Peters (1992) asks us not to take organisations too seriously, with "focus on the charts, the boxes, the job descriptions, the specifiable". Better "to relish a wave-like environment, where relationships are paramount... where *necessary disorganisation* reigns" (pp. 380–1). Clarkson (2002) agrees, "it is possible that under such stimulus, creativity can continue to evolve disruptively rather than dogmatically" (p. 120). Management theorists falling within this domain include Weick (1995), with his concept of 'sensemaking', and Morgan (1993) in his exhortation for organisations to 'imaginise' what they do and wish to become.

Such necessary disorganisation is akin to the chaos inherent in all dynamic systems. "Clouds are not spheres, Mandelbrot is fond of saying.

Mountains are not cones. Lightening does not travel in straight lines. It required a faith that the interesting feature of a lightening bolt's path, for example, was not its direction, but rather the distribution of the zigs and zags" (Gleick 1987, p. 94). Peters (1992) requests the same from senior executives, "The message is clear: (1) trust, (2) 'they' can handle 'it' (*whatever* 'it' is), (3) you're only in control when you're out of control ['head' of a flat, radically decentralised 'organisation']" (p. 759). Such trust in chaos has a mystical quality that I can only describe as the 'wow!' and 'phew!' of things. It is engendered by the kind of kinship spirit or libido (Jung 1998, p. 71) that organisations attempt to create by mission statements, charters and corporate visions. It is present when, for example, different disciplines come together and produce something more than the sum of their expertise ('wow!'), or when deadlines are met after periods of chaos and confusion ('phew!'). "Creativity happens at far from equilibrium conditions, often needing the stimulus of deadlines, emotional turmoil or a change in setting to flourish" (Clarkson 2002, p. 120).

A multi-national consumer goods company was planning an important annual promotional campaign for its main product. I was a consultant observer in several planning meetings, made up of marketing, sales, product and advertising agency executives, each of whom seemed to have a different view of what constituted a strong offer and promotional message. As deadlines approached, panic and desperation crept in as the debates resulted in little creative output. The meetings, led by the marketing chief, became deadlocked, heated and hard work. At this point, I intervened pointing out that individual egos and aims seemed to be getting in the way. I said, "you have to let go of your vested interests; you must stop contriving and really give something, and trust it will work". This brought forth a burst of creativity. The product manager developed ideas for new value-added features, the advertising agency created a related graphic, and the sales manager a pricing proposal. Led by the marketing chief, their ideas came together in a creative synthesis that was manifest in a physical sense of 'wow!' I felt something mystical had happened between and beyond them as a drunken ambience filled the room. This gradually waned into several expressions of 'phew!' as some realised how close to deadlines the planning had gone.

The campaign exceeded expectations, helping the company beat its forecast. It seemed that in the feelings experienced and expressed there was an implicit recognition of the transpersonal; there was a mysterious conjunction (Jung 1946) of ideas that was 'more elusive' or 'bigger' than individual input.

There is a quality to this dimension that cannot be named, and if we were to analyse the relational process I suspect we would identify only the other four relational modes. The transpersonal implies *"a letting go* of skills, of knowledge, of experience, of preconceptions, even of the desire to heal, to be present"* (original italics, Clarkson 1995a, p. 20).

CONCLUSION

Recent authors like Sutton, Goleman and Greenleaf have brought a new emphasis to management concepts that highlight the quality of interpersonal relationship. Clarkson's work is an important contribution to this perspective, describing the relational encounter in a way that both integrates and transcends prevailing theories. The working alliance highlights the importance of defining roles and boundaries, and emphasises the need to work positively with others based on realistic expectations. The transferential dimension helps us understand how we can misconstrue interpersonal relations to fit the patterns of earlier experiences and create relational dynamics detrimental to organisational objectives. The developmentally needed dimension harnesses our human capacity to facilitate others and create as a means of building self-esteem and group cohesion (Hirschorn 1988). The person-to-person mode allows us to be human, with frailties and doubts, and yet still be valued, moderating the distortions of transference. The transpersonal embraces spontaneity and imagination, and symbolises our ability to find meaning in what we do, allowing 'necessary disorganisation'.

This case material illustrates how these modalities have been experienced in organisational settings and coaching practice. Clarkson's framework provides a perspective that management consultants and coaches can use in the design of organisational structures, procedures and roles, and highlights the relational qualities that affect these. It should help coaches' diagnostic skills and interventions, and for organisational psychologists it offers a discipline-related framework for understanding neurotic styles of management and the 'snake-pit organisation'. It provides a coherence by which managers and coaches can understand what relational factors affect performance and happiness, and what qualities bring improvement and change.

CHAPTER 11

SHAME IN THE COACHING RELATIONSHIP: REFLECTIONS ON INDIVIDUAL AND ORGANISATIONAL VULNERABILITY

SIMON CAVICCHIA

A SICKNESS OF THE SOUL

Shame and its milder relation, embarrassment, are particular forms of anxiety which alert us to when we might have transgressed a boundary demarcating the difference between what is generally considered acceptable and unacceptable in a particular culture or context. As such, shame can be seen to have a useful function in maintaining norms and social cohesion. However, for many of us, and our clients, the experience of shame reaches far beyond this function of policing civility and acts as a debilitating force, disrupting our connection to our varied talents and capacities and reducing the quality of our interactions with others. It is these more negative aspects of shame that I shall be exploring in this chapter, particularly how they arise and the impact they can have on client and coach effectiveness and the dynamics of the coaching relationship. I shall end with a series of considerations for those coaches wishing to work with a greater alertness to shame. As shame disturbs our clients' relationship to themselves and what they are capable of, reducing the intensity of shame experiences not only stands to improve their well-being but can contribute to significant improvements in performance.

Gershen Kaufman (1989) describes shame as "the affect of indignity, of transgression, of defeat, of inferiority and alienation" (p. 16). It is experienced as an "inner torment, as a sickness of the soul. It is the most poignant experience of the self by the self, whether felt in the humiliation of cowardice, or in the sense of failure to cope successfully with a challenge. Shame is a wound felt from the inside, dividing us both from ourselves and from one another" (ibid. p. 16).

In the grip of shame "the attention turns inward, thereby generating the torment of self-consciousness" (Kaufman 1989, p. 17). We feel deficient by comparison with others, failures in our own and others' eyes, and so held up to critical scrutiny that we want to sink to the ground and become invisible (Orange 2008).

Gestalt psychotherapy and relational psychoanalysis (e.g. Philippson 2009; Beebe & Lachmann 2002; Philippson 2001; Orange, Atwood & Stolorow 1997; Hycner & Jacobs 1995; Atwood & Stolorow 1992) consider that self-experience, the sense we have of ourselves moment by moment, is a feature of the field conditions we inhabit at any time and our relationship to them. In other words, how we feel, think and act is dependent on the total situation we find ourselves in and our ways of responding based on individual histories and experience.

A BRIEF DEVELOPMENTAL PERSPECTIVE

While some of us may be more prone to shame than others, it is nonetheless an experience most know something of. We all have had the experience of being and feeling small and inadequate in relation to others who are big and powerful (usually, but not exclusively, parents).

Relational development perspectives (Beebe & Lachmann 2002; Stern 1998; Stolorow & Atwood 1992; Winnicott 1965) suggest that the emergence of a coherent and functioning sense of self, which is experienced as resourced and which can adjust fluidly and creatively to individual needs and the demands of the external environment, is bound up with the content and quality of these early relationships.

I wish to concentrate on a series of perspectives which serve to shed light on the dynamics of shame in coaches, clients and organisational life. These are:

- Shame as a result of identification with negative self-images or beliefs

- Shame as a result of a rupture in relationship

- Shame in relation to trying to live up to ideals, self-images and idealised self-images.

IDENTIFICATION WITH NEGATIVE SELF-IMAGES AND BELIEFS

Erskine (1995) and Philippson (2009) describe how, when we are reprimanded as children, we will often identify with the content of criticism. In simple terms, this means that we believe the messages that we are a 'bad' boy or girl, that we are 'greedy' or 'rude' – the specific content is unique to each of us and potentially vast. Identification is an important process. Although what we are taking in are ideas and an other's temporary and partial perspectives about us, identification means that we start to take them for *who* we are in a way that can become fixed and absolute (Kaufman,1989). These ideas then contribute to the vast array of images that we hold about ourselves, who we are, and what we believe and feel we are and are not capable of.

A RUPTURE IN RELATIONSHIP

Whenever parents and significant others fail to respond to us in a way that feels supportive, tuned in and sensitive to our feelings and needs, we experience a rupture in relationship. This disrupts our feeling of being accepted and received for who we are by an 'other' who is important to us. When we feel this acceptance, it is as if a "relational bridge" (Kaufmann 1989) exists between us and the other. The experience of the relational bridge is core to our sense of psychological integrity and well-being. When this bridge is broken by an experience of being profoundly missed, dismissed, humiliated or criticised, the experience is one of shame. We feel unacceptable in the eyes of others, diminished and fundamentally flawed. If this sort of experience is repeated, it can become part of our on-going sense of ourselves and create a susceptibility, which can frequently be reactivated in adult interactions, especially in superior–subordinate interactions at work with their potential to evoke historical parent–child relational templates (Krantz 1993). One only has to think of the anxiety that is evoked for many during annual performance appraisals, to recognise one of many ways in which shame can arise in the context of typical and established organisation processes.

IDENTIFICATION WITH POSITIVE SELF-IMAGES AND THE PURSUIT OF IDEALS

As we experience interaction upon interaction, the feelings and thoughts that we construct as a result of them coalesce into a complex web of beliefs, self-images, feelings and energetic states that give mental and bodily form to who we take ourselves to be. In addition to images based on deficiency, we also develop positive self-images. These can be based on an accurate assessment of our capabilities, or be inflated attempts at compensating for feelings of vulnerability and insecurity as in the case of narcissistic process (Almaas 1996).

It is important to understand that the extent to which we *identify* with these positive images is the extent to which they need to be maintained through our living up to them. Any failure to do this will cause a de-stabilising of the image, and a corresponding ruffle in the fabric of self-experience, feelings and energetic states – in essence, who we take ourselves to be. Ideals and self-images can motivate individuals to achieve great things and behave in ways that are supportive of social functioning. If they are overly and unconsciously identified with, they can tip into workaholism, addictive striving, loss of efficiency and, ultimately, burnout (Casserley & Megginson 2009). There is an important distinction to be made here between what may be actual qualities of capability and competence, which an individual has and can draw upon, and the *image* of being competent and capable with which an individual is identified, and which is threatened every time life-experience calls it, temporarily, into question.

Early experiences contribute to each of us forming a unique, fingerprint-like susceptibility to shame, with some being more prone to and affected by shame than others. Our individual shame templates remain with us in adult life and colour our interactions with others. Just as these templates were originally forged in relational interactions, they go on being potentially evoked and maintained in relationship. The good news is that it is also in relationship that they can be surfaced and re-drawn, in order to reduce their debilitating impacts. I shall now turn my attention to some of the ways shame can arise in the relational, contextual matrix that is an organisation.

SHAME IN ORGANISATIONAL AND EXECUTIVE LIFE

Organisational theory is evolving to conceive of organisations as complex systems of human relationship and interaction (e.g. Gould, Stapley & Stein 2006; Stacey 2001; Wheatley 2006). Understanding the nature and dynamics of these interactions is increasingly informing how organisational development and learning are conceptualised and facilitated. Given the relational nature of shame, understanding the effect of shame on individuals and interactions is an indispensable perspective for coaches and consultants wishing to act as agents of change.

The experience of shame is a potent and palpable reminder of our human need for connection and our vulnerability to its loss. Yet organisations often implicitly and explicitly work to deny vulnerability in favour of outward manifestations of bullish confidence, passionate commitment, privileging and valuing the individual over collaborative relationships between people.

The Western culture of individualism naturally glorifies the lonely hero while denigrating any need for relationships and support, which is seen as infantile or effeminate (Lee & Wheeler 1996). Competition, internal or external to the organisation, whilst motivating for some, contributes to field conditions where anxiety related to success and failure, comparison with others and harsh self-criticism abound. Hierarchies and rank contribute to dynamics where individuals are inevitably compared to one another and compare themselves to those above and below, leading to what Fuller (2004) terms cultures of "somebodies and nobodies". The part emotion and feeling states play in thinking and in determining behaviour is often denied. Instead there is a privileging of knowledge capital, control, partial and 'illusory' certainties, and ideals such as omniscience and omnipotence (Cavicchia 2009; Hirshhorn & Barnett 1993; De Vries 1980). These latter two aspects often act as idealised self-images, which many, with varying degrees of awareness, feel they have to live up to.

The realities of many organisations mean that leaders need to develop resilience and responsiveness in the face of constant, rapid and unforeseeable change. They need to develop the capacity to bear uncertainty, contain anxiety and interact with colleagues to generate new and appropriate responses to complex challenges. This is particularly true where prior learning and 'old' approaches no longer seem fit for purpose (Cavicchia 2009; Wheatley 2006; Stacey 2001; Isaacs 1999).

Experiences of stuckness, confusion and uncertainty, whilst common, undermine the ideals of omniscience and omnipotence and so have to be hidden, from where they then act as silent and private sources of anxiety and shame.

The pursuit of perfection and excellence, which is so established as a cultural norm in organisations, makes it exceedingly difficult for clients to consider the possibility of being what Winnicott (1965) terms "good enough". In fact, when I mention this to my clients, they frequently assume that "good enough" must mean mediocre. Yet with many of the complex challenges executives can face, and the multitude of variables at play, good enough is often the best solution possible. Where leaders are identified with ideals of omnipotence, any thought or intervention which falls short of this ideal will tend to be experienced as a failure.

EFFECTS OF SHAME

The experience of shame disconnects individuals from a realistic assessment of their resources; it can drive a retreat from relationship, where individuals withdraw from conversations if they experience their views not being heard or not being taken seriously; it fuels conflict and splitting in the form of the blaming and scapegoating of others. Here an individual or department experiencing or fearing shame attempts to restore some sense of well-being by finding fault in others. Shame contributes to a contraction of the space for inquiry, dialogue and thinking *together*. Experimenting with new behaviours or imagining new possibilities become extremely difficult to the extent that individuals are often acutely self-conscious, primarily preoccupied with being acceptable and unwilling to risk anything that might make them look bad or simply different (Cavicchia 2009). Thus spontaneity, so essential for creativity, is quickly stifled.

A client of mine, a senior executive in a financial institution, spoke in coaching of feeling flat, confused and lost. She described going blank when faced with the complex day-to-day challenges her role required her to address and resolve. At one point she said "I feel I have nothing to draw on, all my experience has left me." This client had recently been promoted to a new role where she had gone from having a manager she experienced as extremely supportive of her and her ways of thinking to one whom she described as critical and constantly challenging her thought processes. As I knew her to have a track record of significant successes, I was intrigued by her experience.

Over time we were able to see how she was identified with an image of success and potency based on these past experiences. At one point she said "I can't understand what is happening to me, I have been a leader in a FTSE 100 for the past ten years". In the absence of supportive feedback and encouragement from her superior, an *image* of a successful FTSE 100 leader could no longer be maintained in her mind. It was her *identification* with the image, and the fusion of her sense of capacity with that image, that led to her distress and the feeling of being resource-less.

In the course of her coaching she was able to reframe her struggle as being novel (she had never experienced anything like this before at work) and, through my non-judgmental acceptance of her current reality, and my thinking aloud on the organisational context and the nature of shame, she was able to reconnect with her capacity for thought and creativity in service of negotiating a different and improved relationship with her boss. This in turn reconnected her with a sense of agency, capability and well-being. This type of shift involves a movement away from identifying with an image to identifying more with core qualities such as the capacity for reflection and imagination; increasing self-awareness by noticing sensory and emotional, as well as cognitive, processes and becoming fully immersed in the question of how best to respond to a complex situation. "*I am successful*" is a precarious self-image. If it cannot be maintained and supported by specific external evidence, the experience is often one of shameful incapacity. "*I have the ability to feel and think my way through uncharted territory*" came to be a much more sustaining, resourcing and supportive notion for this particular client, particularly as it was congruent with her experience of herself in the course of her coaching and, as a result, in her practice out in the organisation.

SHAME IN THE EXECUTIVE COACHING RELATIONSHIP

Shame is an ever-present potential in the coaching relationship, particularly in organisations where, inevitably, standards and ideals, assessments and feedback, codes of conduct and cultural norms abound. All of these serve to heighten the sensitivity of coaches and coachees as to whether they fit in, or are making and will continue to 'make the grade'. Where, as coaches, we may identify with, or be cast in, the role of expert, coachees can feel inferior in relation to our real (in some areas) and imagined (usually in many areas!) greater expertise. This is particularly the case where coaching may be subtly or overtly construed as remedial in some way. The emphasis coaching places on outcomes and forwarding action can mean that clients who may be struggling to acclimatise to the coaching process, or identify a way forward given the complexities of their current situation, might feel shamed by a coach's insistence on output. In these instances, the pursuit of a solution, however well-intentioned, can come to feel like persecution – and the coach an ever-so-helpful sadist.

The emphasis coaching places on skills and tools can also result in coaches being less sensitised to the quality of relationship with their coachees. Enthusiastic coaches, who might extol the virtues of their particular approach, can assume an air of methodological evangelism. This can alienate coachees whose unique experience may differ, and imply that there is something wrong with them if they fail to benefit from what is presented as some kind of panacea.

I often hear coaches and supervisees talk about particular clients being "uncoachable". This can, of course, occasionally be true, but is often a discounting of the part shame might be playing in informing the quality of relationship between coach and coachee and the insight available to each – as in the following example.

A number of years ago I was coaching a senior HR professional in a manufacturing organisation, whom I shall call 'Mike'. I had gone through a standard contracting process, and spent some time explaining the kind of coach I was and my ways of working. He seemed comfortable with this and we contracted to work on developing his leadership capability and presence.

As we began to explore his current thoughts and approaches to leadership and surface areas for development, he appeared to become less engaged. His responses to my open questions became less detailed and thoughtful, and he seemed to be retreating from contact with me and the coaching process. It is significant that, in spite of noticing this, I found myself unable to think about what this might be saying about our relationship, and became more and more preoccupied with 'coming up with the goods', feeling increasingly responsible for finding a way to engage him. Yet, the harder I tried, the more distant and disconnected he became.

In one session where I experienced him as particularly taciturn, I found myself working extremely hard, thinking about all the different leadership models I had come across. My anxiety was increasing as I trotted out more and more perspectives in the hope of coming up with something that might prove to be of interest, all the while privately doubting myself and my ability to be of use to him. Feeling irritated and stuck, I eventually made a confronting and rather punitive interpretation that he was overwhelmed with the enormity of his challenges, and might be disengaging as a way of managing his anxiety.

He looked at me with fury in his eyes and said with disdain "Oh that's what's happening is it?"!

This pulled me up short. I realised the extent to which I had missed attending to the quality of our relationship and had failed to consider what I was experiencing and how it might be relevant to our work. I saw that, given my own vulnerability and need to feel competent, I had, myself, moved further away from him and an interest in his experience. My comment about his disengagement was infused with this need to save face and also, undoubtedly, a projection of my own withdrawal from relationship! It was then I also remembered that earlier he had mentioned an experience of a coach that had not gone well for him. He described how she had insisted on telling him what he needed to do and how he had felt de-skilled in the process.

I looked at him with mock seriousness and exaggerated gravitas in response to his question.... "Believe me" I intoned firmly, "I have a diploma!"

He looked confused for a moment, then broke into a smile. This built into a deep belly laugh, which I also joined in with. In that moment it felt as if a barrier had dissolved between us and we could share in my self-deprecation and the intended irony of my comment. This moment of humour relaxed something in our relationship, and we were soon talking about how we had perhaps not got off to a very good start. I owned the part I had played in getting busy, and perhaps being over-zealous in my interventions. He was generous enough to disclose that his experience of the other coach had made him suspicious of me and reluctant to engage fully.

This example illustrates the often subtle, yet powerful, unconscious ways in which coaches and coachees can co-create their relationship. Mike's experience of his previous coach and the shame he had felt was in the field at the start. I failed to register the possible significance of this, suggesting that something of my own performance anxiety about doing a good job had reduced my capacity to reflect on information that implied the early stages of our contracting might need to be handled with particular care. Given my own levels of shame at not being 'effective', I was unable to think about Mike's reluctance to engage and resorted to getting busier and busier, becoming, I imagined, a version of the previous coach. I shared this thought with Mike who agreed that I had at times "spookily" resembled her. Out of conscious awareness, both Mike and I had conspired to re-enact something of his earlier coaching relationship. By being willing to turn our attention to the quality of our relating, how we had missed one another and what relevance this might have to our work, we were able to create a new and novel encounter that eventually yielded much learning for both of us.

WORKING WITH SENSITIVITY TO SHAME

Working with sensitivity to shame requires coaches to develop sufficient awareness of their own vulnerabilities (including their own idealised self-images, the ideals of the coaching profession and the extent to which they are identified with them) along with the capacity to monitor, in the moment, how shame may be arising in their relationship with clients.

There is a delicate line to be navigated between, on the one hand, under-standing the debilitating effects of shame and working to reduce these and, on the other, a need to hold in mind the extremely private nature of shame and the shaming potential of overtly and prematurely drawing attention to it in corporate contexts.

A particular challenge arises given the number of our clients who depend for their motivation, often unconsciously, on their identification with ideal-ised self-images and the fear of failing to live up to them. Clients who may be experiencing shame at not performing at the level that is expected, will often, initially, demand that their coach shore up their strengths and self-images and develop strategies for overcoming their anxiety by trying harder or refining their skills. Whilst this *development* strategy may work in the short term, it does not address the nature of shame and the need for clients to examine their relationship to themselves and the organisation context and culture in which they operate, in order to *transform* anxiety into internal reflective support in the face of complexity, of the unknown and the novel. It is in the context of a coaching relationship that is sensitive and attuned to shame that this transformation can be facilitated.

It has long been observed in the fields of psychoanalysis and psycho-therapy that clients achieve transformative change on the basis of their experience of their therapist and their relationship with him or her (Stern 2004; Beebe & Lachmann 2002; Orange, Atwood & Stolorow 1997; Hycner & Jacobs 1995). Relational dynamics are now being considered for what they might have to offer the process of coaching (De Haan 2008c).

The following is a series of pointers for coaches wishing to work with a sensitivity to shame in order to restore and increase their coachees' connection to their own resources.

CONTRACTING FOR RELATIONSHIP

Much contracting in coaching can concentrate on desired outcomes. In working with a sensitivity to shame, it can be beneficial also to turn attention towards the relationship the coach and client might create. Fuller and Fridjhon (2005) suggest a process for designing a "partnership alliance". Here questions such as "what is the culture/atmosphere we want to create together?", "what would help this relationship flourish?" and "how do we want to be together when it gets difficult?" orientate both coach and coachee to the relationship as a dynamic process that calls for conscious and intentional management if it is to become a container in which vulnerabilities can be surfaced and worked through.

STANCE OF THE COACH

Different coaching theories acknowledge the importance of the coach's attitude in contributing to supporting the coachee's development (Palmer & Whybrow 2007; Whitworth, Kimsey-House & Sandahl 1998). Of particular relevance, when shame is in the field, are attitudes such as compassion for self and other; acceptance of what is; playfulness and lightness of touch; detachment and indifference to specific outcome; curiosity and inquiry. Mindell (1995) calls these "metaskills" as opposed to tools and technique. They are vital in evoking an emotional and relational field in which clients are more likely to make use of our interventions.

Crucial to working with shame is a coach's ability to be fully available with all their feelings and responses. This is not easy, as it means coming out from behind the shield of tools and technique. It involves being willing to be impacted by our coachees; paying attention to the present moment of the encounter with all that is arising; negotiating meaning with them, and resisting the pull to impose theory, protocols and procedure onto their experience.

MONITORING THE RELATIONAL DANCE

This involves monitoring the moment-by-moment quality of the relational bridge between coach and coachee, and noting and naming possible ruptures in order to restore connection. The quality of the relational bridge and the coachee's levels of internal support are inextricably linked and help to determine the grading and timing of more confronting interventions. These are a necessary and often extremely powerful component in coaching, yet they must be practiced with sensitivity and alertness to the quality of the relationship, to try and ensure that the coachee can make effective use of them. As coaches we will get it wrong by our clients from time to time. Here it is important to be able and willing to reflect on those moments and own the part we played in whatever rupture might have occurred.

A CONCERN FOR MUTUALITY

Clients can project expertise and authority onto us as coaches. Whilst this may be appropriate at times, we need to be alert to the part these projections can play in making clients feel diminished and emptied of their own resources. Being willing to be human and name our own limitations can be a powerful way of restoring moments of mutuality where unhelpful asymmetrical power relations may have arisen.

EVOCATION AND INDIRECTION

Related to a concern for mutuality is an attitude of gentle and interested inquiry that is based on evocation and indirection. Phillips (1998) describes this as "having a stab at hinting". Here the coach's questions and thoughts are offered in a light way along the lines of "I find myself wondering... might it be possible that... have you thought of...?" It can be of enormous benefit for coaches and coachees if the coach views every intervention as a hint. In this way the coachee is free to pick on what makes sense or resonates and is less likely to feel impinged upon. By viewing interventions as experiments the coach is more likely to be free to discover what the coachee then does, or does not, make of them.

EDUCATION AND NORMALISATION

Shame is experienced as a private and profoundly solitary phenomenon. Finding ways to talk about it and normalise it can go a long way to reducing the tendency for people to believe they are the only ones who suffer in this way. Coachees are, therefore, likely to benefit from feeling less isolated and part of a human race which shares similar experiences, enabling them to think about their own particular experience of shame. This supportive reflexivity can help to relax the internal images and structures that keep shame in place. This represents a departure from trying harder, attempting to force positivity, and doing more, which tends to work in the direction of shoring up self-images. Any experience of success, and its attendant feelings of joy and satisfaction, will always be short-lived and feel precarious if the individual is not able to integrate and normalise inevitable moments of vulnerability and limitation.

MODELLING SUPPORT AND REFLECTION IN THE FACE OF NOT KNOWING

In many corporate environments, coaches can feel under similar pressure to that experienced by their clients to have to know it all, fearing that any admission of vulnerability, confusion or uncertainty on the part of the coach might be perceived as evidence of incompetence. As coaches, we need to be able to trust in our capabilities, the support of supervisors and those professional groups we find nourishing in order to be able to sit with our own limitations. Provided we have done the necessary work on ourselves, we can embody and model a capacity to remain resourced and thoughtful when we are not sure how to proceed, adopting what Staemmler (1997) refers to as an attitude of cultivated uncertainty. As a significant component in the forming of shame experiences is based on internalising negative beliefs and attitudes from others, internalising more positive experiences can go a long way to reducing susceptibility to shame. Over time, coachees are likely to internalise a coach's calm, supportive and reflective attitude, which they will then be able to draw upon in themselves when faced with challenging situations. By also surfacing the role of self-images in creating anxiety in the face of limitation, which deviates from the individual and organisational ideal of omniscience, it is more likely that coachees will be able to integrate the experience of not knowing as a temporary and occasional realm of experience. This acceptance supports the development of trust in their capacity to go on thinking and resourcing themselves in the face of uncertainty. In this way, not knowing need no longer be experienced as catastrophic, a source of defensiveness and shame, but as a necessary pre-cursor to meaning-making, discovery, learning and creativity. This can engender resilience to 'hang in' with complex change processes, and reflect on the experience of chaos and confusion that accompanies individual and organisational transformation.

EMBRACING COMPLEXITY

In working with sensitivity to shame it can be helpful to take a more complex, wider-field perspective on the coachee's presenting issues. Coaching theory and practice still tend to be shaped by the individualistic biases of the organisation and competitive-sports fields out of which they have arisen. This can lead to preoccupation with being right or wrong, winning or losing, and a simplification and reduction in the way meaning is made about the coachee's experience and development. Holding in mind the importance, and possible relevance, of multiple voices and multiple meanings allows coach and client to be less attached to seeking the 'right' answer. Individuals can be supported to make better use of tentative hypotheses, insights and experiments to think and act differently if their experience can be located in a wider context and the effects of system and relational dynamics on their felt sense of worth examined. Far from being a way of avoiding accountability, reducing the fear of exposure and shame can make it easier for individuals to take fuller accountability for the part they have played in any situation, reflect and learn from it.

DIS-IDENTIFICATION WITH INTERNALISED NEGATIVE SELF-IMAGES

There are many approaches to working with negative self-images and beliefs. These include cognitive-behavioural techniques, visualisations, working with affirmations, imagery and anchoring of positive states, externalising and dialoguing with the inner critic, to mention but a few. All potentially have a place. I mention these tools and techniques last because I wish to emphasise the importance of attending to the quality of relationship between coach and coachee in determining the usefulness of these approaches and the fact that, without a sufficiently sensitive and attuned relationship, where shame is concerned, they can become persecutory and ineffective.

CONCLUSION

The dynamics of relating between coach and coachee offer a way of identifying and undoing the historical shame templates and beliefs that are often evoked in organisational and coaching interactions. For coachees, forming an internal image of a supportive, sensitive and reflective coach, along with the feelings and thoughts to which this then gives rise, enables them to develop and draw upon a broader range of internal resources and counter any previous tendency to collapse into incapacitating shame. Whenever a coachee says "I was feeling really stuck and wobbly, then I thought, what would Simon do right now?" they are making use of an internalised set of representations that they can mobilise in service of their own ability to resource themselves and think on their feet. This is not that they are becoming clones of their coach. In fact, they often make thoughtful and creative interventions that would never occur to me! Rather, they are using their experience of being with a coach who can sit with uncertainty to learn to regulate their own anxiety and to activate their own reflective abilities, in order to discover what *they* would do in a novel situation outside of the coaching room.

Tools and technique undoubtedly have their place in coaching. What I am proposing here is an approach that can also make conscious use of relational principles, where the quality of a coach's presence, attunement to the coachee's experience and their shared awareness of what is happening in the coaching relationship contribute to shaping the crucible in which shame phenomena can be surfaced, explored and transformed. This can then lead to a more reflective orientation to when shame arises, and greater acceptance of self, including moments of limitation and not knowing. This stands to cut across the common tendency of individuals in organisations to recoil from the experience of vulnerability and limitation and develop ever-more entrenched ways of covering it up from themselves and others – through, for example, a drive to do more and more to the point of burnout, or the pursuit of perfection to such an extent that procrastination takes the place of action.

Working to unlock the clinch of shame in individuals and organisations seems a key component in supporting a more realistic assessment of presenting problems, creativity and a greater range of response to complex situations and challenges.

CHAPTER 12

DO WE UNDERSTAND EACH OTHER? AN INQUIRY INTO THE COACHING RELATIONSHIP WHEN WORKING IN DIFFERENT LANGUAGES

JANE COX

We live in a world of global networks where the ability to communicate with anyone, in any place at any time has revolutionised the way we do business. It is no longer necessary to establish a company in one country before striding out across the rest of the world like McDonald's golden arches. In our internet world, a global business can be set up *virtually* anywhere and anyone who has the right skills or experience may take a job anywhere in the world, irrespective of where they come from or where they live. With this freedom come new opportunities and challenges for our business leaders who now have global activities to run and virtual teams to manage.

Back in the 1980s and '90s, Hofstede, Trompenaars et al. were writing about the importance of understanding and adjusting to different cultural norms if we are to be successful in managing international business activities. Others such as Rosinski (2003) continue to talk about the importance of recognising cultural difference, but recent advances in communication have brought about huge changes in our business world. Global organisations have become complex fusions of different national cultures and multiple languages and each will develop its own unique culture with its own ways of communicating. Typically it will also adopt a common language in which to conduct its business but that common language does not necessarily originate from its country of origin nor reflect that national culture (e.g. American English that may have more to do with the internet than the USA). We might even describe it as a 'lite' (reduced fat) version of the original since, although it is fit for purpose (i.e. as an effective communication tool), it does not have the same richness as the original.

"So what?" you may be saying, "Surely we must welcome the opportunity and equality that this provides?" Whilst I entirely agree, as an executive coach I also see significant implications for our profession. We have opportunities to work with a far more diverse range of clients and take advantage of many different channels of communication that were not previously available to us. This makes it even more important to focus on the relational aspect of our work. We must not lose sight of the relationship as a critical success factor in coaching, as Wampold (2001) proved in his extensive research. How can we ensure that we are helping our coachees to access deeper levels of understanding or find the language to express themselves in new ways if we only have the 'lite' version of a language to work with? What are the challenges of establishing and maintaining a good working alliance with only a 'lite' language, which may not be the first language for either of us?

As a linguist with a first degree in modern languages, the challenges that cultural and linguistic diversity can bring for both organisations and the people who work within them is an area of particular interest to me. My interest in languages first took me to live and work in France and later to develop a career in international sales. Working "across the language gap" (Stevens & Holland 2008) was a fact of life then and has become so again in my work as an executive coach, for I am often working with global organisations where clients speak many different languages.

My experiences have provided me with some interesting insights into the importance of language as a key aspect of building the coaching relationship and also informed my choice of Inquiry for the Ashridge Master's in Executive Coaching.

In their chapter on international coaching in *The Reflecting Glass*, West & Milan (2001) write that "The development coach's fundamental task is to enter into his/her coachee's frame of reference" (p. 139). They go on to say that coaching allows us to do this as it is non-judgemental. If we accept this as true, we cannot then assume that we know about our coachee's cultural background or that we 'know what they mean' when they express themselves in a language that is not their own. If we do not "freely and wholeheartedly engage with another's subjectivity... while maintaining and being in touch with [our] own" (Fletcher 1998) then we are at risk of inadvertently imposing our own filters and increasing the chance of missing something important.

Wittgenstein (1922) is translated as saying that, "The limits of my language mean the limits of my world." As a relational coach, I believe that I have a role to play in helping my coachees to transcend the limits of their language and to explore beyond the limits of their world.

172

In this chapter, I use case studies to explore what might happen when we are building our *working alliances* (Greenson 1965) and whether the language we use makes a difference. I start by analysing what happens when the coach is embarking on a working relationship with a coachee who shares the same native language. I then explore what might be different when the common language is native to only one of the participants, or when both coach and coachee are working in a shared language that is not native to either of them.

BUILDING THE COACHING RELATIONSHIP BASED ON SHARED NATIVE LANGUAGE

When we meet a coachee from our own culture, language is probably not the first thing on our mind. Perhaps we assume it as a basic condition of communicating, if we consider it at all, since we are likely to be more concerned with understanding our coachee's issues and focusing on the practicalities of setting up the coaching contract. We may know little about each other apart from what we have been told by another, so we start by taking tentative steps towards finding out.

The coach consciously takes the lead in building the relationship by asking questions that invite the coachee to open up. Thus encouraged, we hope that the coachee will begin to talk about himself and offer us a glimpse of his world. At this stage, we are each using our own words, our own version of the language we both speak. We may assume that the other understands our meaning as we do not yet have evidence to the contrary. We are, however, consciously or unconsciously also paying attention to all those subtle unspoken non-verbal signals to gauge how well we are getting our message across, how well we are being received. The coach wants her coachee to learn to trust her and shows this by offering her undivided attention and actively listening to what her coachee is saying. The coach may also be tapping into her wider knowledge, perhaps assessing the coachee's personality type or behavioural style (e.g. Jung 1998; Myers & Myers 1980) to inform the way she communicates. The coach is proactively encouraging in her approach as the coachee may still be fearful of exposing himself to this comparative stranger, even though his hope is to be able to trust the coach with his innermost thoughts. Our starting points are inevitably different as we begin to communicate and try to understand each other. We are embarking on a new relationship from different directions; entering uncharted waters and hoping to find firm ground to stand on – common ground.

Both parties begin by looking for areas of commonality. Gradually, we start to mirror each other and develop a mutual understanding, a shared language, using words, phrases and gestures that we both understand. We may even start to "make leaps or take shortcuts in language as (we) know that the other native speaker can generally follow (our) logic" (Boyes 2006, p. 96). If the coachee perceives that he can trust the coach, he will gradually reveal more of himself. The coach gains closer insights into the coachee's world, is allowed into his 'frame of reference' (West & Milan 2001) and the relationship starts to develop.

Once this mutual bond of understanding has been established, communication between the two parties starts to flow more easily and we move, as if in a dance, matching each other's language, both verbal and non-verbal. We are able to dip beneath the surface of the spoken language to access deeper intuitive levels of communication. We have moved on from our asymmetric start points and created a space of mutuality, a space where we can safely start to explore patterns and mental models in the *here and now.*

It is only once we have achieved this state of trust and mutual understanding that the coach can start to challenge her coachee's thinking and assumptions. The relationship between the two is strong enough to withstand such challenge as the coachee has learned that he is in safe hands.

Now the coach can start to use language rather differently, exploring why the coachee uses certain words and what meanings might be buried in the way he uses his own version of this common tongue. The coach may focus on highlighting the difference between herself and her coachee – the difference in how each of them may be using or understanding the same language – so as to help the coachee to greater insights.

Coach and coachee may experience moments of discord where they diverge in their understanding, but if the relationship is strong, they will come together again as new meaning emerges for the coachee. As the coachee shares his meaning making, mutual understanding is restored. It is the coach's responsibility to ensure that her coachee feels supported so that they can be bold enough to explore the unknown, the un-thought or the un-expressed, and know that they are not risking irrevocable rupture. This is the relationship at work.

In the diagram below I have attempted to capture the pattern of this developing communication.

The linguistic pattern of the developing coaching relationship

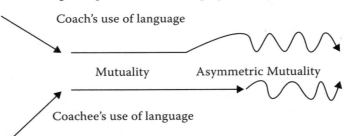

The following case study illustrates this process in action.

'A' was the MD of an engineering company and at our first meeting he told me that he wanted help to sort out his senior management team and the structure of the business. I encouraged him to start by giving me some background: "tell me about yourself so that I can get a clearer picture of your challenges". I listened very attentively and spoke little but when I did speak it was to seek clarification and to show him that I had understood his meaning by summarising what he was telling me. I deliberately repeated the words that he himself had used: "So you say that the senior team need sorting out – tell me a bit more about what you mean exactly." Together we were beginning to create a shared understanding of the situation as he allowed me to see into his world.

After a while, A revealed his underlying anxiety that he was not the right person to lead the business. He seemed very relieved to have finally admitted this to someone and this signalled to me that he was now feeling he could trust me and that we had laid the foundations of an effective working relationship. We went on to talk about how we might work together and I asked him to reflect on what he really wanted to achieve. This he did for our second session: "I have been thinking about that and I realise I really need you to grill me... to help me think through in detail what my purpose is as MD... and what sort of leader I want to be". This further confirmed to me that he now trusted me with his real problem.

Our sessions from then on became an increasingly animated and intellectually stimulating dance. He welcomed my challenges to his thinking, finding that they helped him to clarify his thoughts. "That's a great challenge – I never thought about it like that...".

Six months into our coaching, the relationship is robust and dynamic. It is also caring and supportive, often punctuated with laughter. We explore together, I can challenge him, he can take risks but we always end up agreeing on his next steps. This is the language of our coaching relationship.

WHAT IF WE DON'T SPEAK THE SAME LANGUAGE?
What might be different about building a relationship with a coachee whose native language is not the same as our own? I am an English native and as this is often the common language used by the organisations I work with, it would be easy to assume that we all use this common language in the same way and understand each other perfectly.

I started to become aware that this might not always be the case a few years ago when I took on an assignment that involved coaching the French design director of a large Japanese car corporation based in London. The original presenting issue for this coachee was his leadership style, specifically how he communicated with his team and colleagues.

I particularly welcomed the assignment as I spoke French fluently, having lived and worked in France, and felt I was well placed to understand my coachee's 'frame of reference'. In fact we would often talk French for a while at the beginning of our coaching sessions, even though the coaching was to be conducted in English. The coachee spoke English well but because of my strong command of *his* language, if he was struggling for a word I would encourage him to say it in French and then we would discuss the English translation or simply accept that we both understood. I often recognised the French phraseology he used when expressing himself in English and I believe that my facility in his language helped him to feel understood, "You are the only person who really listens to me – seems to understand me". Some of his challenges with his team did indeed seem to stem from their apparent lack of patience with him when he tried to explain the finer details of something in English.

In our coaching sessions we developed a language that was neither entirely English nor French but a sort of amalgam of the two. This mutually created language was the common ground on which our relationship was based, but reflecting on the work later, I wondered if I was making too much of an assumption about how well I understood *his* culture and language. Perhaps I was taking shortcuts at the expenses of thoroughly exploring his meaning. If I had *not* spoken French, might I have been more vigilant?

It was some of these emerging questions that I decided to explore further through some informal research that I carried out for one of my clients and which gave me some useful experiences to share here. I was invited to set up a series of individual coaching sessions for a representative group of international managers based at a head office in the Netherlands. All the sessions were to be conducted in English, the common language of the business, and they would each be asked for structured feedback on their experience.

The HR director was Indian and she was to be my first volunteer coachee. I was mindful of paying particular attention to the linguistic aspect of building our coaching relationship and I was consciously enunciating more clearly than I generally might, using simpler language and trying to find different ways of saying the same thing. I found myself deliberately checking my understanding and listening very attentively with all my senses to make sure I grasped her meaning.

In this way, our communication became increasingly 'fluent'. Not only was I beginning to use words that she used but I also noticed that she started to copy my language and phrasing. We were mirroring each other in other ways too, picking up each other's gestures and non-verbal communications. I did not feel that the session was particularly challenging or that she achieved any great breakthrough, as she reflected quite tactfully in her slightly stilted feedback on our session, "I appreciated the neutral approach which was nevertheless based on a strong relational aspect." We had, however, achieved an intuitive working relationship and she obviously picked up on the non-judgemental approach which I believe to be core to my coaching.

The second coachee had previously received his 360-degree feedback from me and this helped to ease the first few minutes of our session as we were able to pick up on our previous conversation. He was Danish and he wanted to use the session to explore how to share the feedback with his team. The issue of language arose when he asked me for feedback about what he planned to say to them. He was surprised when I told him that his words sounded quite abrasive. This was not what he intended but he realised that it was perhaps a cultural difference, acknowledging that the Danes could be quite forthright. Since his team was all English, we talked about how they might interpret his message and how he might express himself more effectively to get his true meaning across without upsetting people. He went away with some very specific actions to take and was satisfied to have achieved his objective.

The third coachee was Spanish and on the fast-track management scheme. He told me he had sufficient command of English to manage at work (the 'lite' version) but that he found it difficult to build a social life outside because of his lack of fluency in the local language. He wanted to work on identifying his next career move but he was struggling to find the right words in English. I took an intuitive but deliberate decision to try a non-verbal NLP technique to help free him from the constraint of trying to express himself fully in a language that was not his own. The technique involved him in visualising a "well-formed outcome" (Boyes 2006, p. 90) and then working out the seven steps he needed to take to achieve it. Physically moving from one position to another and visualising each step of his journey gave him the freedom to frame his thoughts in his head and describe it to himself before he had to find English words to explain it to me. He found this process liberating and it certainly enabled him to clear the blockage of how to approach his next challenge.

In the course of my Inquiry, I also coached a Swedish international business consultant who offered to give me feedback about his experience of my coaching from the perspective of a non-native English speaker. The first conversation took place on the phone so we did not have all the non-verbal signals at our disposal.

Our agenda was to help him see a situation from a new perspective: "I am stuck in my own thinking". I found myself summarising regularly – partly to confirm my understanding, partly to help keep him focused and realise the implications of what he was saying. At one point this helped him make a link which he later described as being a really significant moment for him. "Yes I know what I can do now... talking to you about this has helped me... I just have to find some other options... find my way in this context – I want to grow and be challenged". Eventually he resolved to go away and think creatively, "because I can and I like to do this. Well, this is good – I need to get more creative."

When I asked this coachee how he had experienced the session, he said, "I felt that you really listened to me... summarising helped me to make sure I understood the language as well as it being a coaching technique. It helped me find the right words (because I heard how you said something). If I am not able to find the right words in English, it stops me from exploring something in myself – I can't work all the way through in the subtleties".

By concentrating on trying to find a way of expressing himself, he often felt impeded from thinking more deeply about something. So my technique of clarifying my own understanding and reflecting back what he was saying gave him a shortcut to verbalising something, leaving space for new ideas to emerge.

So what did I learn from working with these coachees who were speaking my first language but not their own? Above all, I enjoyed finding a way into each coachee's frame of reference, paying particular attention to our different linguistic starting points and then the mutual 'language' we subsequently developed. I found that I accentuated my natural habit of summarising and seeking clarification and I was aware of trying to avoid using my own familiar colloquialisms whilst using more simple constructs to express myself clearly and deliberately. At times it felt that I was perhaps compromising my command of my own language in order to meet my coachee in a more mutual space. On reflection, I thought this might sound condescending but the coachees' feedback confirmed that this simplification was useful as it helped them navigate a potential impediment to expressing themselves fully.

In the face-to-face meetings, I was aware of my heightened emphasis on non-verbal communication. Intuitively "matching and mirroring" each person's behaviour was a deliberate attempt on my part to communicate at every level with my coachees. "Matching or mirroring another person's communication is the way to build rapport by becoming like the other person at a deep unconscious level" (Boyes 2006, p. 73). During my telephone sessions I did not have access to the visual signals but by concentrating hard and listening intently, I was still able to pick up many non-verbal signals and we achieved a deep level of communication.

The common thread in all these examples is that the coach is deliberately paying attention to the language used, right from the beginning of the conversation. Although this takes more effort at the outset, it enables us to develop a shared understanding with each coachee. In effect we are constructing our own version of a language that we can both use. This opens the way to building an effective coaching relationship in which we are both fully present and open for change to emerge.

However, we do not always pay such careful attention and this may have disastrous consequences, as I discovered to my cost during a conversation with a Dutch colleague. This was not specifically a coaching conversation, but it alerted me to the possibility that a simple misunderstanding could inadvertently trigger a powerful "critical moment" (De Haan 2011).

My colleague and I were discussing coaching and I was sharing some of my early thoughts about working across languages. At one point I described the practical implications of my speaking "proper English" when this was not my coachee's first language. Unwittingly I had hit a nerve. Some time later, my colleague told me that he thought I was criticising *him* when I used the words "proper English" as he was also a non-native speaker. It was certainly not my intention to criticise his English. I simply meant to highlight that as a native speaker one has full command of one's own first language, but that is not how he interpreted my words because he heard them through his own filter. Careless use of my language had created a sense of inequality which might have resulted in an irrevocable rupture, had my colleague not shared his reaction with me. By talking it through, we arrived at a better understanding of each other which probably strengthened our relationship although things might have turned out very differently.

WHAT HAPPENS WHEN NEITHER COACH NOR COACHEE IS SPEAKING IN THEIR OWN LANGUAGE?

The third scenario I wish to explore occurs when coach and coachee are using a common language that is not native to either of them.

Let me draw on another recent coaching experience. Here the coachee was a Swiss German who engaged me to help her work out her next career move. We agreed to work in French as this was the only language we had in common.

At the outset, this arrangement seemed to work well enough even though our communication felt somewhat stilted. We were relying heavily on non-verbal signals to check our understanding of each other and I found myself wondering how this would affect the coaching.

As we explored her motivations and what was blocking her from achieving her objectives, she started to stumble over her words and look perplexed. Alerted as I was to the possible issues of language, I asked if she was having trouble expressing her meaning. She nodded and burst into tears. When she recovered herself she told me that she wasn't quite sure what I was asking her or what she should say. It was in this moment that I sensed I had seen a manifestation of her real anxiety about her issue. She seemed to be imagining that I was feeling irritated and impatient with her and thereby projecting her own frustration onto me. There seemed to be a clear parallel between my lack of understanding and the lack of understanding she was experiencing at work. I sensed she had subconsciously revealed the root of her problem about her next career move and wanted me to explore this with her gently, but I struggled to find a way of expressing what I would have said in my own language. We were both stuck because neither of us could find the right words for what turned out to be a turning point in the coaching.

For a while no words were spoken, but something was clearly passing between us. Eventually, in her faltering French, she verbalised exactly what I had been thinking. "I understand now what has been holding me back. Because I do not understand what is expected of me, I feel impotent. I don't know what to do. You have helped me to understand this – thank you".

What was it that passed between us and helped her understand this? On the surface of it, we were held back by our lack of fluency in the common language which became a limiting factor as we could not find the words to express the subtleties of our thoughts and feelings. On another level, however, the lack of linguistic fluency forced us to focus on other, more intuitive, channels of communication that provided a powerful catalyst for change. We did not at that critical moment need a spoken language as we had found another language in which to communicate.

CONCLUSIONS

Having explored the issue of language in coaching from the perspectives of asymmetry (where only one party is working in their first language) and mutuality (where both or neither party shares the same native language), I come to the conclusion that paying careful attention to our use of language is a critical success factor in any coaching relationship. The spoken aspect of any language is the way we first make contact, the currency we use to start the process of building a relationship.

Nevertheless, most of the coaches I spoke to reported that they did not regard language or their level of fluency as a great problem in their practice. Whichever language they work in, they assured me that a lack of 'first-hand understanding' or 'total fluency' can actually be a benefit in coaching. This can slow down the conversation and allow for more reflection as well as bringing out idiomatic expressions, literal meanings and other curious properties of language which are as worthy of deeper exploration as the (Freudian) slips that might occur in our own language.

If we share the same native language, however, we may automatically assume that we are both using it in the same way. We may overlook the importance of how our coachee is using his version until we are deeper into the relationship, and only then start to explore the meaning of his words with a view to allowing his deeper thoughts, feelings and emotions to surface.

So whichever language(s) we are using in our coaching, we might do well to assume that we are always speaking entirely different languages and slow down, reflect, make sense and inquire into use of language from the word go.

Certainly, where there is linguistic asymmetry, we are more likely to pay attention to language from the outset. As the native speaker we may still overlook the other's command of our language, particularly if they are speaking fluently, but if we are aware of the possibility for misinterpretation or of evoking a feeling of inferiority in the other person, then we can work with this to make sure that the emerging relationship starts off on an equal footing.

The same would be true if we are both working out of our comfort zone, as we are far less likely to make assumptions about the use of language if we ourselves are not easily able to verbalise all our thoughts and feelings.

Speaking at a seminar in 2008, Charlotte Sills said that "The process of coaching can be thought of as an individual's attempt to find a new language to express and make sense of herself". If the coachee is looking for a new way of expressing "herself" then whatever language we start with serves only as a facilitator for creating the conditions that will allow this *new* language to emerge. Whatever the starting point, both coach and coachee have an equal part to play in creating these unique conditions precisely because the new language can only be *co-created.*

This new language is not dependent on the words we use, but is a much more complex 'interweaving' of all the different ways we have of communicating with each other. It is something so deeply shared that it cannot be expressed solely in words and yet it can be universally understood. "Meaning arises in the relations between units of language" (Derrida quoted by Collins & Mayblin 1996, p. 58). If new meaning emerges in the relational space between what we say, it can only be co-created and therefore is unique to each coaching relationship. So it doesn't matter which language we speak because the coaching relationship itself provides us with our own new, shared language.

PART V

QUANTITATIVE RESEARCH INTO THE COACHING RELATIONSHIP

This section of the book contains the following chapters:

Chapter 13 – Erik de Haan and Anna Duckworth – The coaching relationship and other 'common factors' in executive coaching outcome

Chapter 14 – Jeffrey Jackson, Lisa Boyce and Laura Neal – eHarmony, match.com, plentyoffish: have you considered matching to support your client–coach relationships?

Chapter 15 – Louis Baron and Lucie Morin – The working alliance in executive coaching: its impact on outcomes and how coaches can influence it

The final part of the book provides a continuation of an amazing track record in outcome research in the helping professions, with three pioneering outcome-research papers on factors of effectiveness in coaching.

The research has been carried out in three different countries and in three different contexts: one paper's research was carried out in a large private corporation; another's in the U.S. military, a public body; and the third's in a myriad of independent companies.

Each of these independent research articles demonstrates that it is the coaching *relationship* that has the highest claim to effectiveness in coaching. Moreover, two of three articles show that the relationship actually *mediates* the effects of other factors: in other words, it seems that the significance of the effective ingredient 'relationship' helps to explain those other ingredients as well.

In the unfolding journey of the book, this part represents the climax, in other words a 'eureka' moment that gives further support to the idea that the coaching relationship lies at the root of understanding, matching, experimentation and effectiveness.

CHAPTER 13

THE COACHING RELATIONSHIP AND OTHER 'COMMON FACTORS' IN EXECUTIVE COACHING OUTCOME

Erik de Haan and Anna Duckworth

Abstract

This is a quantitative study of executive coaching to determine the key factors or 'active ingredients' which contribute to its effectiveness.

Data collected from 156 client–coach pairs participating in formally contracted, external executive coaching was analysed to examine the impact on coaching outcome of the following: client self-efficacy, client personality and client–coach personality match (in terms of the Myers–Briggs Type Indicator – MBTI), perceived coach interventions and the strength of the client–coach relationship (using the working alliance inventory).

Strong indications were found for the prediction of coaching outcome by: (1) the coaching relationship in terms of a working alliance, as experienced by the client; (2) the self-efficacy of the client; and (3) generalised coaching technique as experienced by the client. The client–coach relationship (working alliance) strongly mediated the impact of self-efficacy and technique on coaching outcomes, suggesting that the perception of working alliance by the client was the key factor in coaching outcome. Personality or personality matching did not correlate with coaching outcome.

From this research it seems that the so called 'common factors' of coaching conversations – i.e. those aspects which are not related to specific coaching technique, approach or philosophy – indeed play a role in influencing the outcome for the client. As a result, it appears most important at all times to attend to and develop the coaching relationship as seen by the client.

INTRODUCTION

It is our experience that coaches tend to be caring people who are passionate about their field. The chance to help others achieve their dreams is often seen by them as a vital opportunity to contribute to all that is good in this world and to find personal fulfilment. This is just one reason why most executive coaches constantly seek to learn and grow their coaching capability and increase its effectiveness and versatility so that they can deliver the best possible service to each of their unique clients.

This research study was carried out with this motive. We wanted to explore what different clients say about what actually works most effectively for each of them to achieve their various chosen outcomes. From our own earlier research (De Haan et al. 2011), our intuition and experience as practising executive coaches and our literature searches into both the relatively new field of coaching outcome research and the established field of psychotherapy outcome research (Duckworth et al. 2012), we concluded that our energy would be best spent exploring the impact of various 'common factors' (Wampold 2001) in order to deduce which of these contribute most significantly to successful outcomes for the client.

Based on findings from our literature survey (see Duckworth et al. 2012) and the prevailing idea (see the Introduction to this book) that common factors and in particular the coaching relationship are likely to have a differential, high impact on coaching outcome, we hypothesised the following:

H1. The strength of the coaching relationship (as measured by the Working Alliance Inventory) will predict coaching outcomes, both (a) as measured by clients of coaching and (b) as measured by their coaches.

This follows findings of Allen et al. (2004), Boyce, Jackson & Neal (2010) and De Haan et al. (2011), as described in Duckworth et al. (2012).

H2. Personality differences (as characterised by the MBTI profile) will predict coaching outcomes.

This follows the results of Scoular & Linley (2006), also summarised in Duckworth et al. (2012). We acknowledge that the Myers–Briggs Type Indicator has only 'sufficient' levels of reliability and validity and has been shown to be a poor predictor of, for example, managerial effectiveness, job performance and employee commitment (Gardner & Martinko 1996). On the other hand, the MBTI is still the instrument most frequently used by practitioners and has been used by previous researchers.

H3. General self-efficacy of the client will predict coaching outcomes.

Research by Anderson and Betz (2001) shows that the expectations individuals have about their self-efficacy – or in other words their beliefs that they are capable of performing in a certain manner to attain certain goals – directly influence their personal and career development. Personal self-efficacy expectations are often regarded as primary determinants of behavioural change (Sherer et al. 1982). Within the coaching outcome literature, Stewart et al. (2008) have shown that general self-efficacy predicts coaching outcome.

H4. All (perceived) coach techniques – all coaching behaviours as reported by clients – will predict coaching outcomes approximately equally.

This follows the results of De Haan et al. (2011).

H5. The strength of the coaching relationship mediates: (a) the impact of client–coach personality differences on coaching outcome, as stated by H2; (b) general self-efficacy of the client impact on coaching outcome, as stated by H3; and (c) perceived coach techniques impact on coaching outcome, as stated by H4.

This follows the results of Boyce, Jackson & Neal (2010), summarised in Duckworth et al. (2012).

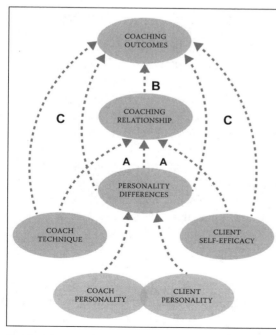

A graphical depiction of the various 'common factors' and their relationship to coaching outcome, as studied by us. Our independent variables were coach technique, personality differences and client self-efficacy. Our dependent variable was coaching outcome. In this study we investigate both direct influence of the independent variables on coaching outcome (dependencies B and C), and the probability of mediation of this influence through the strongest dependency, the coaching relationship (dependency A plus B as compared to C).

Figure 1

Figure 1 shows the various common factors (Wampold 2001) that we hypothesise to have a positive impact on the outcome of coaching conversations. The figure also shows how a mediation of the impact of these common factors through the relationship, as predicted by Hypothesis 5, may take place.

METHOD

PARTICIPANTS

The coaches who participated in this study were experienced and qualified and were employed by different institutions, such as Ashridge Business School and the Oxford School of Coaching and Mentoring. About one-third of the sample of coaches was self-employed. Each coach completed an on-line 'coach survey' and then invited their clients to complete an on-line 'client survey'. It was made clear to both coaches and clients that "All responses to this questionnaire will be treated in strictest confidence and no individual respondent will be identified."

The response rate to the questionnaire for the coaches was 78.6% and for clients it was 58.4%. We attribute these high response rates to the personal approach used to select respondents. With 34 coaches and 156 clients participating in the survey, we were able to study a total of 156 coaching relationships. The average experience of the coach was 10.3 years, the minimum experience was 3 years and the maximum was 20 years. The SSRs of the coaching clients' MBTI scores were mostly similar to the large database of Ashridge clients' SSRs, i.e. they had a bias towards 'NT' of about 2–6 but when normalised against the database of all Ashridge clients, there was a bias of about 2–6 towards 'F'. Clients were mostly senior and middle managers in large organisations, with a very small minority being coaches or consultants themselves. The number of sessions that coach and client had undertaken at the point data was collected ranged from one to around a hundred with a mean of 8.6. Session lengths ranged from around 75 to 120 minutes. Data collection took place over a 12-month period from August 2008 to August 2009. Approximately 60% of clients and approximately 80% of coaches were UK based, whilst all coaches and clients were based in (wider) Europe. 60% of clients were male and 40% female. 49% of coaches were male, 51% were female.

QUESTIONNAIRES

The coach questionnaire could be completed in five minutes and the client questionnaire in no more than 20 minutes. After establishing the relevant background information on gender, MBTI type and coaching credentials, the coach questionnaire asked coaches to rate the quality of their relationships with each of their different clients by scoring the statement "I have a very good relationship with this client" on a seven-point Likert scale. Using the same scale, they were asked several control questions to establish the extent to which they tend to adapt their style (either deliberately or subconsciously) to meet the needs of the client. This was done so that the data could be filtered to prevent distortion from those samples where the coach modifies their style away from their own natural type preferences. They were asked about their personal preferences for a range of coaching styles and techniques and finally we asked them for any comments regarding (1) whether they had noticed different responses to particular approaches from the differing client personality types and (2) whether they adapted their own coaching style to different personalities.

The client questionnaire asked for background information and was then split into four sections. The first section contained questions requiring answers on a seven-point Likert scale about perceived outcomes: "your overall coaching experience", "coaching adding value", "impact coaching on your performance at work" and "coaching helps to achieve what you want to achieve", with 'average effectiveness' being calculated as the averaged score from these four values. In this section we also asked respondents about their prior expectations of the likely benefit from coaching and the extent to which the organisational context supported the coaching objectives. The second section explored the extent to which clients perceived they get a range of different inputs from their coach and the extent to which they might value different inputs. This section was based upon the well-known Heron (1975) model comprising six categories of counselling intervention. The third section contained an adapted full version of the well-established Working Alliance Inventory (Horvath & Greenberg 1989). This instrument is used widely in therapy for measuring the quality of the relationship between therapist and patient and was adapted here to measure the coach–client relationship. In the fourth section, we used another well-founded instrument to establish the client's self-efficacy (Schwarzer, Mueller & Greenglass 1999). All sections included space for comments or clarification and there was a final text box asking for respondents' perceptions of the effectiveness of the coaching they were engaged in.

PROCEDURE

The main dependent variable was 'average effectiveness' (the average of four different outcome variables rated by the client), and the independent variables were the coaching relationship (as assessed by coach and client independently), the difference in Myers–Briggs 'type' of coach and client, the self-efficacy of the client, and six generalised coaching behaviours. Due to the relatively small numbers of coaches, we were unable to use coach MBTI type as an independent variable.

RESULTS
DESCRIPTIVE STATISTICS

Firstly, we looked at the mean values for our key variables. The dependent variable, 'average effectiveness', had a mean value of 5.97 with a standard deviation of 0.79 and a range of 2.5 to 7. The mean score for the coach's assessment of the relationship (scored by the coach) was 6.07, with a standard deviation of 0.92 and a range of 3 to 7, where 7 is the highest possible score. The mean value for the working alliance between coach and client was 71.6 out of a possible 84, with a standard deviation of 8.4 and a range of 37.3 to 84. The mean value for self-efficacy was 22.9 out of a possible 30, with a standard deviation of 3.9 and a range of 11 to 30.

We carried out reliability measurements on all of the scales. The Cronbach's Alpha for the four items in 'average effectiveness' was 0.90. Cronbach's Alpha for Total Working Alliance Inventory of 36 items was 0.94, with figures for the three subscales of working alliance (each containing 12 items); Task, Bond and Goal being 0.86, 0.83 and 0.88 respectively. The Cronbach's Alpha for Self Efficacy was 0.83. All of these reliability tests demonstrate good internal consistency as they are all above 0.8.

We looked at the influence of client gender on perceived outcome of coaching. A T-test comparing the male and female distributions of perceived outcome did not produce a significant difference ($t = -.63$, $df = 153$, $p = .53$). However, interestingly, a 2x2 ANOVA to look at the impact of coach–client gender pairings on Average Effectiveness reveals a slight but significant difference in perceived outcome by 'gender match' for female clients, i.e. female coaches coaching female clients are slightly more effective than male coaches coaching female clients (mean effectiveness scores of 6.2 and 5.7 respectively). This is only true for female clients and coaches; no other significant differences are found in comparing male/female coaches with male/female clients. The increased effectiveness for female coaches working with female clients chimes with what Ragins, Cotton & Miller (2000) found with regard to formal mentoring programmes.

Through inspecting all the background information, a correlation between reported number of sessions and average effectiveness found no significant linear correlation. There was, however, a small but highly significant correlation ($r = 0.28^{**}$) between perceived outcome and the extent to which the client believes their organisational context supports the coaching objectives. There was no significant correlation ($r = .10$) between clients' reported prior expectations of coaching and perceived outcome.

Testing the hypotheses H1 – H5
H1: Strength of coaching relationship predicts coaching outcomes

We found strong and consistent correlations between working alliance as measured by the client and our client outcome measures, but no correlations between the coaches' measure of the relationship and outcome (see Table 1). Hypothesis 1, therefore, was confirmed with regard to the client's rating of the relationship, for all aspects of the standard Working Alliance Inventory. This supports the studies by Boyce, Jackson & Neal (2010) and Baron & Morin (2009), albeit that these studies also found some evidence of positive correlation between coaches' ratings of the relationship and coaching outcome. Our result is similar to what has been found in psychotherapy, see, for example, Horvath & Symonds (1991) where client ratings (and not therapist ratings!) of the alliance are the best predictor of outcome. It appears from our results that the correlation with outcome is slightly higher for the task-aspects of the relationship (clarity and mutual agreement on the tasks, strength of collaboration, etc.). Broadly, all the correlations with the working alliance in Table 1 count as a large effect size (r around 0.5) according to accepted definitions of effect size (Cohen 1988) and this is little affected when controlling for self-efficacy.

Table 1

Pearson product correlations between measures of the working alliance as perceived by coach and client and outcome measures as registered by clients. Please note that the client and coach measures of relationship strength: Working Alliance Inventory (WAI) and coach relationship assessment, do not correlate ($r = 0.12$, $p = 0.19$) and that client WAI correlates significantly with self-efficacy ($r = 0.38**$) whilst the coach measure of relationship strength does not correlate with self-efficacy ($r = 0.12$, $p = 0.17$).

Working Alliance Measures	Outcome measures:				
	Overall coaching experience	Coaching adding value	Impact on performance	Achieving your objectives	Average effectiveness
Task	0.62**	0.55**	0.47**	0.54**	0.62**
Goal	0.55**	0.48**	0.44**	0.51**	0.57**
Bond	0.56**	0.44**	0.32**	0.38**	0.48**
Total WAI:	0.63**	0.54**	0.45**	0.52**	0.61**
Coaches' relationship assessment	0.09	0.15	0.09	0.13	0.13
Self-efficacy	0.20*	0.23**	0.25**	0.18*	0.25**

H2: PERSONALITY DIFFERENCES PREDICT COACHING OUTCOMES

To our surprise, Hypothesis 2 was not borne out in any way. Firstly, using t-tests, we looked for differences in the reported outcome of coaching for each of the Myers–Briggs client personality dichotomies, E/I, S/N, T/F and J/P (Myers 1998) and found none. We then used correlation to look for evidence of differences in outcome depending on degrees of separation between coach and client types on the Myers–Briggs type table (as a measure of personality mismatch) and found none. We also used a t-test to investigate the impact of matching and mismatching the coach and client MBTI 'temperaments' (Briggs Myers et al. 1998) and found no difference. We filtered out those coaching relationships where the coach reported that they consciously modify their style once they know the client's type and repeated these tests, but again no differences were found. This discrepancy with the results found by Scoular and Linley (2006) may be due to differences in the design of the two studies: our data comes from longer-term coaching relationships whereas the data from Scoular and Linley (2006) came from one-off 30-minute sessions, where it is possible that the impact of matching might be more significant.

H3: SELF-EFFICACY OF THE CLIENT PREDICTS COACHING OUTCOMES

Hypothesis 3 was supported in that significant correlations between the clients' self-efficacy measures and the client outcome measures were found (see Table 1). Again, this confirms well-established results in a related field: significant correlation between self-efficacy and perceived outcome in self-regulated learning (see, for example, Schunk 1990).

H4: ALL (PERCEIVED) COACHING TECHNIQUES PREDICT OUTCOMES APPROXIMATELY EQUALLY

Hypothesis 4 was partially supported in that the techniques and behaviours people perceive they get in their coaching affect the outcome similarly, for 4 out of 6 coach behaviours. These results are shown in Table 2 using correlations and the important feature to draw out here is not so much the values themselves (because if a client reports a positive experience overall, they are quite likely to give high scores on all aspects of it – see, for example, De Haan, Culpin & Curd 2011) but that there is considerable variation across the values.

Table 2

Pearson product correlations between the extent to which the client perceives that they get different things from the coach and average coaching effectiveness as registered by clients. The first six descriptors are based on Heron's six categories of counselling intervention (Heron 1975) and the other five are based on our own experience of what clients are looking for in executive coaching engagements.

What the client perceives they get	Correlation with Average Effectiveness
To be advised or told what to do by my coach	.06
For my coach to provide me with information	.22*
For my coach to challenge my thoughts or actions	.37**
For my coach to help me to make discoveries	.42**
For my coach to support me	.39**
For my coach to help me to release emotions	.28**
Significant progress on my issues through step-by-step change	.31**
Significant progress on my issues through critical moments of insight or realisation	.51**
Significant growth relating to outcomes/doing	.53**
Significant growth relating to behaviours/being	.48**
Explicit focus on my most important goals	.46**

H5: THE STRENGTH OF THE COACHING RELATIONSHIP MEDIATES THE OTHER VARIABLES

Hypothesis 5 stated that the strength of the coaching relationship mediates the influence of (a) personality differences, (b) client self-efficacy and (c) perceived coaching behaviours on coaching outcomes. Personality differences were shown not to predict outcome, so hypothesis 5(a) is not relevant and cannot be supported. When self-efficacy and working alliance were regressed on reaction, the working alliance was significantly related to coaching outcome and self-efficacy score became non-significant at the $p<0.01$ level. The result of Sobel's test showed that the parameter estimate for the relationship between the self-efficacy and generalised outcome was significantly lower in the mediated condition than in the non-mediated condition $Z = 3.87$, $p < 0.0001$, indicating that relational processes fully mediated the relationship between client self-efficacy and coaching outcome

(Baron & Kenny 1986). This provides support for Hypothesis 5(b). Similarly, when perceived coach behaviours and working alliance were regressed on reaction, the working alliance was significantly related to coaching outcome and all coaching behaviours scores (except for two: perceived explicit focus on goals and perceived help with making discoveries) became non-significant at the $p<0.01$ level. The result of Sobel's test showed that the parameter estimates for the relationship between coaching behaviours and generalised outcome was significantly lower in the mediated condition than in the non-mediated condition, $Z > 3.26$, $p < 0.01$ for all 6 coaching behaviours, indicating that relational processes significantly mediated the relationship between coach techniques and coaching outcome (for interest, perceived help with making discoveries remained significant after mediation at the $p<0.05$ level). This provides support for Hypothesis 5(c). This result is similar to those of Baron & Morin (2009) and Boyce, Jackson & Neal (2010) who also found that the relationship mediates significantly the other independent variables that correlate with coaching outcome.

DISCUSSION
IMPLICATIONS OF FINDINGS
The research confirms Hypothesis 1(a), Hypothesis 3, Hypothesis 4 and Hypothesis 5 (b and c) on the impact of common factors on coaching outcome. We have found strong indications that the coaching relationship (or to be more precise, the working alliance), as rated by the client, predicts coaching outcome to a considerable degree. We have also found indications that client self-efficacy and perceived coach behaviours predict coaching outcome. The findings here support the general principle of coaching; that asking questions and helping the client to gain new insights and make their own discoveries is reported to be more effective than providing instruction, advice and information.

We have found no evidence for a differential impact of either client personality or coach–client personality matching. This means our results confirm those of Boyce, Jackson & Neal (2010) and Baron & Morin (2009) regarding the coaching relationship and those of Stewart et al. (2008) in the area of self-efficacy, whilst we have not been able to confirm the findings in the area of personality matching by Scoular & Linley (2006).

We are now in a situation where we have strong indicators for the importance of certain common factors in executive coaching, in particular the coaching relationship as seen by the client, whilst the importance of *objective matching* between two personalities as it is usually done might be overstated. From a buyer's perspective, it might be more important to focus on coach selection – in terms of qualifications, accreditation and supervision records

– than on client matching, as Wycherley & Cox (2008) also suggest. The only form of matching between coach and client for which this research has found any support is *subjective matching*: where client and coach physically meet each other and have an interview or a trial session, after which the client determines whether to proceed with that coach, on the basis of his or her first impression of the strength of the coaching relationship.

In contrast to these findings related to personality characteristics, we have found no indications that the importance of the coaching relationship (as judged by the client) has been overstated in the coaching profession: the working-alliance scores by clients in this study predict an impressive 25% of total proportion of variance of coaching outcome (see Table 1). Whilst the quality of the experienced relationship seems to be crucial, the ability to self-motivate ('general self-efficacy') also seems to be significant (this amounts to around 4% of proportion of variance according to Table 1).

Although this has been found before in psychotherapy (see, for example, Horvath & Symonds 1991), we think it is fascinating that despite the high predictive value of the client's view of the strength of the coaching relationship, the coach's estimate of that same relationship bears no relationship with either the coaching outcomes or the strength of the relationship as estimated by the client. However much we emphasise the importance of the coaching relationship for effectiveness, we need to emphasise as well that clients and coaches have completely independent perspectives on that relationship, so coaches have no certain way of knowing how well they are doing in this regard. Finding out the client's view, by using the version of the Working Alliance Inventory and encouraging frankness, appears to be a way of resolving that dilemma (see Miller et al. 2005).

However, for a coach to inquire into the client's perspective on the relationship also has an impact on that relationships as coaches and clients are both not only observers but also key participants within the coaching relationship. Moreover, clients might be polite, defensive, avoidant or otherwise unfocused in their answers to their coaches. For convenience, the coaching literature speaks about 'the coaching relationship', an expression that suggests that there are relational aspects that client and coach hold in common. However, 'the' relationship between coach and client only exists in their respective minds (and in the minds of outside observers), where 'it' will be represented in a completely independent way and moreover be evaluated completely independently and according to highly personal criteria and expectations. Research into 'the' therapeutic relationship shows time and time again that there is no one thing called '*the* helping relationship' as it is perceived and evaluated independently by clients, therapists and indeed observers (see, for example, Horvath & Marx 1990; Horvath & Symonds 1991).

LIMITATIONS OF THIS RESEARCH

Although our key findings seem fairly robust, there are certain limitations which lead to our recommendation of further research. One limitation affects practically all coaching research including ours. It is that in this emerging profession of executive coaching researchers have not been able to achieve the 'gold standard' of therapy outcome research, namely, randomised control trials (Wampold 2001). In this particular study this means that we have not been able to suggest objective criteria for outcome, such as the assessment by independent outsiders on a well-validated instrument. Another limitation of our design was that every coaching relationship studied was measured only once and at a random stage of its development. Finally, we employed different scales for the assessment of the working alliance for coaches and their clients.

We believe there is certainly more research needed into coaching outcome, in particular in the area of personality of coach and client, and personality matching. Next, it would be helpful to have more findings with greater statistical power on the impact of the relationship, so that we can look more closely into key aspects of the coaching relationship, such as 'task', 'goal' and 'bond' as seen by clients and coaches.

CONCLUSION

This is one of the first studies to explore systematically and compare the contribution of various factors which are deemed to contribute to coaching effectiveness, the so-called 'common factors'. It has found fresh evidence for the importance of the quality of the working relationship (the 'working alliance') as seen from the perspective of the client, and for the importance of general self-efficacy of the client who comes to the coaching relationship. Also, it shows that personality factors and personality matching are likely to play a lesser role as a predictor of success in executive coaching. These are important findings that may guide both the development of the profession and the choices that are made in the recruitment, development, deployment and matching of executive coaches.

CHAPTER 14

EHARMONY, MATCH.COM,
PLENTYOFFISH: HAVE YOU
CONSIDERED MATCHING TO
SUPPORT YOUR CLIENT–COACH
RELATIONSHIPS?

R. JEFFREY JACKSON, LISA A. BOYCE
AND LAURA J. NEAL

eHarmony, match.com, plentyoffish and many other on-line dating services claim to use a scientific approach to match singles that results in millions of satisfied customers. While not for love, the idea of matching clients and coaches to develop professional relationships for the purpose of promoting effective outcomes is gaining interest. However, such a decision is not trite. Many issues need to be considered, including why matching would be particularly relevant to developmental relationships, what factors are relevant to consider in matching and who or which programs are more suited to matching – as well as how a matching process is implemented. Despite the strong rationale for a central role of matching in coaching outcomes, we find that coaching relationship processes have a strong direct effect on results, while matching plays an important role in enabling the favourable effects of the coaching processes. We supplemented our combined fifty-plus years of coaching experience with research-supported insights into these issues. As matching to promote developmental relationships is a relatively new practice, we hope to broaden the discussion and excite empirically driven decisions to achieve successful coaching outcomes by developing effective relationships from successfully matching clients and coaches.

MATCHING TO MEET CHALLENGES IN
DEVELOPMENTAL RELATIONSHIPS

Coaching is a developmental relationship for leaders interested in learning interrelated skills and abilities to enhance their effectiveness and expand their leadership capacity. By the very nature of this process, there is a gap being addressed between current capability and desired levels. Even though this gap doesn't necessarily signify a derailing risk, it nonetheless indicates that something more is expected – the current level of performance is not perfect and may especially need expanding for higher levels of leadership (Drotter & Charan 2001). Some coaching approaches challenge those being coached to create deliberately a state of disequilibrium and, by design, move clients beyond current routines and out of their comfort zones (McCauley & Van Velsor 2004). As a result, the process of being coached is inherently destabilising, although geared to foster development and effectiveness. Further, a common coaching objective is increased self-awareness, which can be threatening since it exposes blind spots and bursts the bubble of positive illusions. Sherman and Freas (2004) describe this phenomenon as outsourced candour! The revelation of secrets and exposure of known and unknown limitations in the presence of and by a coach, an intimate stranger early in the relationship, can be quite unsettling.

In addition to the specific challenges coaching presents for clients, there are several general challenges concerning the very different nature of tasks and behaviours that are valued and rewarded in the work environment versus those that are desired and expected in the coaching context. At work, the client is expected to be broadly competent with specific expertise manifested in self-confidence. In coaching, clients are in a learning and developing mode that can involve self-questioning and exploration of personal limitations. Coaching also involves open disclosure, transparent self-presentation and reflection, processes that are very different from a fast-paced action orientation. Thus, the factors that frequently contribute to work success are different and sometimes even opposed to those that are activated in coaching. This difference compounds the challenges of being in a coaching relationship and reflects ubiquitous tensions experienced in coaching for leadership development.

In short, there are several coaching challenges in a developmental relationship which may be positively influenced by matching clients with coaches. Using the definition of matching as an attempt to identify a coach tailored to meet the needs of an individual client (Wycherley & Cox 2008), there are several ways this match can be beneficial. For example, matching may promote familiarity with coaches so they don't seem like total strangers to the client, accelerate the development of a working relationship by building from shared characteristics, facilitate more openness as a result of early bonding, support earlier developmental risk taking by creating a strong basis for trust and enhance client's self-efficacy through more knowledge about the coach. These examples indicate that matching could be a powerful tool in creating the conditions for a strong coaching relationship. In turn this relationship supports key coaching processes expected to lead to favourable coaching outcomes.

MATCH FACTORS TO ENHANCE COACHING RELATIONSHIPS

Consistent with other developmental relationships, a quality coaching relationship may be the single most important factor for successful coaching outcomes (e.g. Asay & Lambert 1999; Kampa-Kokesch & Anderson 2001; O'Broin & Palmer 2006) and a crucial factor in sustaining the opportunity for development (Thompson et al. 2008). The coaching relationship as depicted by Boyce and Hernez-Broome (2010) is influenced by the independent characteristics of the coach and client; it is predicated on the sets of experiences, backgrounds, styles and general histories that each brings; and is further influenced by the level of organisational support (see Figure 1). The degree of match between the participants can act as a catalyst for specific coaching processes that substantially move the client toward planned outcomes. For a discussion of the process and outcome components of the model, please see Boyce, Jackson & Neal (2010). Of particular relevance, the client–coach match consists of three characteristics: commonality, compatibility and credibility.

COMMONALITY

Commonality refers to the client and coach sharing common characteristics, attributes, backgrounds or experiences. There are three categories of these common characteristics or experiences: biographical, professional and personal. Biographics refer to surface-level attributes such as race, ethnicity, gender and age. Professional background encompasses past work experiences as well as education and professional training. Personal background broadly subsumes interests, hobbies, volunteer activities and religious and sexual orientation.

Matching a coach who is similar to a client in terms of demographics and professional and personal backgrounds is based on the belief that rapport and trust will be more quickly and effectively established in the coaching relationship. On a basic level, the similarity-attraction hypothesis provides support for this idea, maintaining that similarity is a major source of attraction between individuals and a variety of physical, social, and status traits are

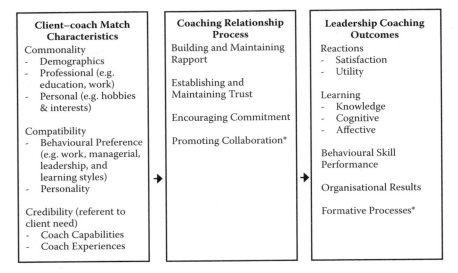

Client–coach Match Characteristics	Coaching Relationship Process	Leadership Coaching Outcomes
Commonality - Demographics - Professional (e.g. education, work) - Personal (e.g. hobbies & interests) Compatibility - Behavioural Preference (e.g. work, managerial, leadership, and learning styles) - Personality Credibility (referent to client need) - Coach Capabilities - Coach Experiences	Building and Maintaining Rapport Establishing and Maintaining Trust Encouraging Commitment Promoting Collaboration*	Reactions - Satisfaction - Utility Learning - Knowledge - Cognitive - Affective Behavioural Skill Performance Organisational Results Formative Processes*

* Introduced in latest revisions of the model, Framework for Leadership Coaching Research (Boyce & Hernez-Broome 2010)

Figure 1. Conceptual framework for understanding the impact of client–coach matching on coaching relationships and coaching outcomes

used for inferring similarity in attitudes and beliefs (Byrne 1971; Harrison, Price & Bell 1998). Because of these core similarities, the coach and client share perspectives and understanding of relevant issues.

On a deeper level, social identity theory maintains that social identification and self-categorisation help individuals establish a sense of belonging to particular groups – they are "matches to the relevant ingroup" (Hogg 2001, p. 187; Hogg, Terry & White 1995). The social comparison process of identifying with others fulfils a basic need for self-esteem and belonging and enables a connection to those who are viewed as prototypical expressions of oneself. The identification process is comforting in that it reduces uncertainty about others since the attitudes, behaviours and feelings of ingroup members are familiar and predictable.

As a result, social identity theory relates to matching through commonality via a rapid social comparison process – by defining the relationship in a connected 'we' and 'us' fashion rather than a differentiated or individuated 'I' and 'you' interaction (Bizumic et al. 2009). By quickly gaining clarity about 'who' we are as a dyad, the coaching relationship has a foundation to move to other tasks.

200

COMPATIBILITY

Compatibility is the appropriate combination of client and coach behavioural preferences. Behavioural preferences are the characteristics that influence client and coach cognitions and behaviours in various situations and can include personality traits as well as managerial, leadership and learning styles. While commonality addresses the issues of 'who' is working together, compatibility concerns 'how' the coach and client will interact.

Coaches matched to clients based on compatible personality and behavioural styles are expected to have a better working relationship, particularly with securing commitment and supporting collaboration. Although compatibility is a broad concept, a few studies support the idea that similarity promotes coaching processes and outcomes. Matching was found to enhance rapport and goal attainment (Wycherley & Cox 2008), reduce personality mismatches/ conflicts that result in premature termination (Gerstein 1985; Hunt & Michael 1983) and produce a greater likelihood of a client feeling supported in a mentoring relationship (Wanberg, Kammeyer-Mueller & Marchese 2006).

Although these results support similarity, they don't contribute sufficient clarity to the concept of compatibility. Similarity doesn't necessarily represent compatibility. In fact, too much similarity can limit the long-term benefit of learning since there is less opportunity to challenge assumptions, perspectives, and experiences (Scoular & Linley 2006; Wycherley & Cox 2008). In a therapy context, 'mismatching' therapist directiveness to client resistance actually improves outcomes (Norcross & Lambert 2006). Complementary styles, not just similar styles, are important in relationship compatibility.

Framing compatibility within a broader theory suggests the degree of overlap between the views of the client and coach about how they will work together and what they work towards may be a primary factor for deep-level compatibility in coaching. Their shared mental models – in this case, linked beliefs about coaching and the coaching relationship – may be more important than other dimensions of compatibility (e.g. personality, values, motivation) and may explain why 'opposites attract'. In other words, these shared mental models create such strong compatibility that it actually allows a coach and client with otherwise dissimilar styles and personalities to employ their individual strengths to achieve higher outcomes.

The shared-mental-models literature addresses many of the processes by which partners work and their ensuing performance. Shared mental models are used to form expectations, draw inferences, make predictions, understand experiences and co-ordinate actions to adapt to others and their situation (Mathieu et al. 2000) which help to anticipate others' needs, retrieve and share relevant information, and synchronise behaviours toward objectives (DeChurch & Mesmer-Magnus 2010). Particularly relevant to compatibility in the coaching relationship, shared teamwork schema support key interactional dimensions related to roles and responsibilities, interaction patterns, communication, attitudes, preferences and tendencies that allow individuals to build on differences. Thus, compatible mental models enhance the ability to "be 'in sync,' whereas differences in mental models would likely result in greater process loss and ineffective team processes" (Mathieu et al. 2000, p. 275).

CREDIBILITY

Credibility refers to a coach possessing the necessary credentials to meet client needs. Credentials include evidence of coaching competence as well as requisite experience. Credibility addresses the 'what' question for clients: Does the coach have what it takes to assist the client in being successful?

Matching a credible coach to a client in terms of their coaching needs establishes trust and confidence in the coaching relationship and openness to the coaching process. The client's perception of the coach's qualifications and experiences influences the degree to which trust is enhanced. In turn, trust helps the client "accept vulnerability based upon positive expectations of the intentions or behaviour of another" (Rousseau et al. 1998, p. 395). This openness is a critical condition enabling other coaching processes.

Credibility also supports the activation of a beneficial factor that is regarded as common or non-specific in helping relationships. The instillation and then maintenance of hope is essential to maintain the relationship, which then allows other beneficial factors to take hold (Yalom 1980). The credibility of the coach can help generate hope and support client trust, thereby establishing a critical platform from which coaching can proceed (Asay & Lambert 1999).

Match factors shown to contribute to credibility include coaching competence, expertise in business, management, leadership, particular industries, and politics (Alvey & Barclay 2007; Kampa-Kokesch & Anderson 2001; Sue-Chan & Latham 2004). In contrast, Kauffman & Coutu (2009) indicated neither certification nor prior experience as a therapist was deemed as particularly important for buyers of coaching services.

In summary, matching is a multidimensional process involving three distinct constructs. Commonality is a similarity match based on both surface- and deep-level characteristics indicating that coach and client are alike. It supports a rapid partnership through social identification with common personal characteristics, attributes, backgrounds and experiences. Compatibility is not necessarily based on behavioural similarity as it rests instead on the idea of sharing an understanding of the relationship process. These shared mental models reflect an understanding of the processes or styles engaged in the relationship allowing complementary styles to flourish.

Credibility relates to an attraction based on professional qualifications when the coach meets client expectations as a legitimate source of help. Collectively these support the client through familiarity and predictability about who will be working with them, how the coaching work will unfold and what the coach brings to the coaching relationship. Commonality, compatibility and credibility positively impact coaching relationship processes by building and maintaining rapport, establishing and maintaining trust, encouraging commitment, and promoting collaboration.

MATCHING TO MAXIMISE BENEFIT

For the reasons identified, matching clients and coaches appears to be a useful practice to build the critical foundation for the coaching relationship and to use that foundation to leverage coaching processes (e.g. rapport, trust, commitment and collaboration) and techniques (e.g. gap analyses, goal setting and accountability partnerships). Matching is especially valuable in certain conditions and contexts, involving all three key constituents: the coach, client and organisation.

Regarding coaches, matching may set inexperienced coaches up for success. Any helping relationship is a complex endeavour, so external assistance in building the coaching foundation reduces complexity. Through matching, the inexperienced coach can rely on the relational conditions already being met, reducing requirements to attend to these processes and supporting the opportunity to focus on core issues. For example, rather than searching for commonality or pressing to establish credibility, the coach can take a more direct – and relaxed – approach to understanding the client's goals and objectives.

From the other perspective, ambivalent clients with a strong match may more readily resolve their approach-avoidance conflict and engage. This engagement may be particularly enhanced if the client has a role in the matching process. Extrapolating from the psychotherapy context, half of the clients drop out by the third session and 35% don't follow-up after the first appointment (Barrett et al. 2008). While there are a variety of factors for not continuing, certainly one factor is the quality of the relationship. In fact, there is a moderate relationship between dropouts and the quality of the therapeutic alliance (Sharf, Primavera & Diener 2010) illustrating the potential value of matching as a strategy for supporting the relationship and reducing client uncertainty.

The organisational structure related to the coaching program is also a factor in leveraging the benefits of a well-developed matching process. Organisations whose coaching program has scheduled start dates, time-limited coaching and/or variability in coach qualifications can promote a solid coaching relationship by matching. Organisations using external coaching pools would benefit from having key information to guide the match. Otherwise the relationship is essentially a random connection rather than an informed decision. Finally, and for similar reasons, organisations building a coaching program that employs matching processes demonstrate a systematic approach to developing the coaching relationship and supporting a culture of leadership development.

In summary, matching can be useful to support coaches, clients and the organisation. Matching may be particularly helpful to inexperienced coaches and hesitant clients. By externally creating a strong foundation for rapport and trust, both can approach the relationship more comfortably. Matching provides a similar benefit to organisations, particularly when the scope of coaching has expanded to include a large pool of both coaches and clients and when coaching programs begin as a group. Under such conditions, the ability to match participants efficiently and effectively using an informed and systematic process can increase the likelihood of a robust relationship between coach and client.

MATCH LOGISTICS TO SUPPORT PRACTICES

While potentially beneficial, matching doesn't occur without challenge. Even our framework employing commonality, compatibility and credibility may lack the specificity valued by other organisations. Matching can include other dimensions, like organisational program objectives, personal values, scheduling availability, location and even medium. As these important dimensions compound, the matching process becomes increasingly demanding and complex. This is particularly the case if matching is performed by a well-intended co-ordinator attempting to retain information from hand-written records or basic spreadsheets, and even more challenging if there are assessments that need to be scored and varying weights assigned to matching dimensions.

One method for managing the complexity is to automate the process. Boyce & Clutterbuck (2010) describe a range of software support for matching that can be entirely computer driven. In this case, the software is designed to identify best-fit matches based on specified criteria. There are also programs with less sophisticated algorithms allowing co-ordinators to use computer-generated parameters to support the matching decision. Automation clearly can be used to support the matching process but, like other elements of coaching programs, it requires organisational support.

RESEARCH EXAMINING MATCHING IN A LEADERSHIP COACHING PROGRAM

Based on our conceptual model and the supporting literature, we examined the impact of client–coach pairs systematically matched on commonality, compatibility and credibility, hypothesising that they would evaluate coaching outcomes more positively than client–coach pairs randomly assigned by indicating: 1) a higher degree of coaching satisfaction and utility, 2) a higher perceived leadership performance effectiveness and 3) more favourable perceptions of the coaching program. Similarly, effective relationships processes (rapport, trust and commitment) were expected to result in positive coaching outcomes. In addition to these direct effects on outcomes, we predicted three mediated or indirect relationships based on matching: relationship processes mediate client–coach match for 1) commonality, 2) compatibility and 3) credibility on the three levels of coaching outcomes.

METHOD

Participants. Volunteers included 145 cadet clients and 85 senior leader coaches participating in a leadership-development coaching program at a United States military academy. Pre- and post-data were available for 74 clients.

The cadet sample comprised undergraduates between the ages of 17 and 24, 66% were male and 87% were white. The senior leaders were faculty members or squadron commanders responsible for academic instruction or military guidance. These military (86%) and civilian (14%) volunteers were between the ages of 26 and 58, 75% were male and 81% were White.

Procedure. The cadet coaching program, LEAD, develops leadership competencies to improve effectiveness in current and future leadership roles while building life-long learning skills through a coaching relationship. The program framework includes Partnering, Assessment, Action and Transition. Coaches and clients met both face-to-face and virtually, as needed, with 77% of the clients communicating with their coaches at least once every two weeks, including an average of eight face-to-face meetings lasting between 10 and 90 minutes.

Potential clients and coaches completed an application on-line during an open enrolment period. During the two cycles of data collection, the number of applicants exceeded the availability of coaches, so 47 (55%) of the available coaches agreed to support at least two clients. Clients were randomly divided into two groups such that coaches accepting two clients were randomly assigned to one and systematically matched to the other. Coaches electing to support only one client were randomly selected to either receive a random or systematically matched client.

Criteria for systematic matching included commonality, compatibility and credibility. Matches were completed using Excel spreadsheet calculations, potential client–coach pair score comparisons on each match criteria and workable schedules for both coach and client.

Clients and coaches completed end-of-program (EOP) surveys, which included the relationship and outcome measures as well as additional process items relating to the coaching, such as mechanics, program content and tools/techniques. The survey was administered on-line following the termination of the coaching engagement.

Measures

The application and EOP surveys included both historic items for trend analyses as well as items developed specifically to operationalise the relationship issues. The measures were divided into three sections: the predictors (commonality, compatibility and credibility), the relationship process mediators (rapport, trust and commitment) and the criterion outcomes (satisfaction, leadership-development behavioural and program).

Commonality. A composite score was developed by comparing coach and client across 18 responses (gender, ethnicity, state of record, academic major and 14 hobbies/interests); 62% of pairs had at least two or more commonalities.

Compatibility. Coaches completed Clark's (1998) 18-item Leadership Questionnaire to identify a senior leader's managerial preference style on two axes: concern for people or for tasks. Clients completed Soloman and Felder's (2005) 44-item Index of Learning Style Questionnaire, with results identifying a client's learning preference style also on two axes: tasks and emotional processes. The similarity between these two-dimensional models provided the compatibility score, such that client–coach pairs scoring similarly on the task dimension (high or low) and process dimension (high or low) received a higher compatibility score than client–coach pairs in opposite quadrants. Scores ranged from 0 to 4 with higher scores indicating greater compatibility.

Credibility. Coaching credibility examined coach's requisite ability to meet the client's developmental need by comparing the overlap in the competencies clients identified as a developmental need and the self-rated expertise of a coach in that competency area. Military credibility, similar to business acumen or sector knowledge in the public domain, was determined by the coach's military-assignment history and military status, with higher score indicating greater military experience.

Rapport. Rapport was assessed with two Likert scale, client-centered and two coach-centered items on the EOP survey (e.g. "I felt a strong connection with my LEAD coach/client") with scale reliabilities greater than .85 for client and coach ratings.

Trust. The client and coach responded to one trust item, "I trusted my LEAD coach and the coaching process", or "My LEAD client was honest and candid" on the five-point Likert scale.

Commitment. Clients rated coach commitment on three items (e.g. "My coach was committed to my personal leadership development") and coaches rated client commitment on two corresponding items; scale reliabilities were greater than .85.

Outcomes. The evaluation items were based on Kirkpatrick's (1996) criteria. Reaction combined satisfaction with the leadership coaching experience and utility items. Two leadership performance items were completed by clients. Finally, organisational outcomes focused on the *coaching program* and was measured using three client items and three parallel coach items. All scale reliabilities ranged from .81 to .92.

Manipulation check. Three items to assess if the systematic matching produced perceptions of commonality, compatibility and credibility.

RESULTS

The manipulation checks revealed significant differences between random and systematic matches commonality scores (t(121) = 4.14, p <.01), compatibility scores (t(121)= 2.54, p <.05) and credibility scores (t(121)=5.02, p <01). However, when the three scores were compared using only the 74 client–coach pairs with outcome data, there was no longer a significant difference between client–coach pairs randomly and systematically matched on compatibility (t(66) = .57, n.s.) and a smaller, although still significant effect with commonality (t(66) = 2.40, p < .05; Cohen's d .75 to .59). Also, when compared with the manipulation check items, there were no correlations with matched and random pairs and their perceptions of commonality, compatibility and credibility (r = .17, .09, .02; n.s., respectively). This suggests that the matching intervention was not successful for the reduced population of respondents. Therefore, it was not surprising that there were no significant differences between systematically matched and randomly assigned client–coach pairs found in coaching outcomes as rated by clients (satisfaction t(70) = .95, n.s.; leadership performance t(70) = .04, n.s.; program t(70) = .80, n.s.) or coaches (satisfaction t(746) = .29, n.s.; program t(46) = .32, n.s.).

However, examining the data through a regression window, the relationship processes did predict coaching outcomes (see Table 1). Specifically, results revealed the overall models were significant (satisfaction F(3,66) = 34.51, p< .01; leadership performance F(3,66) = 19.16, p< .01; program F(3, 66) = 20.40, p< .01) with a good fit and 61%, 47% and 48% of the variance explained in the client's satisfaction, leadership development and program outcomes, respectively.

In terms of the best predictors, rapport, trust or commitment, the regression analyses suggest that client–coach rapport (t(66) = 3.47, p <.01) and trust (t(66) = 2.80, p <.01) but not commitment (t(66) = 0.35, n.s.) predict client satisfaction, while commitment (t(66) = 1.97, p <.05) but not rapport (t(66) = 0.74, n.s.) or trust (t(66) = 1.08, n.s.) predicts leadership performance. Further, trust (t(66) = 2.22, p <.05), not rapport (t(66) = 1.71, n.s.) or commitment (t(66) = 0.91, n.s.), predicted program outcomes for clients.

Table 1.

Regression Results: Standardised Regression Coefficients (β) Between Predictors and Leadership Coaching Outcomes

Relationship Processes	Coaching Outcomes		
	Client Ratings		
	Reaction	Leadership Performance	Program
Client Rating	R^2= .61**	R^2= .47**	R^2= .48**
Rapport	.42**	.10	.24
Trust	.38**	.21	.35**
Commitment	.06	.42*	.17

* p< .05 (two-tailed); ** p < .01 (two-tailed)

Our remaining hypotheses suggested that relationship processes mediate the influence of client–coach match conditions (commonality, compatibility and credibility) on coaching outcomes (satisfaction/utility, leadership performance and coaching program; Table 2). When client–coach compatibility and relationship processes were regressed on reaction, the relationship (β = .58, t(65) = 7.44, p < .01) was significantly related to coaching satisfaction and the compatibility score became non-significant (β = .03, t(65) = 1.83, n.s.). The result of Sobel's test showed that the parameter estimate for the relationship between compatibility and satisfaction was significantly lower in the mediated condition than in the non-mediated condition, z = 2.01, p < .05 (Preacher & Leonardelli 2001), indicating that relationship processes fully mediated the relationship between client–coach compatibility scores and coaching satisfaction.

Similar results were found when credibility (military experience) and relationship process were regressed on satisfaction, leadership performance and program outcomes. The relationship was significantly related to coaching satisfaction (β = .61, t(63) = 7.47, p < .01), leadership performance (β = .44, t(63) = 4.79, p < .01), and program outcomes (β = .68, t(63) = 7.33, p < .01) while credibility became non-significant (β = .07, t(63) = 1.23, n.s.), (β = .13, t(63) = 2.13, n.s.), (β = .11, t(63) = 1.22, n.s.), respectively. The Sobel test results (z = 3.02, p < .01; z= 2.72, p < .01; z =3.00, p < .01) provide statistical support for the fully mediated relationship. Therefore, relationship processes did mediate coach credibility on all three coaching outcomes but, as noted, didn't mediate the impact of commonality and only mediated the impact of compatibility for client satisfaction/utility.

Table 2.

Mediated Regression Results with Standardised Regression Coefficients (β)

Predictor (IV)	Mediator	Coaching Outcome (DV)	Predictor (IV)	Mediator	Coaching Outcomes (DV)		
	Relationship	Satisfaction/ Utility (Client Rating)		Relationship	Satisfaction/ Utility (Client Rating)	Leadership Performance	Program (Client Ratings)
Step 1			**Step 1**				
Compatibility		-.06**	Credibility		.25**	.23**	.21**
R²		.11**	R²		.14**	.18**	.14**
Step 2			**Step 2**				
Compatibility	.05*		Credibility	.25**			
R²	.06*		R²	.15**			
Step 3			**Step 3**				
Compatibility	-.03		Credibility	.07	.13*	.11	
Relationship		.58**	Relationship	.61**	.44**	.68**	
R²		.52**			.54**	.40**	.54**
F (df)		34.82** (2, 65)			37.62** (2, 63)	20.61** (2,63)	36.33** (2,63)
Sobel test		2.01*			3.02**	2.72**	3.00**

* *p*< .05 (two-tailed); ** *p* < .01 (two-tailed)

Discussion

Our fundamental premise is that the coaching relationship represents both an extraordinarily complex and important interpersonal interaction and theoretical construct. As depicted in the broad coaching relationship framework, the relationship includes characteristics of the coach and client, the particular interaction of the two in terms of a match, and the processes engaged in as part of the relationship. Given these dynamics and the inherent ambiguity, underlying evaluative component and 'stretch' expectations involved in coaching, the anticipated benefits of matching clients and coaches for commonality, compatibility and credibility seem to justify rigorous matching efforts.

Our analysis lends evidence to the idea that a favourable match relates to favourable outcomes. Matching emerges as an important factor because it serves as an enabling condition for promoting effective relationship processes, which drives positive coaching outcomes. In particular, compatibility and credibility provide a foundation upon which to build and develop critical levels of trust, rapport and commitment. Our research indicates that matching is a useful tool because clients with credible coaches in a compatible partnership are able to perform important relationship processes that lead to successful coaching outcomes. However, we acknowledge that to the extent other mechanisms are able to develop productive relationship processes, sophisticated matching can be a timely and/or costly endeavour and it is not likely to be the only mechanism to deliver functional coaching relationships. Matching does not appear to be an absolutely necessary condition for successful coaching outcomes. It is the coaching processes that directly impact effective outcomes. Specifically rapport, trust and commitment are central features in relationships and, when perceived by clients, they predict positive outcomes, a finding consistent with helping relationships like psychotherapy. Together the findings provide useful clarity on the components and processes of coaching and offer direction to coaches and organisations invested in the effectiveness of coaching.

Further, our results indicate that these coaching processes have specific rather than uniformly positive effects. More precisely, rapport predicted positive reactions regarding satisfaction and program utility, whereas commitment predicted behavioural change in terms of leadership performance. Trust seemed to emerge as a foundational quality, predicting both positive reactions and a generally positive evaluation of the program. Clearly these are all beneficial in coaching. In terms of coaching processes overall, we do concur with Wycherley and Cox (2008) to train coaches to build rapport and extend this to generate trust and commitment.

Considering that our results showed positive and direct influence for coaching processes, it might be tempting to forego the many challenges of creating a successful matching process while investing more heavily in coach training. We believe this type of binary decision is too narrow and premature. We would like to highlight that clients who felt the client–coach relationship was compatible and credible also reported favourable outcomes. Specifically, compatibility was associated with client perceptions of the program as satisfactory and useful. This was also true with perceptions of credibility and, in addition, credibility was associated with higher ratings of leadership performance and program value. Further, the relationship processes mediated client–coach match compatibility on client coaching outcomes (coaching satisfaction and utility) as well as credibility with all three coaching outcomes. In other words, it seems to be the case that coaching pairs that are compatible and credible engage in effective coaching processes (rapport, trust and commitment) and this in turn promotes favourable coaching outcomes. In short, matching influences coaching processes creating a positive coaching experience. However, unlike personal relationships, clients might regard coaching as a true working relationship that doesn't require the same strong degree of commonality to promote it fully or sustain it. The emphasis is on a professional outcome and not a long-term interaction.

The theoretical implications of these results are important as they support the idea that coaching relationships are complex, different in some ways from personal relationships, yet still influenced by some of those same, fundamentally interpersonal dynamics. The client–coach relationship and, particularly, those relationship-building processes are critical to coaching effectiveness. Even so, the fit between the client and coach personal characteristics should be considered when pairing a client with a coach. Obviously, more research examining predictors of effective client–coach relationships is warranted.

LIMITATIONS AND FUTURE RESEARCH
Although the results provide insight into some of the complexities of the coaching relationship, our conclusions are tempered by certain shortcomings. There are external validity issues based on our military sample of junior leaders with similar demographic characteristics, our coaches who served as volunteers and the academic context of coaching program. Future research should investigate coaching relationships in business situations unrelated to traditional leadership development courses and in different industries.

Another limitation involves common method bias. Method effects, however, were hopefully minimised by collecting mediator and criterion measures using different scale formats (five-point versus seven-point Likert scale). Future research needs to incorporate alternative outcome data, such as peer or supervisor ratings of change in leadership performance, organisational performance and future coaching involvement.

We acknowledge that building and maintaining rapport, trust and commitment occur within the context of other relationship processes (e.g. collaboration) and other coaching processes (e.g. mechanics, tools and techniques). These are also likely to influence coaching outcomes and need to be investigated systematically. We also encourage future research to measure the purpose of the relationship, client affective factors, the client–coach relationship within a virtual or e-environment, and variables that may impact different stages of an evolving dynamic client–coach relationship. Finally, we suggest that technology be examined as a tool for identifying and creating optimal and minimal client–coach matches.

Conclusion

This study represents one of the first attempts to examine client–coach relationships systematically. Our study contributes to the scientific and practitioner literature by providing empirical findings regarding the impact of the coach–client relationship on coaching. Further, our results support the understanding of factors influencing client–coach relationships, which allows us to develop selection tools to better match clients with coaches, increase the quality of the relationship between the client and coach, and ultimately improve coaching outcomes.

We urge practitioners to consider not only the potential benefits of matching and relevant match factors but also the context or situations when matching may be most beneficial, the relationship with coaching processes, as well as the logistical issues in implementing matching processes before they undertake such efforts. Finally, as organisations continue to adapt and grow leadership coaching programs, it is imperative that researchers continue work that will close the scientist–practitioner gap with respect to design and delivery of coaching and remain sensitive to the very human element that is involved in this relationship. Can matching support client–coach relationships in your coaching program? Unlike on-line dating services, we can't offer a guarantee but it's worth considering.

CHAPTER 15

THE WORKING ALLIANCE IN EXECUTIVE COACHING: ITS IMPACT ON OUTCOMES AND HOW COACHES CAN INFLUENCE IT

LOUIS BARON AND LUCIE MORIN

INTRODUCTION

Executive coaching has come to play a key role in the field of management development. In regard to the conditions favouring effective coaching, a good working alliance between the coach and the coachee has been proposed as a key success factor. However, very few empirical studies have investigated this proposition. The primary purpose of this chapter is to present an empirical study that was conducted to examine the working alliance in a real organisational setting*. Specifically, our research aimed to answer the following questions: What role does the working alliance play in the relationship between coaching and its outcomes? Which coaching skills are associated with the coachee's perception of the working alliance? What happens when the coach and the coachee have a different perception of the working alliance between them?

The chapter is structured as follows: first, we present the conceptual framework supporting our empirical study. Then, we detail the method used to answer our research questions, this being followed by our results. Finally, we conclude with a discussion including theoretical and practical implications.

---

* This chapter rests on two articles published in *Human Resource Development Quarterly* (Baron & Morin 2009) and in *Journal of Management Development* (Baron, Morin & Morin 2011)r.

CONCEPTUAL FRAMEWORK

Results from the few rigorous empirical studies that have investigated executive coaching have shown that it is associated with many positive impacts (for a review, see Baron & Morin 2010). Yet, we still know little about why it works. Many authors have proposed that the working alliance between the coach and coachee is an essential condition of coaching success (Kampa & White 2002; Lowman 2005).

The concept of working alliance has its roots in the psychotherapy literature. Broadly speaking, working alliance refers to the "quality and strength of the collaborative relationship between client and therapist in therapy" (Horvath & Bedi 2002, p. 41). This definition highlights the interdependence of the therapist and the client in the development of the alliance. According to Bordin (1979), the strength of the working alliance rests on the existing agreement between the client and the therapist concerning the following three aspects: the objectives of the therapy, the tasks required to reach those objectives, and the bond that develops between the client and the therapist. A wide range of empirical evidence has consistently shown a significant positive relationship between the strength of the working alliance and therapy's success. Two meta-analyses estimated that the therapeutic alliance accounts for somewhere between 7% and 17% of the variance in therapy outcomes, and effect sizes for this relationship range from .22 to .26 (Horvath & Symonds 1991; Martin, Garske & Davis 2000).

With respect to executive coaching, very few empirical studies have examined the concept of working alliance. Indeed, there are scarcely any reported studies that make a link between the working alliance and the effectiveness of executive coaching or examined the correlates of the coach–coachee working alliance. Among the rare results on these issues, some revealed that the quality of the relationship with the coach is perceived by the coachee as critical to the success of coaching (McGovern et al. 2001) and that there is a significant positive relationship between the quality of the coaching offered (as assessed by the coach's interpersonal and communication skills, and the instrumental support offered by the coach) and the coachee's self-efficacy (Dingman 2004). The goal of this study is then partially to fill that gap in the literature.

Our first research question investigates the role the working alliance plays in the relationship between executive coaching and its outcomes. Specifically, we seek to know if the link between the number of coaching sessions received and coaching effectiveness is influenced by the quality of the working alliance and, if so, whether the working alliance acts as a moderator or a mediator. In other words, is the working alliance a 'nice-to-have' characteristic in a coaching process or does it have a direct effect on coaching outcomes, being thus a prerequisite? Due to the lack of support in the scientific literature either for the moderating or the mediating role, we did not formulate any hypothesis. To answer this research question, the outcome we used (the dependant variable) was the coachee's self-efficacy. Self-efficacy is defined as a person's belief of being capable of accomplishing a given task (Bandura 1997). Results from numerous studies have revealed a positive relationship between self-efficacy and various organisational outcomes (Judge et al. 2007; Stajkovic & Luthans 1998). Self-efficacy has also been extensively studied in the training literature. Among other things, findings indicate that training can enhance one's self-efficacy (Gaudine & Saks 2004; Mathieu, Martineau & Tannenbaum 1993). In regard to coaching, Malone (2001) has suggested that executive coaching can enhance self-efficacy since it naturally uses techniques aimed at its determinants, i.e. self-thought, mastery experiences, modelling, social persuasion and psychological states management (see Bandura 1997; Stajkovic & Luthans 1998).

Our second research question investigates the correlates of the coach–coachee working alliance. This question has never been addressed so far in the coaching literature. However, studies in psychotherapy indicate that some therapists are more helpful than others and that these differences seem to be more related to the therapist's skills than to the treatment methods. Along the same lines, a review of the literature indicated that many attributes (e.g. flexibility, warmth, interest, openness) and techniques used by the therapist (e.g. behaviours that promote a sense of connection with the client and favour in-depth reflection and exploration) are associated with the development and maintenance of the alliance (Ackerman & Hilsenroth 2003).

In light of this literature, we decided in this study to focus on three specific coaching skills: relational skills (e.g. empathy, respect, trust, presence and availability), inquiry skills (e.g. questioning, reformulating, reinforcing and confronting) and the ability to facilitate learning and results (e.g. establishing a development plan, assessing learning and identifying obstacles). In consequence, the following three hypotheses were formulated:

Hypothesis 1a. The coach's relational skills are positively associated with working alliance.

Hypothesis 1b. The coach's inquiry skills are positively associated with working alliance.

Hypothesis 1c. The coach's facilitating learning and results skills are positively associated with working alliance.

Finally, our third research question is related to the impact of a discrepancy between the coachee's rating and the coach's rating of the working alliance. In the psychotherapy literature, Bedi, Davis & Williams (2005) suggest that clients and therapists can diverge in their perceptions of what elements are important in the development of the therapeutic alliance. Findings from empirical studies have indicated that the client's view of the working alliance is a better predictor of the success of a therapy than the therapist's view (Horvath & Bedi 2002). Results have also shown that similarity or low discrepancy between client and therapist alliance ratings in the middle and late phases of treatment is a consistent predictor of positive outcomes (Hersoug et al. 2002; Kivlighan & Shaughnessy 1995).

In light of this information, we argue that the impacts of a discrepancy in alliance ratings noted in psychotherapeutic contexts might also be observed in an executive coaching context. If so, divergent assessments of the alliance could present a problem. For instance, a coach's inaccurate assessment may lead him or her to neglect to work on critical relational issues. Moreover, a coach's over- or underestimation might mean that the coach is not in tune with his or her coachee or that he or she is not able to recognise the client's perspective about their relationship, the objectives they are pursuing, the tasks required to reach those objectives or the bond that has developed between them.

A useful framework for examining the issue of discrepancy in perceptions of the working alliance in coaching is the self–other agreement paradigm from the leadership literature. Although the evaluation of the working alliance does not constitute in itself an evaluation of the coach, the latter may feel a greater responsibility in facilitating the developmental exercise than the coachee. Self–other agreement represents the degree to which individuals see themselves as others see them (see Atwater et al. 1998; Whittington et al. 2009). Typically, "difference scores are used to represent the congruence between two constructs, which is then treated as a concept in its own right" (Edwards 2001, p. 265). Difference scores can be treated as a continuous variable, or categorised into one of three agreement groups: over-estimators, accurate estimators and under-estimators of a coach's leadership behaviours in comparison with ratings from his/her followers (Atwater, Roush & Fischthal 1995; Atwater & Yammarino 1992). Empirical evidence has shown that self–other agreement can be used to predict performance as well as work-related perceptions, such as organisational commitment, job satisfaction and trust (Alimo-Metcalfe 1998; Atwater et al. 1998; Atwater et al. 2005; Atwater & Yammarino 1992; Bass & Yammarino 1991; Day et al. 2002; Furnham & Stringfield 1994; Sosik & Megerian 1999; Van Velsor, Taylor & Leslie 1993; Whittington et al. 2009). In short, overestimation leads to diminished outcomes, accurate estimation leads to enhanced performance and underestimation is associated with mixed outcomes.

In line with the above literature, one can argue that, relative to coachees' estimates, coaches who overestimate or underestimate the working alliance will not foster as good coaching outcomes as coaches who accurately estimate the working alliance. In consequence, coachees who work with over- or under-estimators will develop less than coaches who work with accurate estimators. As such, we formulated the following hypothesis:

> **Hypothesis 2.** Coachees who work with a coach who is an accurate estimator – in relation to coachees' ratings – will develop more than coachees who work with a coach who is an under- or an over-estimator.

METHOD

FIELD SETTING AND COACHING

Our empirical study was conducted in a large North American manufacturing company that offered its junior and mid-level managers an eight-month leadership development program addressing various topics, such as leadership and interpersonal communication. In that program, executive coaching consisted of face-to-face, 75-minute sessions with a certified internal coach. During the first coaching session, managers were asked to establish three main goals they wanted to work on. These goals had to be related to the skills addressed in the leadership development program. Although the program suggested one coaching session every two weeks, the specific scheduling was left to the discretion of coaches and coachees. Overall, managers received between three and eleven coaching sessions during eight months, representing a mean of 5.77 sessions. Qualitative data indicated that lack of time and schedule conflicts were the two main reasons for not attending coaching.

PARTICIPANTS

The participants in this study were divided into two groups: coachees (n=127) and internal coaches (n=64). Our final sample was composed of 73 coachees (63 men, 10 women) who answered the two questionnaires (response rate: 57.5%). The average age of the coachees was 38 years, 63% had a university-level education and their average number of years as a manager was 4.7. Results from statistical analyses showed no significant differences between the 73 managers who completed all the questionnaires and the others who did not, in regard to age, sex, education, number of years as a manager and pre-coaching self-efficacy.

The internal coaches were senior managers (n=64) who had participated in a coaching certification program. Prior to the start of the leadership-development program followed by the coachees, these senior managers had received two days of coaching training by an outside consultant. They then completed their certification by participating in four two-hour individual meetings with a 'master coach' and four four-hour action-learning workshops. Among these participants, 24 (21 men, 3 women) returned the questionnaire that was sent to them at the end of the program, for a response rate of 37.5%. The average age of the coaches was 41 years, 79% had a university-level education and their average number of years as a manager was 9.3.

In total, 30 coach–coachee dyads were formed, whereby some coaches were paired with two coachees for the duration of the program. Pairings were arranged to ensure that no coach had a pre-existing organisational authority over the managers he or she coached. Results from statistical analyses showed no significant differences between the 30 coachees with data from their coach and the 43 coachees without data from their coach in regard to age, gender, education, number of years as a manager as well as pre-coaching and post-coaching self-efficacy.

DATA COLLECTION

Our study rests on the following data-collection procedure: prior to coaching, we collected an initial measure of the coachees' self-efficacy as well as some socio-demographic data on both coaches and coaches; and, at the end of the coaching, we collected a second measure of the coachees' self-efficacy as well as a measure of the working alliance from both coaches and coachees. For a complete description of the measures used, see Baron & Morin (2009) and Baron, Morin & Morin (2011).

MEASURES

Executive coaching. The variable was measured by the number of coaching sessions received by each coachee. Data were provided by the HR department.

Coachees' self-efficacy. This variable was assessed by an 8-item, 11-point Likert scale developed specifically for this study (e.g. "Today, as a manager, I feel confident in my ability to help my employees learn lessons from the difficulties and setbacks they may encounter").

Working alliance. This variable was measured using the Working Alliance Inventory – short version (Horvath & Greenberg 1989; Tracey & Kokotovic 1989), a 12-item, 7-point Likert scale. In this study, the wording of the original version was slightly adapted to fit the coaching context (e.g. "coach" instead of "therapist" and "development needs" instead of "problems").

Coach's self-efficacy in regard to coaching skills. The coach's self-efficacy was measured by an 18-item, 11-point Likert scale developed for this study (e.g. "Today, as a coach, I feel confident in my ability to help the individual to acknowledge his responsibility toward coaching and the power he has with respect to the situation").

Working-alliance discrepancy. To measure this variable, coaches were categorised into one of the three agreement groups, relative to the ratings of coachees. The rating difference for each coach–coachee dyad was computed and then each coach's difference score was compared to the mean difference score. Three groups were formed: over-estimators (one-half of a standard deviation or more above the mean difference), under-estimators (one-half of a standard deviation or more below) and accurate estimators (within one-half of a standard deviation).

RESULTS
RESEARCH QUESTION #1 – THE WORKING ALLIANCE:
MEDIATOR OR MODERATOR?

The descriptive statistics of the variables related to our three research questions are presented in Baron & Morin (2009) and Baron, Morin & Morin (2011). Our first research question was: What role does the working alliance play in the relationship between coaching and its outcomes? In the scientific literature, there is no clear support for either a moderating or a mediating role (see Baron & Morin 2009 for a review on that question). We began our analysis by looking at the conditions required for mediation analysis (Baron & Kenny 1986). Results from a paired *t*-test analysis indicated that there was a significant increase in the coachees' self-efficacy between the beginning and the end of the training program ($t_{72} = 6.27, p < .01$). Then, findings from partial correlation matrix – after controlling for the coachees' pre-training self-efficacy – revealed that executive coaching is positively and significantly related with coachees' post-training self-efficacy ($r_p = .24, p < .05$) as well as with working alliance ($r_p = .32, p < .01$). Finally findings showed that working alliance is positively and significantly related to post-training self-efficacy ($r_p = .48, p < .01$). Thus, all conditions were met.

To test for mediation and moderation, we used the method of multiplying regression coefficients (MacKinnon et al. 2002). This method gives good statistical power and a low incidence of type-1 error. The hierarchical regression results for the coachees' self-efficacy presented in Table 1 indicate that when coaching and working alliance are both entered together in the regression equation, the working alliance holds a significant coefficient whereas coaching does not. In addition, a Sobel's test (1982) confirmed that the association between the number of sessions of executive coaching and the development of self-efficacy is mediated by the working alliance ($z = 2.31, p < .05$). Further, our results demonstrate that the mediation is complete, as the association between executive coaching and self-efficacy becomes non-significant when working alliance is added. In regard to moderation, the results from Step 4 of the regression analysis indicate a non-significant inter-active effect of working alliance and the number of coaching sessions received. In short, our results suggest that the working alliance plays a medi-ating role rather than a moderating role in the relationship between executive coaching and its outcomes.

Table 1

Hierarchical regression of coachee's self-efficacy – After (standardised ß)

	Step 1	Step 2	Step 3	Step 4
Variables	ß	ß	ß	ß
Coachee SE – Before	,49**	,49**	,44**	,44**
Coaching received		,21*	,08	,07
Working alliance			,39**	,39†
Coaching * alliance				,02
Adjusted R^2	,231	,265	,398	,389
Δ adjusted R^2		,034*	,133**	-,009

N=73, $^{†}p < .10$, $^{**}p < .01$, $^{*}p < .05$

RESEARCH QUESTION #2 – COACHING SKILLS ASSOCIATED WITH WORKING ALLIANCE

Our second question was: Which coaching skills are associated with the coachee's perception of the working alliance? The correlation matrix of the correlates of the working alliance reveals that the coach's self-efficacy with respect to relational ($r = .07$, n.s.) and inquiry skills ($r = .00$, n.s.) had no significant link with working alliance. Hypotheses 1a and 1b were thus rejected. In contrast, self-efficacy with regard to facilitating learning and results showed a significant positive correlation with the working alliance ($r = .42$, $p < .01$). Hypothesis 1c was thus confirmed.

RESEARCH QUESTION #3 – IMPACT ON OUTCOMES OF WORKING-ALLIANCE RATING DISCREPANCIES

Our third research question was: What happens when the coach and the coachee have a different perception of the working alliance between them? We hypothesised that coachees who work with a coach who is an accurate estimator – in relation to coachees' ratings – will develop more than coachees who work with a coach who is either an under- or an over-estimator. Table 2 presents the means for working-alliance ratings and post-coaching self-efficacy for the three categorisations.

Table 2

Means for working alliance and post-coaching self-efficacy

Group	N	Mean coachees' working alliance ratings (SD)	Mean coaches' working alliance ratings (SD)	Mean post-coaching self-efficacy* (SD)
Under-estimators	9	6.33 (.77)	5.43 (.72)	8.61 (.57)
Accurate estimators	11	6.03 (.60)	5.97 (.67)	8.05 (.51)
Over-estimators	10	5.37 (.35)	6.25 (.42)	7.28 (.44)

* adjusted means

To test our hypothesis, a one-way analysis of covariance (ANCOVA) was conducted with post-coaching self-efficacy as the dependant variable (DV) and pre-coaching self-efficacy and coachee's working alliance assessment as the two covariates. Since the correlation between coachees' working alliance assessment and our DV is very strong (rp = .51, p < .01), using the former variable as a covariate controlled for the effect it might have on another correlation, namely the correlation between working-alliance discrepancy and the DV. After all, according to our results, if coachees rate their alliance as high, they are most likely to present a high score on their self-efficacy post-coaching, and their coaches are more likely to be categorised as under-estimators. The independent variable, namely the working-alliance discrepancy, was composed of the following three groups: under-estimators, accurate estimators and over-estimators. Table 3 presents the results of the ANCOVA.

Table 3

ANCOVA analysis results

Source of variation	Sum of squares	Df	Mean square	F statistics	Prob.
Corrected model	10.245	4	2.561	10.492	.001
Intercept	5.680	1	5.688	23.299	.001
Pre-coaching self-efficacy	.794	1	.794	3.253	.08
Working alliance – Coachee	.102	1	.102	.417	.52
Working-alliance discrepancy (three groups)	4.673	2	2.336	9.570	.001
Error	6.103	25	.244		
Total	1918.391	30			
Corrected total	16.348	29			

First, results show no significant effects for our two covariates. Second, findings indicate a significant group effect on post-coaching self-efficacy. Results also show a very strong relationship between the working-alliance discrepancy and self-efficacy. Follow-up tests (Holm's sequential Bonferroni) were conducted to evaluate pairwise differences among the adjusted means of the three groups. Contrast analysis revealed that coachees in the over-estimators group had a significantly different post-coaching self-efficacy than coachees in the under-estimators group (contrast estimates = 1.34, $p <$ .001) and coachees in the accurate estimators group (contrast estimates = 0.77, $p <$ .001). There was also a significant difference between the accurate estimators group and the under-estimators group (contrast estimates = -0.53, $p <$ .05). Thus, our hypothesis that predicted that the accurate estimator would be best is not supported. Rather, our results suggest a negative linear relationship: the more a coach overestimates the working relationship compared to the person he or she coaches, the less that person develops.

DISCUSSION

Our objective was to investigate working alliance in an organisational setting. We tried to answer three key questions: What role does the working alliance play in the relationship between coaching and its outcomes? Which coaching skills are associated with the coachee's perception of the working alliance? And what happens when the coach and the coachee have a different perception of the working alliance between them?

Our results first indicate that the coach–coachee relationship does play a mediating role in the association between the number of coaching sessions received and the development of a manager's self-efficacy. The theoretical implication of this result is important, because it suggests that it is by its effect on the coach–coachee relationship that the amount of coaching received influences the development of the coachee. The coach–coachee relationship thus constitutes a prerequisite for coaching effectiveness. Our findings also reveal that the number of coaching sessions received is a significant determinant of the coach–coachee relationship. This result is consistent with the psychotherapy literature, which shows that the working relationship between the therapist and his client increases with the number of therapy sessions (Kivlighan & Shaughnessy 1995).

Our second research question aims to investigate the relationship between coaching skills, as assessed by the coaches, and the working alliance, as assessed by the coachees. Our findings indicate that only the ability to facilitate learning and results – which includes the ability to establish a development plan, to track learning progress, to use a structured approach, to help make connections and to identify obstacles – was significantly correlated to the working alliance. Although this result helps to understand better what may influence the working relationship between a coach and a coachee, it contradicts previous findings in psychotherapy which indicate that the therapist's attributes have a greater influence on the relationship than do the techniques employed (Horvath 2005). This result may be explained by the fact that the characteristics of the executive-coaching clientele and their goals differ from those of the clientele in psychotherapy (Peltier 2001). Indeed, the general goal of executive coaching is professional-skill development rather than the re-establishment of a healthy functioning level of interaction with the world, as is often the case in therapy. This result suggests that a manager's development can occur in spite of less introspection than in psychotherapy, as long as the coachee is actively involved in reaching her development goals. The coach's skills in facilitation of learning and results seem to encourage putting learning into practice. The context in which the data were collected – i.e. an industrial setting very focused on following procedures and obtaining results and largely composed of managers with a background in engineering – might be a possible explanation for these results. These characteristics may help explain why the more pragmatic coaching skills, related to structuring the process and attaining results, for example, had a larger impact on working alliance than did relational or inquiry skills.

At last, in regard to our third research question, our findings reveal the following negative linear relationship: the more a coach overestimates the working relationship compared to the person he or she coaches, the less that person develops. Thus, in this study, coaches' underestimation of the working alliance is the best predictor of post-coaching self-efficacy in coachees. This result differs from findings in the psychotherapy literature, which have shown that similarity or low client–therapist rating discrepancies in working alliance is the best predictor of positive therapy outcomes (Hersoug et al. 2002; Kivlighan & Shaughnessy 1995).

One possible explanation for our findings comes from de Haan (2008c, p. 104), who advances that "coaches all have the tendency to want to eliminate doubts and anxieties. ...The more we coach, the more we ourselves build up long-term defenses against our tensions and existential doubts without realising it. This is perhaps the main reason why inexperienced therapists often appear to perform better than experienced ones (Dumont 1991). They set to work with more enthusiasm, involvement and vulnerability". In consequence, this author encourages coaches to coach with an "on-going and deliberately maintained doubt as their only certainty" (de Haan 2008c, p. 106). According to this argument, coaches who overestimate the alliance with their coachee may feel overconfident about the coaching they are providing, which might lead them to be less sensitive to signs of what the coachee is experiencing and not take the initiative to verify the coachee's comfort level with the way coaching is proceeding. On the other hand, coaches who underestimate the alliance with their coachee may be more humble and have more doubts about their capacity to support the development of others. This stance may lead them to pay closer attention to what the client is experiencing and, consequently, to offer a coaching that is more person-centered than problem-centered. Since the "only thing the coach can use to exert albeit an indirect influence on the outcome of coaching is the relationship between coach and coachee" (De Haan 2008c, p. 53), a coach who puts greater emphasis on the coaching relationship might provide better support to the development of others and, in so doing, facilitate the enhancement of others' self-efficacy.

Our results also underline the importance in certification programs to sensitise coaches to the working relationship, by making them conscious of how they influence its development and the obstacles they may encounter. To maximise success, coaches can also take into account advice given to therapists (Safran et al. 1990; Safran et al. 2001). First, therapists should be aware that patients often have negative feelings about the way therapy is going or the therapeutic relationship but, fearing the negative reactions of their therapist, are reluctant to address them. Secondly, it is important for clients to have the opportunity to express negative feelings about the therapeutic process, should they emerge. Thirdly, when this takes place, therapists should adopt an open, non-defensive stance and accept responsibility for their contribution to the interaction, while empathising with the client's experience, though it may be an uncomfortable or threatening experience for them – "one that activates concerns around competency as a [coach]" (Safran et al. 1990, p. 164). In summary, a coach should exercise caution about his or her perceptions of what is going on in the coaching room and not take for granted the satisfaction of his or her client.

LIMITATIONS AND CONCLUSION

A first limitation of this study is the sample size affecting the statistical power. Low statistical power increases the chance of having a Type II error, or in other words, saying that there is no effect when in fact there is one. We encourage researchers in coaching interested in studying dyads to continue their quest toward larger samples, which could permit the application of more sophisticated statistical analyses, for instance polynomial regression (see Edwards 1994).

A second limitation has to do with the generalisation of our findings. First, the context of this study was rather unique, in that it was conducted in a field setting that used recently trained internal coaches, who may differ significantly in competencies from external coaches. In general, external coaches have extensive coaching training, either in psychology or in coaching per se, or an expertise developed from multiple situations and organisational contexts they've encountered. For a description of pros and cons associated with the utilisation of internal vs. external coaches, see Wasylyshyn (2003) and de Haan (2008).

Despite these limitations, the present study makes several noteworthy contributions that shed light on the coaching process. Furthermore, it confirmed the theoretical and practical importance of the working-alliance factor in the field of coaching. Given organisations' increasingly prominent use of executive coaching, understanding the conditions under which coaching works best is highly relevant (Paradise & Mosley 2009).

Authors

EDITORS:

Erik de Haan, PhD is organisation-development (O.D.) consultant, executive coach and supervisor. He is the Director of the Ashridge Centre for Coaching and programme leader of AMEC, the Ashridge Master's (MSc) in Executive Coaching, and ACOS, the Ashridge Postgraduate Certificate in O.D.-Consulting and Coaching Supervision. Erik is also Professor of Organisation Development and Coaching at the VU University of Amsterdam. He has written more than a hundred articles and six books in different languages, among which *Fearless Consulting* (2006), *Coaching with Colleagues* (2004; with Yvonne Burger), *Relational Coaching* (2008) and *Supervision in Action* (2011).

Charlotte Sills is a coach and coach supervisor and co-director of the Coaching for Organisation Consultants programme at Ashridge Business School, UK. She is a visiting professor at Middlesex University and was for many years head of the Transactional Analysis Department at Metanoia Institute, UK where she is still a senior tutor and supervisor. She has published several books and numerous articles in the fields of psychotherapy, coaching and supervision, including, with Phil Lapworth, *An Introduction to Transactional Analysis* (2011) and *Integration in Counselling and Psychotherapy* (2001/2010), and *Skills in Gestalt Counselling and Psychotherapy* (2001/2010) with Phil Joyce.

OTHER CONTRIBUTING AUTHORS:

Louis Baron, PhD is Assistant Professor at the Department of Organization and Human Resources and Director of the MBA in Management Consulting at University of Quebec in Montreal, Canada. His research interests include leadership development, executive coaching, authentic leadership and action learning methods. He has a PhD in industrial/organizational psychology and a master's degree in clinical psychology. He is a chartered psychologist and practices as a coach and psychotherapist.

Lieutenant Colonel Lisa A. Boyce, MSc, PhD is the Reserve Scientist and Deputy Site Commander at the European Office of Aerospace Research and Development in London for the United States Air Force. Dr Boyce has 20 years of industrial/organizational (I/O) psychology research, teaching, consulting and coaching experience for the United States and Australian militaries as well as private and non-profit organisations. With over fifty publications and presentations, her current research interests focus on leadership development and technology application. Lisa earned her PhD and M.S. in I/O Psychology from George Mason University and St. Mary's University, respectively, and B.S. in Behavioral Science from the USAF Academy.

Michael Carroll, PhD is a chartered counselling psychologist. He is an accredited executive coach and an accredited supervisor of executive coaches with APECS (Association for Professional Executive Coaches and Supervisors). Michael is Visiting Industrial Professor in the Graduate School of Education, University of Bristol and the winner of the 2001 British Psychological Society Award for Distinguished Contributions to Professional Psychology. He is the author/editor of eight books. Michael has worked both nationally and internationally as a trainer and facilitator and has run a counselling service for young people, taught at university and is now self-employed.

Simon Cavicchia, BA (Hons) (Oxon), MA, MSc, MSc (Gestalt Psychotherapy), UKCP is an executive coach, coach supervisor, organisational consultant and psychotherapist. He is joint programme leader of the MA/MSc in Coaching Psychology at the Metanoia Institute in London and was, for six years, a visiting lecturer on the MSc in Change Agent Skills and Strategies at the School of Management, University of Surrey. He has consulted at all levels in organisations, and is particularly interested in integrating relational perspectives from psychotherapy into coaching theory and practice, and researching how these perspectives can be used creatively in organisational settings.

Jane Cox, BA, MSc, Dip.Grad.Sec.Linguists is an experienced executive development coach and facilitator of change. She is accredited by Ashridge Business School as an organisational coach, has an MSc in Executive Coaching and just completed a Postgraduate Certificate in Advanced Coaching & Organisational Supervision. In her work as a development coach, group facilitator and supervisor for both internal and external coaches, Jane draws on her experience in international sales and business relationship management and her underpinning belief in the coaching relationship as a facilitator of change.

Bill Critchley, MBA, MSc, Clinical Dip. in Psychotherapy, Dip. in Org. Consulting practises as an organisation consultant, an executive coach and psychotherapist. He is founder and director of the Ashridge Master's in Organisation Consulting, the Ashridge Coaching for Organisation Consultants programme and the Ashridge Professional Doctorate in Organisation Consulting. He is also a visiting Professor at Middlesex University. Bill has worked for 20 years facilitating organisational change, coaching executives, and facilitating small and large groups engaged in change activity. Bill focuses on raising awareness of the real issues in the here and now. His purpose is to increase 'liveliness' in organisations.

Andrew Day, BSc (Hons), MSc, C.Psychol, D.Psych is an executive coach and organisation development consultant with Ashridge Consulting Ltd. He is also a member of faculty for the Ashridge Master's in Executive Coaching and the Ashridge Master's in Organisation Consulting. His research and consulting interests including helping organisations and their leaders manage complex transitions, the dynamics of collaboration in organisations and organisation dynamics that arise in environments of uncertainty. He is a Chartered Occupational Psychologist and holds a Professional Doctorate in Occupational Psychology. He is currently completing his second Professional Doctorate, in Counselling Psychology.

Billy Desmond, MBA, MSc, UKCP is a gestalt-orientated executive coach, organisation development consultant, coach supervisor and registered psychotherapist. He is also a member of faculty for the Ashridge Master's in Executive Coaching and the Ashridge Master's in Organisation Consulting. His interest as a practitioner–researcher is focused on supporting sustainable and generative change with individuals, groups and organisational clients who often struggle to make healthy and nourishing contact with others around issues of personal and strategic importance, particularly when holding perspectives that appear counter-cultural in the communities, society and organisations in which they participate. Billy also has a private psychotherapy and supervision practice in London, primarily working with clients from minority and disadvantaged groups.

Anna Duckworth, MA, PhD, C.Phys, MAPM, MABNLP, MICF is director of Duckworth Coaching Associates and is a qualified and experienced executive coach. With a background in science and engineering, she has over twenty years of experience working within industry and has been coaching professionally at a senior level since 2001. She is also a faculty coach-mentor with the OCM Group Ltd. Her interest in coaching research stems from applied physics research during her doctorate and early career, and her fascination with psychology and what really helps people to grow. She is currently writing a book about healthy leadership which includes emotional intelligence, TA, personal strengths and mindfulness.

Jeff Jackson is a tenured Associate Professor in the Department of Behavioral Sciences and Leadership at the United States Air Force Academy. His primary responsibilities involve teaching and program evaluation related to leadership development and effectiveness. Originally a clinical psychologist, Jeff's interest shifted from behavioural change practices to coaching changes that improve leadership and effectiveness of organisations. His doctoral and master's degrees were granted by Loyola University, Chicago; his undergraduate degree is from Duke University. Dr Jackson has published in the areas of anxiety, airsickness, personality and leadership. He serves as adjunct faculty for the Center for Creative Leadership.

Kathleen King is a business director with Ashridge Consulting and programme director for the Ashridge Master's and Doctorate in Consulting. Kathleen consults to private, public, charitable and not-for-profit organisations and works as an executive coach. From her very first work with children and women, she has been motivated to support people to engage with the world and with life in a way that is generative, rewarding and sustainable at a deep level. Her interest in the Academy, learning and research is one manifestation of her investment in a sustainable future.

Robert M. Moore, DPsych is a registered psychoanalytic psychotherapist with the Irish Council for Psychotherapy and a certified group psychotherapist with the American Group Psychotherapy Association. He is currently working in private practice in Belfast in psychotherapy, supervision and organisational consultancy. Bobby is also Director of Supervision Training at the International College for Personal and Professional Development in Athlone and External Examiner for the Master's in Group Psychotherapy at CHT in London. A founding member of the Supervisors' Association of Ireland, Bobby currently serves as Vice Chair.

Lucie Morin has a PhD in human resources management/organizational behavior from University of Toronto. She is Professor at the Department of Organization and Human Resources at University of Quebec in Montreal,

Canada. Her research interests focus mainly on employee training & development at both the micro level of analysis (e.g. how can we maximise transfer of training) and the macro level (e.g. what are the links between training & development practices and employees' retention). She teaches at the undergraduate and graduate levels, supervises graduate students on a regular basis and works with organisations on training & development issues.

Laura J. Neal is a Leadership Training Specialist in the Department of Behavioral Sciences and Leadership at the United States Air Force Academy. Laura has over ten years' experience in leadership training and assessment including as Director of the Leadership Enrichment and Development Program, the cadet leadership coaching program; Director of the Dean's Faculty Organizational Climate Survey and Graduation Survey programs; and Director of Assessment Program. Ms Neal also provides assessments, teambuilding and personal consultations to outside agencies.

John Nuttall, PhD, MA, ADipPsy, DIA, DipM, UKCP is Head of the School of Psychotherapy and Counselling Psychology at Regent's College, London. After studying industrial administration and organisation theory at Aston University he followed a long career in international senior management and consultancy in industry and finance. He is a certified management consultant and chartered marketer, and a professional psychotherapist in private practice. He has written widely on management and psychotherapy and his special interests include psychotherapy integration, organisation theory and the provision of psychotherapy in the community. He is also honorary psychotherapist and Chair of Trustees of West London Centre for Counselling, a charitable provider of therapeutic counselling in primary care.

David Skinner was awarded the Ashridge Master's in Executive Coaching in 2010. He founded Leadership Systems Limited with a partner in 1993 to focus on organisational development and coaching interventions internationally. Since then he has worked on assignments in 43 countries and is particularly interested in cultural differences in terms of their impact on communication and business-related behaviour. David considers himself to be very fortunate in continuing to work today with organisations who were his first clients when he originally started his company in 1993.

Max Visser, MA, PhD has worked as a consultant and researcher inside and outside academia. Currently he is an assistant professor at Nijmegen School of Management, Radboud University, the Netherlands. His research interests include consistency, learning and communication in organisations, on which subjects he has published in *Academy of Management Review, System Dynamics Review, Journal of the History of the Behavioral Sciences* and *Human Resource Management Review*, among others.

Rob Watling, BA (Hons), MSc, PhD is a qualified leadership coach whose work is informed by 30 years' experience as a leader, manager and researcher in the public and voluntary sectors. He has worked at the BBC; the Universities of Nottingham and Leicester; for government departments, community groups, Arts Councils and Trade Unions; and as a consultant for the BBC World Service Trust. He now runs Momentum Associates, which provides coaching and consultancy for leaders in these fields. He enjoys coaching leaders through complex transitions and has a long-standing interest in the relationships between professional knowledge, power and change.

References

ABBS, P., 2003. *Against the Flow Education, the Arts and Postmodern Culture.* London: RoutledgeFalmer /z-wcorg/. ISBN 0203401905 9780203401903.

ACKERMAN, S. and HILSENROTH, M., 2003. A Review of Therapist Characteristics and Techniquest Positively Impacting the Therapeutic Alliance. *Clinical Psychology Review*, vol. 23, pp. 1–33.

ALEXANDER, R., 2011. The Dark Side of Emotional Intelligence. *Management Today*, 04, pp. 46–50 ISSN 00251925.

ALIMO-METCALFE, B., 1998. 360 Degree Feedback and Leadership Development. *International Journal of Selection and Assessment*, 01, vol. 6, no. 1, pp. 35–44 ISSN 0965-075X; 1468–2389.

ALLEN, J.A.R., 2011. Relational practice and interventions: neuroscience underpinnings. In: H. Fowlie & C. Sills (eds), *Relational Transactional Analysis – principles in practice*. London: Karnac, pp. 221–32.

ALLEN, T.D., et al., 2004. Career Benefits Associated with Mentoring for Protégés: A Meta-Analysis. *Journal of Applied Psychology*, 02, vol. 89, no. 1, pp. 127–136 ISSN 00219010.

ALMAAS, A.H., 1996. *The Point of Existence: Transformations of Narcissism in Self-Realization*. Berkeley, CA US: Diamond Books /z-wcorg/. ISBN 0936713097 9780936713090.

ALVESSON, M. and SKOLDBERG, K., 2000. *Reflexive Methodology*. London: Sage.

ALVEY, S. and BARCLAY, K., 2007. The Characteristics of Dyadic Trust in Executive Coaching. *Journal of Leadership Studies*, vol. 1, no. 1, pp. 18–27.

ANDERSON, S.L. and BETZ, N.E., 2001. Sources of Social Self-Efficacy Expectations: Their Measurement and Relation to Career Development. *Journal of Vocational Behavior*, 02, vol. 58, no. 1, pp. 98–117 ISSN 0001-8791.

ARGYRIS, C., 1970. The organization: what makes it healthy? In: Sexton, W.P. (ed.), *Organization Theories*. Ohio: Merrill Publishing, pp. 191–208.

ARGYRIS, C., 1991. Teaching Smart People how to Learn. *Harvard Business Review*, May, vol. 69, no. 3, pp. 99–109 ISSN 00178012.

ARGYRIS, C. and SCHÖN, D.A., 1978. *Organizational Learning: A Theory of Action Perspective*. Massachusetts: Addison-Wesley.

ARMSTRONG, D., 1979. The Institution in the Mind. *Free Associations*, vol. 7, no. 48.

ARON, L., 1996. *A Meeting of Minds: Mutuality in Psychoanalysis*. Hillsdale, NJ: Analytic Press, Inc ISBN 0-88163-159-0.

References

ASAY, T.P. and LAMBERT, M.J., 1999. The empirical case for the common factors in therapy: Quantitative findings. In: M.A. HUBBLE, et al. eds, *The heart and soul of change: What works in therapy*. Washington, DC: American Psychological Association. *The Empirical Case for the Common Factors in Therapy: Quantitative Findings*, pp. 23–55 ISBN 1-55798-557-X.

ASSAGIOLI, R., 1985. *The Act of Will*. Wellingborough: Turnstone Press.

ATWATER, L.E., OSTROFF, C., YAMMARINO, F.J. and FLEENOR, J.W., 1998. Self-Other Agreement: Does it really Matter?. *Personnel Psychology*, 09, vol. 51, no. 3, pp. 577–598 ISSN 00315826.

ATWATER, L., ROUSH, P. and FISCHTHAL, A., 1995. The Influence of Upward Feedback on Self- and Follower Ratings of Leadership. *Personnel Psychology*, Spring95, vol. 48, no. 1, pp. 35–59 ISSN 00315826.

ATWATER, L., WALDMAN, OSTROFF, ROBIE and JOHNSON, 2005. Self-Other Agreement: Comparing its Relationship with Performance in the U.S. and Europe. *International Journal of Selection and Assessment*, 03, vol. 13, no. 1, pp. 25–40 ISSN 0965-075X; 1468-2389.

ATWATER, L.E. and YAMMARINO, F.J., 1992. Does Self-Other Agreement on Leadership Perceptions Moderate the Validity of Leadership and Performance Predictions?. *Personnel Psychology*, Spring92, vol. 45, no. 1, pp. 141–164 ISSN 00315826.

ATWOOD, G.E. and STOLOROW, R.D., 1984. *Structures of Subjectivity; Explorations in Psychoanalytic Phenomenology*. Hillsdale, NJ: The Analytic Press.

ATWOOD, G.E. and STOLOROW, R.D., 1992. *Contexts of Being – The Intersubjective Foundations of Psychological Life*. Hillsdale NJ: The Analytic Press. ISBN 0-88163-388-7.

AUTHUR, N. and COLLINS, S. (2009) Culture-Infused Counselling Supervision. In: Pelling, N., Barletta, J. and Armstrong, P. (eds), *The practice of clinical supervision*. Brisbane, Australia: Australian Academic Press.

BALINT, M., 1968. *The Basic Fault*. London: Tavistock.

BANDURA, A., 1997. *Self-Efficacy: The Exercise of Control*. New York, NY US: W.H. Freeman.

BARON, R.M. and KENNY, D.A., 1986. The Moderator-Mediator Variable Distinction in Social Psychological Research: Conceptual, Strategic, and Statistical Considerations. *Journal of Personality and Social Psychology*, vol. 51, no. 6, pp. 1173–82 /z-wcorg/. ISSN 0022-3514.

BARON, L. and MORIN, L., 2009. The Coach–Coachee Relationship in Executive Coaching: A Field Study. *Human Resource Development Quarterly*, Spring2009, vol. 20, no. 1, pp. 85–106 ISSN 10448004.

BARON, L. and MORIN, L., 2010. The Impact of Executive Coaching on Self-Efficacy Related to Management Soft-Skills. *Leadership & Organization Development Journal*, vol. 31, no. 1, pp. 18–38 ISSN 0143-7739.

BARON, L., MORIN, L. and MORIN, D., 2011. Executive Coaching: The Effect of Working Alliance Discrepancy on Coachees' Self-Efficacy. *Journal of Management Development*, 30 (9), pp. 847–864.

BARRETT, M.S., CHUA, CRITS-CHRISTOPH GIBBONS, CASIANO and THOMPSON, 2008. Early Withdrawal from Mental Health Treatment: Implications for Psychotherapy Practice. *Psychotherapy: Theory, Research, Practice, Training*, 06, vol. 45, no. 2, pp. 247–267 ISSN 0033-3204; 1939-1536.

BARRY, D. and HANSEN, H., 2008. *The SAGE Handbook of New Approaches in Management and Organization*. Los Angeles; London: SAGE /z-wcorg/. ISBN 9781412912181 1412912180 9781412912198 1412912199.

BASS, B.M. and YAMMARINO, F.J., 1991. Congruence of Self and Others' Leadership Ratings of Naval Officers for Understanding Successful Performance. *Applied Psychology: An International Review*, 10, vol. 40, no. 4, pp. 437–454 ISSN 0269-994X; 1464-0597.

BATESON, G., 1963. Exchange of Information about Patterns of Human Behavior. In: W.S. FIELDS and W. ABBOTT (eds), *Information storage and neural control*. Springfield, IL: Thomas Books, pp. 173–186.

BATESON, G., 1972. *Steps to an Ecology of Mind: Collected Essays in Anthropology, Psychiatry, Evolution, and Epistemology*. San Francisco: Chandler Pub. Co. /z-wcorg/. ISBN 0810204479 9780810204478 0345273702 9780345273703.

BATESON, G. and JACKSON, D.D., 1968. Some Varieties of Pathogenic Organization. In: D.D. JACKSON (ed.), *Communication, Family and Marriage*. Palo Alto, CA: Science and Behavior Books, pp. 200–216.

BAVELAS, J.B., 1990. Behaving and Communicating: A Reply to Motley. *Western Journal of Speech Communication*, vol. 54, no. 4, pp. 593–602.

BAVELAS, J.B., 2007. Writing with Paul. *Journal of Marital and Family Therapy*, 07, vol. 33, no. 3, pp. 295–297 ISSN 0194-472X. DOI 10.1111/j.1752-0606.2007.00027.x.

BECK, A.T., 1976. *Cognitive Therapy and the Emotional Disorders*. New York, NY US: International Universities Press /z-wcorg/. ISBN 0823609901 9780823609901.

BEDI, R.P., DAVIS, M.D. and WILLIAMS, M., 2005. Critical Incidents in the Formation of the Therapeutic Alliance from the Client's Perspective. *Psychotherapy: Theory, Research, Practice, Training*, vol. 42, no. 3, pp. 311–323 ISSN 0033-3204; 1939-1536.

BEEBE, B. and LACHMANN, F.M., 2002. *Infant Research and Adult Treatment: Co-Constructing Interactions*. Hillsdale (N.J.): the Analytic press /z-wcorg/. ISBN 0881632457 9780881632453.

BEISSER, A.R., 1970. The paradoxical theory of change. In: J. Fagan and I. Shepherd (eds), *Gestalt Therapy Now*. Palo Alto: Science and Behaviour, pp. 77–80.

BEM, D.J., 1967. Self-Perception: An Alternative Interpretation of Cognitive Dissonance Phenomena. *Psychological Review*, 05, vol. 74, no. 3, pp. 183–200 ISSN 0033-295X; 1939-1471.

BERG, M.E. and KARLSEN, J.T., 2007. Mental Models in Project Management Coaching. *Engineering Management Journal*, 09, vol. 19, no. 3, pp. 3–13 ISSN 10429247.

BERGLAS, S., 2002. The very Real Dangers of Executive Coaching. *Harvard Business Review*, 06, vol. 80, no. 6, pp. 86–93 ISSN 00178012.

BERMAN, W.H. and BRADT, G., 2006. Executive Coaching and Consulting: 'Different Strokes for Different Folks'. *Professional Psychology: Research and Practice*, 06, vol. 37, no. 3, pp. 244–253 ISSN 0735-7028; 1939-1323.

BERNE, E., 1962. Classification of Positions. *Transactional Analysis Bulletin*, vol. 23.

BERNE, E., 1966/1994. *Principles of Group Treatment*. Menlo Park, CA: Shea Press.

BEUTLER, L.E., CRAGO, M. and ARIZMENDI, T.G., 1986. Therapist variables in psychotherapy process and outcome. In: S.L. Garfield and A.E. Bergin (eds), *Handbook of psychotherapy and behaviour change 3rd Edition*. New York: Wiley.

BEUTLER, L.E., MACHADO, P.P.P. and NEUFELDT, S.A., 1994. Therapist variables. In: A.E. BERGIN, S.L. GARFIELD, A.E. BERGIN and S.L. GARFIELD (eds), *Handbook of psychotherapy and behavior change* (4th ed.).Oxford UK: John Wiley & Sons. *Therapist Variables*, pp. 229–269 ISBN 0-471-54513-9.

BIBERMAN, J. and WHITTY, M., 1997. A Postmodern Spiritual Future for Work. *Journal of Organizational Change Management*, vol. 10, no. 2, pp. 130–138 ISSN 0953-4814.

BION, W. R. (1961) *Experiences in Groups*. Tavistock.

BIZUMIC, B., et al., 2009. The Role of the Group in Individual Functioning: School Identification and the Psychological Well-being of Staff and Students. *Applied Psychology: An International Review*, 01, vol. 58, no. 1, pp. 171–192 ISSN 0269-994X; 1464-0597.

BLUCKERT, P., 2005a. The Similarities and Differences between Coaching and Therapy. *Industrial & Commercial Training*, 03, vol. 37, no. 2, pp. 91–96 ISSN 00197858.

BLUCKERT, P., 2005b. Critical Factors in Executive Coaching – the Coaching Relationship. *Industrial & Commercial Training*, 10, vol. 37, no. 6, pp. 336–340 ISSN 00197858.

BOLTON, G., 2001. *Reflective Practice: Writing and Professional Development*. London; Thousands Oaks, CA US: Paul Chapman /z-wcorg/. ISBN 0761967281 9780761967286 076196729X 9780761967293.

BORDIN, E.S., 1979. The Generalizability of the Psychoanalytic Concept of the Working Alliance. *Psychotherapy: Theory, Research & Practice*, vol. 16, no. 3, pp. 252–260 ISSN 0033-3204.

BOWLBY, J., 1977. The Making and Breaking of Affectional Bonds: I. Aetiology and Psychopathology in the Light of Attachment Theory. *British Journal of Psychiatry*, 03, vol. 130, pp. 201–210 ISSN 0007-1250; 1472-1465.

BOWLBY, J., 1988. *A Secure Base: Clinical Applications of Attachment Theory*. London: Routledge.

BOYCE, L.A., 2011. *Advancing Executive Coaching: Setting the Course for Successful Leadership Coaching*. San Francisco: Jossey-Bass /z-wcorg/. ISBN 9780470553329 0470553324 9780470902264 0470902264 9780470902363 0470902361.

BOYCE, L.A. and CLUTTERBUCK, D., 2010. E-Coaching: Accept it, It's Here, and It's Evolving. In: G. HERNEZ-BROOME and L.A. BOYCE (eds), *Advancing Executive Coaching: Setting the Course for Successful Leadership Coaching*. San Francisco: Jossey-Bass, pp. 285–315.

BOYCE, L.A. and HERNEZ-BROOME, G., 2010. E-coaching: Consideration of leadership coaching in a virtual environment. In: D. CLUTTERBUCK, Z. HUSSAIN, D. CLUTTERBUCK and Z. HUSSAIN (eds), Virtual coach, virtual mentor. Greenwich, CT US: IAP Information Age Publishing. *E-Coaching: Consideration of Leadership Coaching in a Virtual Environment*, pp. 139–174 ISBN 978-1-60752-308-6; 978-1-60752-309-3; 978-1-60752-310-9.

BOYCE, L.A., JACKSON, R.J. and NEAL, L.J., 2010. Building Successful Leadership Coaching Relationships: Examining Impact of Matching Criteria in a Leadership Coaching Program. *Journal of Management Development*, vol. 29, no. 10, pp. 914–931 ISSN 0262-1711.

BOYES, C., 2006. *NLP.* London: Collins /z-wcorg/. ISBN 9780007216550 0007216556.

BROWNELL, P., 2008. *Handbook for Theory, Research, and Practice in Gestalt Therapy.* Newcastle: Cambridge Scholars Pub. /z-wcorg/. ISBN 9781847186072 1847186076.

BUBER, M., 1947/1965. *Between Man and Man.* Trans. R.G. Smith, New York: The Macmillan Co.

BUBER, M., 1958. *I and Thou.* New York, NY US: C. Scribner's /z-wcorg/.

BUBER, M. and FRIEDMAN, M.S., 1965. *The Knowledge of Man: A Philosophy of the Interhuman.* New York, NY US: Harper & Row /z-wcorg/.

BURKE, R., 2006. Leadership and Spirituality. *Foresight*, vol. 8, no. 6, pp. 14–25 /z-wcorg/. ISSN 1463-6689.

BYRNE, D.E., 1971. *The Attraction Paradigm.* New York, NY US: Academic Press /z-wcorg/. ISBN 9780121486501 0121486508.

CAMERON, K.S., DUTTON, J.E. and QUINN, R.E., 2003. *Positive Organizational Scholarship: Foundations of a New Discipline.* San Francisco, CA: Berrett-Koehler /z-wcorg/. ISBN 1576752321 9781576752326.

CARROLL, M., 1996. *Counselling Supervision: Theory, Skills and Practice.* London: Cassell /z-wcorg/. ISBN 0304329363 9780304329366.

CARROLL, M. and GILBERT, M., 2005. *On Becoming a Supervisee: Creating Learning Partnerships.* London: Vukani Publishing.

CASSERLEY, T. and MEGGINSON, D., 2009. *Learning from Burnout: Developing Sustainable Leaders and Avoiding Career Derailment.* Amsterdam; Boston: Elsevier/Butterworth-Heinemann /z-wcorg/. ISBN 0750683872 9780750683876.

CAVICCHIA, S., 2009. Towards a Relational Approach to Coaching – Integrating the Disavowed Aspects. *International Gestalt Journal*, vol. 32, no. 1, pp. 49–80.

CLARK, D.R., 1998. *Leadership Questionnaire.* Available from: www.nwlink. com/~Donclark/leader/bm_model.html#Notes.

CLARKSON, P., 1995a. *The Therapeutic Relationship: In Psychoanalysis, Counselling Psychology and Psychotherapy.* Philadelphia, PA US: Whurr Publishers ISBN 1-897635-87-7.

CLARKSON, P., 1995b. *Change in Organisations.* Philadelphia, PA US: Whurr Publishers ISBN 1-897635-33-8.

REFERENCES

CLARKSON, P., 2002. *The Transpersonal Relationship in Psychotherapy: The Hidden Curriculum of Spirituality.* Philadelphia, PA US: Whurr Publishers ISBN 1-86156-249-7.

CLARKSON, P. and NUTTALL, J., 2000. Working with Countertransference. *Psychodynamic Counselling*, 08, vol. 6, no. 3, pp. 359–379 ISSN 13533339.

COHEN, J., 1988. *Statistical Power Analysis for the Behavioral Sciences.* Hillsdale, NJ: L. Erlbaum Associates /z-wcorg/. ISBN 0805802835 9780805802832.

COLLINS, J. and MAYBLIN, B., 1996. *Derrida for Beginners.* Icon Books.

COX, C. and MAKIN, P., 1994. Overcoming Dependence with Contingency Contracting. *Leadership & Organization Development Journal*, vol. 15, no. 5, pp. 21–26 ISSN 0143-7739.

CRAIG, R.L. and AMERICAN SOCIETY FOR TRAINING AND DEVELOPMENT, 1996. *The ASTD Training and Development Handbook: A Guide to Human Resource Development.* New York, NY US: McGraw-Hill /z-wcorg/. ISBN 007013359X 9780070133594.

CRITCHLEY, B., 2010. Relational Coaching: Taking the Coaching High Road. *Journal of Management Development*, 12, vol. 29, no. 10, pp. 851–863 ISSN 02621711.

CRITS-CHRISTOPH, P. and MINTZ, J., 1991. Implications of Therapist Effects for the Design and Analysis of Comparative Studies of Psychotherapies. *Journal of Consulting and Clinical Psychology*, 02, vol. 59, no. 1, pp. 20–26 ISSN 0022-006X; 1939-2117.

CROCKER, S.F. and PHILIPPSON, P., 2005. Phenomenology, existentialism, and Eastern thought in Gestalt therapy. In: A.L. WOLDT, S.M. TOMAN, A.L. WOLDT and S.M. TOMAN (eds), *Gestalt therapy: History, theory, and practice.* Thousand Oaks, CA US: Sage Publications, Inc. *Phenomenology, Existentialism, and Eastern Thought in Gestalt Therapy*, pp. 65–80 ISBN 0-7619-2791-3.

CULLARI, S. and REDMON, W.K., 1982. Bateson and Behaviorism. *The Psychological Record*, vol. 32, no. 3, pp. 349–364 ISSN 0033-2933.

CYERT, R.M. and MARCH, J.G., 1963. *A Behavioral Theory of the Firm.* Upper Saddle River, NJ US: Prentice Hall/Pearson Education.

DANIEL, J.L., 2010. The Effect of Workplace Spirituality on Team Effectiveness. *Journal of Management Development*, vol. 29, no. 5, pp. 442–456 ISSN 0262-1711.

DAY, D.V., SHLEICHER, D.J., UNCKLESS, A.L. and HILLER, N.J., 2002. Self-Monitoring Personality at Work: A Meta-Analytic Investigation of Construct Validity. *Journal of Applied Psychology*, 04, vol. 87, no. 2, pp. 390–401 ISSN 0021-9010; 1939-1854.

DE BEAUVOIR, S., 1973. *The Second Sex.* London: Vintage Books

DE BOARD, R., 1995. *The Psychoanalysis of Organizations: A Psychoanalytic Approach to Behaviour in Groups and Organizations.* London [u.a.]: Routledge /z-wcorg/. ISBN 0415051754 9780415051750.

DE HAAN, E., 2008a. I Doubt therefore I Coach: Critical Moments in Coaching Practice. *Consulting Psychology Journal*, vol. 60, no. 1, pp. 91–105 /z-wcorg/. ISSN 1065-9293.

DE HAAN, E., 2008b. Becoming Simultaneously Thicker and Thinner Skinned: The Inherent Conflicts Arising in the Professional Development of Coaches. *Personnel Review*, 10, vol. 37, no. 5, pp. 526–542 ISSN 00483486.

DE HAAN, E., 2008c. *Relational Coaching: Journeys Towards Mastering One-to-One Learning.* Chichester: John Wiley /z-wcorg/. ISBN 9780470724286 0470724285.

DE HAAN, E. and BURGER, Y., 2005. *Coaching with Colleagues: An Action Guide to One-to-One Learning.* Houndmills, Basingstoke, Hampshire; New York, NY US: Palgrave Macmillan /z-wcorg/. ISBN 1403943230 9781403943231.

DE HAAN, E., CULPIN, V. and CURD, J., 2011. Executive Coaching in Practice: What Determines Helpfulness for Clients of Coaching?. *Personnel Review*, 02, vol. 40, no. 1, pp. 24–44 ISSN 00483486.

DE HAAN, E. and SILLS, C., 2010. Guest Editorial. *Journal of Management Development*, vol. 29, no. 10, pp. 845–850.

DECHURCH, L.A. and MESMER-MAGNUS, J., 2010. Measuring Shared Team Mental Models: A Meta-Analysis. *Group Dynamics: Theory, Research, and Practice*, 03, vol. 14, no. 1, pp. 1–14 ISSN 1089-2699; 1930-7802.

DENHAM-VAUGHAN, S., 2010. The Liminal Space and Twelve Action Practices for Gracious Living. *British Gestalt Journal*, vol. 19, no. 2, pp. 34–45 /z-wcorg/. ISSN 0961-771X.

DESMOND, B., 2011. Effective Group Development: A Paradoxical Appraoch for Action Learning Facilitators. *OD Practitioner*, vol. 43, no. 1, pp. 29–34.

DEURZEN-SMITH, E.v., 1997. *Everyday Mysteries: Existential Dimensions of Psychotherapy.* London: Routledge. /z-wcorg/. ISBN 0415087058 9780415087056.

DEYOUNG, P.A., 2003. *Relational Psychotherapy: A Primer.* New York, NY US: Brunner-Routledge ISBN 0-415-94432-5; 0-415-94433-3.

DIAMOND, M.A., 1991. Stresses of group membership: Balancing the needs for independence and belonging. In: M.F.R. KETS DE VRIES (ed.), *Organizations on the couch: Clinical perspectives on organizational behavior and change.* San Francisco, CA US: Jossey-Bass. *Stresses of Group Membership: Balancing the Needs for Independence and Belonging*, pp. 191–214 ISBN 1-55542-384-1.

DIGMAN, J.M., 1990. Personality Structure: Emergence of the Five-Factor Model. *Annual Review of Psychology*, 02, vol. 41, no. 1, p. 417 ISSN 00664308.

DINGMAN, M.E., 2004. *The Effects of Executive Coaching on Job-Related Attitudes.* /z-wcorg/.

DIXON, J., 2009. The Supervisory Relationship. In: PELLING, N., BARLETTA, J. and ARMSTRONG, P. (eds), *The practice of clinical supervision.* Brisbane, Australia: Australian Academic Press.

DONAVON, A. no date. *A Relational Model of Supervision (Private Paper).*

DROTTER, S.J. and CHARAN, R., 2001. Building Leaders at Every Level: A Leadership Pipeline – Building Lessons into Different Levels of Responsibility Will Help an Organization Sustain a Pipeline of Capable Leaders. *Ivey Business Journal*, vol. 65, no. 5, p. 21 /z-wcorg/. ISSN 1481-8248.

DRUCKER, P.F., 1964. *Managing for Results: Economic Tasks and Risk-Taking Decisions.* London: Heinemann /z-wcorg/.

References

DUCKWORKTH, A., DE HAAN, E., BIRCH, D., HARDMAN, P. and JONES, C., 2012. Executive Coaching Outcome Research: The Contribution of Common Factors such as Relationship, Personality Match and Self-Efficacy. *Consulting Psychology Journal: Practice and Research*, 2012 (in press).

DUMONT, F., 1991. Expertise in Psychotherapy: Inherent Liabilities of Becoming Experienced. *Psychotherapy: Theory, Research, Practice, Training*, vol. 28, no. 3, pp. 422–428 ISSN 0033-3204; 1939-1536.

DUNCAN, B.L. and MILLER, S.D., 2000. *The Heroic Client: Doing Client-Directed, Outcome-Informed Therapy*. San Francisco, CA US: Jossey-Bass ISBN 0-7879-4725-3.

EBY, L.T., et al., 2008. Does Mentoring Matter? A Multidisciplinary Meta-Analysis Comparing Mentored and Non-Mentored Individuals. *Journal of Vocational Behavior*, 04, vol. 72, no. 2, pp. 254–267 ISSN 0001-8791.

EDWARDS, J.R., 1994. Regression Analysis as an Alternative to Difference Scores. *Journal of Management*, Fall94, vol. 20, no. 3, p. 683 ISSN 01492063.

EDWARDS, J.R., 2001. Ten Difference Score Myths. *Organizational Research Methods*, 07, vol. 4, no. 3, pp. 265–287 ISSN 1094-4281; 1552-7425.

ELLIS, A., 1998. How rational emotive behavior therapy belongs in the constructivist camp. In: M.F. HOYT and M.F. HOYT (eds), *The handbook of constructive therapies: Innovative approaches from leading practitioners*. San Francisco, CA US: Jossey-Bass, pp. 83–99 ISBN 0-7879-4044-5.

ENGLISH, F., 1975. The Three-Cornered Contract. *Transactional Analysis Journal*, 10, vol. 5, no. 4, pp. 383–384 ISSN 0362-1537.

ERSKINE, R.G., 1995. A Gestalt Therapy Approach to Shame and Self-Righteousness: Theory and Methods. *British Gestalt Journal*, vol. 4, no. 2, pp. 107–117 /z-wcorg/. ISSN 0961-771X.

ERSKINE, R.G., 2010. *Life Scripts: A Transactional Analysis of Unconscious Relational Patterns*. London: Karnac /z-wcorg/. ISBN 9781855756625 1855756625.

EVERS, W.J.G., BROUWERS, A. and TOMIC, W., 2006. A Quasi-Experimental Study on Management Coaching Effectiveness. *Consulting Psychology Journal: Practice and Research*, vol. 58, no. 3, pp. 174–182 ISSN 1065-9293; 1939-0149.

FAGAN, J. and SHEPHERD, I.L., 1970. *Gestalt Therapy Now: Theory, Techniques, Applications*, Palo Alto, CA US: Science and Behavior Books /z-wcorg/. ISBN 0831400234 9780831400231.

FAIRBAIRN, W.R.D., 1952. *An Object-Relations Theory of Personality*. New York, NY US: Basic Books.

FAYOL, H., 1949. *General and Industrial Management*. London: Pitman /z-wcorg/.

FELDER, R.M., 2004. *Index of Learning Styles*. /z-wcorg/.

FELDMAN, D.C. and LANKAU, M.J., 2005. Executive Coaching: A Review and Agenda for Future Research. *Journal of Management*, 12, vol. 31, no. 6, pp. 829–848 ISSN 0149-2063; 1557-1211.

FINEMAN, S., 2000. *Emotion in Organizations*. London ; Thousand Oaks, CA US: Sage Publications /z-wcorg/. ISBN 0761966242 9780761966241 0761966250 9780761966258.

FLETCHER, J.K., 1994. Castrating the Female Advantage. *Journal of Management Inquiry*, 03, vol. 3, no. 1, pp. 74–82 ISSN 10564926. FLETCHER, J.K., 1998. Relational Practice. *Journal of Management Inquiry*, 06, vol. 7, no. 2, pp. 163–186 ISSN 10564926.

FLETCHER, J.K., 1999. *Disappearing Acts: Gender, Power and Relational Practice at Work.* Cambridge, MA US: MIT Press /z-wcorg/. ISBN 058507819X 9780585078199. FRANKL, V.E., 1969. *The Will to Meaning: Foundations and Applications of Logotherapy.* New York, NY US: New American Library /z-wcorg/.

FRANKL, V.E., 1978. *The Unheard Cry for Meaning: Psychotherapy and Humanism.* Oxford UK: Simon & Schuster ISBN 0671228919.

FRANKL, V.E., 1992. *Man's Search for Meaning*, 4th edition. Originally published in 1959 under the title *From Death-camp to Existentialism.* Boston, MA US: Beacon Press.

FREDRICKSON, B.L., 2003. Positive emotions and upward spirals in organizational settings. In CAMERON, K., DUTTON, J. and QUINN, R. (eds), *Positive Organizational Scholarship.* San Francisco: Berrett-Koehler.

FRENCH, R. and VINCE, R., 1999. *Group Relations, Management, and Organization.* Oxford [etc.]: Oxford University Press /z-wcorg/. ISBN 0198293674 9780198293675 0198293666 9780198293668.

FREUD, S., 1905. *Fragment of an Analysis of a Case of Hysteria.* Standard Edition Vol. 7th ed. London: Hogarth /z-wcorg/.

FULLER, F. and FRIDJHON, M., 2005. *Developing the Partnership Alliance – Unpublished Training Materials from the Center for Right Relationship.*

FULLER, R.W., 2004. *Somebodies and Nobodies: Overcoming the Abuse of Rank.* Gabriola, BC Canada: New Society Publishers /z-wcorg/. ISBN 0865714878 9780865714878.

FURNHAM, A. and STRINGFIELD, P., 1994. Congruence of Self and Subordinate Ratings of Managerial Practices as a Correlate of Supervisor Evaluation. *Journal of Occupational & Organizational Psychology*, 03, vol. 67, no. 1, pp. 57–67 ISSN 09631798.

GARDNER, W.L. and MARTINKO, M.J., 1996. Using the Myers–Briggs Type Indicator to Study Managers: A Literature Review and Research Agenda. *Journal of Management*, Spring96, vol. 22, no. 1, p. 45 ISSN 01492063.

GAUDINE, A.P. and SAKS, A.M., 2004. A Longitudinal Quasi-Experiment on the Effects of Posttraining Transfer Interventions. *Human Resource Development Quarterly*, Spring2004, vol. 15, no. 1, pp. 57–76 ISSN 10448004.

GEIDMAN H.K. and WOLKENFELD F., 1980. The Parallelism Phenomenon in Psychoanalysis and Supervision: Its Reconsideration as a Triadic System. *The Psychoanalytic Quarterly*, vol. 49, no. 2, pp. 234–255 /z-wcorg/. ISSN 0033-2828.

GERGEN, K.J., 1999. *An Invitation to Social Construction.* London; Thousand Oaks, CA US: SAGE.

GERGEN, K.J., 2009. *Relational being: Beyond Self and Community.* New York, NY US: Oxford University Press ISBN 978-0-19-530538-8.

GERHARDT, S., 2004. *Why Love Matters: How Affection Shapes a Baby's Brain.* Hove, East Sussex; New York, NY US: Brunner-Routledge /z-wcorg/. ISBN

1583918167 9781583918166 1583918175 9781583918173 9780203499658 0203499654.

GERSON, S., 2004. The Relational Unconscious: A Core Element of Intersubjectivity, Thirdness, and Clinical Process. *The Psychoanalytic Quarterly*, 01, vol. 73, no. 1, pp. 63–98 ISSN 0033-2828.

GERSTEIN, M., 1985. Mentoring: An Age Old Practice in a Knowledge-Based Society. *Journal of Counseling & Development*, 10, vol. 64, no. 2, p. 156 ISSN 07489633.

GILBRETH, F.B., 1912. *Primer of Scientific Management*. New York, NY US: D. Van Nostrand company /z-wcorg/.

GILLIGAN, C., 1993. *In a Different Voice: Psychological Theory and Women's Development*. Cambridge, MA US: Harvard University Press.

GLASERSFELD, E.v., 1995. *Radical Constructivism: A Way of Knowing and Learning*. London; Washington, DC US: Falmer Press /z-wcorg/. ISBN 0750703873 9780750703871.

GLEICK, J., 1987. *Chaos: Making a New Science*. London: Sphere Books /z-wcorg/. ISBN 0747404135 9780747404132.

GLESO, C.J. and CARTER, J.A., 1985. The Relationship in Counselling and Psychotherapy: Components, Consequences and Theoretical Antecedents. *The Counselling Psychologist*, vol. 13, no. 2, pp. 155–243.

GODDARD, A., 2010. *The Clients' Experience of the Executive Coaching Relationship*. Oxford: Oxford Brookes.

GOLDBERG, C., 1977. *Therapeutic Partnership: Ethical Concerns in Psychotherapy*. New York, NY US: Springer Pub. Co. /z-wcorg/. ISBN 0826123503 9780826123503 0826123511 9780826123510.

GOLEMAN, D., 1996. *Emotional Intelligence: Why it can Matter More than IQ*. London: Bloomsbury /z-wcorg/. ISBN 0747528306 0747529825 9780747529828 0747526222 9780747526223 9780747528302.

GOLEMAN, D., 1998. *Working with Emotional Intelligence*. London: Bloomsbury /z-wcorg/. ISBN 0747539847 9780747539841.

GOULD, L.J., 1991. Using psychoanalytic frameworks for organizational analysis. In: M.F.R. KETS DE VRIES (ed.), *Organizations on the couch: Clinical perspectives on organizational behavior and change*. San Francisco, CA US: Jossey-Bass. *Using Psychoanalytic Frameworks for Organizational Analysis*, pp. 25–44 ISBN 1-55542-384-1.

GOULD, L., STAPLEY, L.F. and STEIN, M., 2006. *The Systems Psychodynamics of Organizations: Integrating the Group Relations Approach, Psychoanalytic, and Open Systems Perspectives*. London: Karnac Books /z-wcorg/. ISBN 185575441X 9781855754416.

GOULDING, M.M. and GOULDING, R.L., 1979. *Changing Lives through Redecision Therapy*. New York: Grove Press.

GRAY, D.E., 2006. Executive Coaching: Towards a Dynamic Alliance of Psychotherapy and Transformative Learning Processes. *Management Learning*, 12, vol. 37, no. 4, pp. 475–497 ISSN 1350-5076; 1461-7307.

GRAY, J.L., 1979. The Myths of the Myths about Behavior Mod in Organizations: A Reply to Locke's Criticisms of Behavior Modification. *Academy of Management Review*, 01, vol. 4, no. 1, pp. 121–129 ISSN 03637425.

GREENBERG, J.R. and MITCHELL, S.A., 1983. *Object Relations in Psychoanalytic Theory.* Cambridge, MA US: Harvard University Press /z-wcorg/. ISBN 0674629752 9780674629752.

GREENBERGH, L. and PINSOFF, W., 1986. *Psychotherapeutic Processes: A Research Handbook.* New York, NY US: Guilford Press.

GREENLEAF, R.K. and SPEARS, L.C., 1998. *The Power of Servant-Leadership: Essays.* San Francisco, CA US: Berrett-Koehler Publishers /z-wcorg/. ISBN 1576750353 9781576750353.

GREENSON, R.R., 1965. The Working Alliance and the Transference Neurosis. *The Psychoanalytic Quarterly*, vol. 34, no. 2, pp. 155–179 ISSN 0033-2828.

HALEY, J., 1963. *Strategies of Psychotherapy.* Oxford UK: Grune & Stratton.

HALL, D.T., OTAZO, K.L. and HOLLENBECK, G.P., 1999. Behind Closed Doors: What really Happens in Executive Coaching. *Organizational Dynamics*, Winter99, vol. 27, no. 3, p. 39 ISSN 00902616.

HARRISON, D.A., PRICE, K.H. and BELL, M.P., 1998. Beyond Relational Demography: Time and the Effects of Surface- and Deep-Level Diversity on Work Group Cohesion. *Academy of Management Journal*, 02, vol. 41, no. 1, pp. 96–107 ISSN 00014273.

HAWKE, C., 1996. Book Review of the Therapeutic Relationship, by Clarkson. *British Journal of Psychotherapy*, vol. 12, no. 4, pp. 405–407.

HAWKINS, P. and SHOHET, R., 1989. *Supervision in the Helping Professions: An Individual, Group, and Organizational Approach.* Milton Keynes, UK; Philadelphia: Open University Press /z-wcorg/. ISBN 0335098541 9780335098545 0335098339 9780335098330.

HAWKINS, P. and SMITH, N., 2006. *Coaching, Mentoring and Organizational Consultancy: Supervision and Development.* Maidenhead: Open University Press /z-wcorg/. ISBN 9780335218165 0335218164 0335218156 9780335218158.

HERNEZ-BROOME, G., BOYCE, L.A. and ELY, K., 2009. The coaching relationship: A glimpse into the Black Box of coaching. Anonymous. In L.A. Boyce and G. Hernez-Broom (Chair), *The Client–Coach relationship: Examining a critical component of successful coaching. At the 24th Annual Conference of the Society for Industrial and Organizational Psychology.* New Orleans, LA US.

HERON, J., 1975. *Helping the Client.* London: Sage Publications.

HERON, J., 1996. *Co-Operative Inquiry: Research into the Human Conditon.* Thousand Oaks, CA US: Sage Publications, Inc ISBN 0-8039-7683-6; 0-8039-7684-4.

HERON, J. and REASON, P., 1997. A Participative Inquiry Paradigm. *Qualitative Inquiry*, vol. 3, no. 3.

HERSOUG, A.G., MONSEN, J.T., HAVIK, O.E. and HØGLEND, P., 2002. Quality of Early Working Alliance in Psychotherapy: Diagnoses, Relationship and Intrapsychic Variables as Predictors. *Psychotherapy and Psychosomatics*, 01, vol. 71, no. 1, pp. 18–27 ISSN 0033-3190; 1423-0348.

243

REFERENCES

HERZBERG, F., 1968. *Work and the Nature of Man.* London: Staples Pr.: /z-wcorg/.

HIRSCHHORN, L., 1988. *The Workplace within: Psychodynamics of Organizational Life.* Cambridge, MA US: MIT Press /z-wcorg/. ISBN 0262081695 9780262081696.

HIRSCHHORN, L. and BARNETT, C. K., 1993. *The Psychodynamics of Organizations.* Philadelphia: Temple University Press /z-wcorg/. ISBN 1566390206 9781566390200 1566390214 9781566390217.

HOCHSCHILD, A.R., 1983. *The Managed Heart: Commercialization of Human Feeling.* Berkeley: University of California Press /z-wcorg/. ISBN 0520048008 9780520048003.

HOFSTEDE, G.H., 1991. *Cultures and Organizations: Software of the Mind.* London; New York, NY US: McGraw-Hill /z-wcorg/. ISBN 0077074742 9780077074746.

HOGG, M.A., 2001. A Social Identity Theory of Leadership. *Personality & Social Psychology Review (Lawrence Erlbaum Associates),* 08, vol. 5, no. 3, pp. 184–200 ISSN 10888683.

HOGG, M.A., TERRY, D.J. and WHITE, K.M., 1995. A Tale of Two Theories: A Critical Comparison of Identity Theory with Social Identity Theory. *Social Psychology Quarterly,* 12, vol. 58, no. 4, pp. 255–269 ISSN 0190-2725.

HOLLAND, J.G. and SKINNER, B.F., 1961. *The Analysis of Behavior: A Program for Self-Instruction.* New York, NY US: McGraw-Hill.

HOLLOWAY, E.L., 1995. *Clinical Supervision: A Systems Approach.* Thousand Oaks, CA US: Sage Publications, Inc ISBN 0-8039-4223-0; 0-8039-4224-9.

HOLTI, R., 1997. Consulting to organisational implications of technical change. In: J. NEUMANN, K. KELLNER and A. DAWSON-SHEPHERD (eds), *Developing Organisational Consultancy.* Brunner-Routledge.

HOPFL, H., 2008. Maternal Organization. In: D. BARRY and H. HANSEN (eds), *New Approaches in Management and Organization.* London: Sage.

HORVATH, A.O., 2005. The Therapeutic Relationship: Research and Theory: An Introduction to the Special Issue. *Psychotherapy Research,* 01, vol. 15, no. 1–2, pp. 3–7 ISSN 1050-3307; 1468-4381.

HORVATH, A.O. and BEDI, R.P., 2002. The Alliance. In: J.C. NORCROSS and J.C. NORCROSS (eds), *Psychotherapy relationships that work: Therapist contributions and responsiveness to patients.* New York, NY US: Oxford University Press, pp. 37–69 ISBN 0-19-514346-9.

HORVATH, A.O. and GREENBERG, L.S., 1989. Development and Validation of the Working Alliance Inventory. *Journal of Counseling Psychology,* 04, vol. 36, no. 2, pp. 223–233 ISSN 0022-0167; 1939-2168.

HORVATH, A.O. and MARX, R.W., 1990. The Development and Decay of the Working Alliance during Time-Limited Counselling. *Canadian Journal of Counselling,* 10, vol. 24, no. 4, pp. 240–260 ISSN 0828-3893.

HORVATH, A.O. and SYMONDS, B.D., 1991. Relation between Working Alliance and Outcome in Psychotherapy: A Meta-Analysis. *Journal of Counseling Psychology,* 04, vol. 38, no. 2, p. 139 ISSN 00220167.

HOUSTON NEUROLOGICAL SOCIETY, FIELDS, W.S. and ABBOTT, W., 1963. *Information Storage and Neural Control.* Springfield: Charles C. Thomas /z-wcorg/.

HUCZYNSKI, A. and BUCHANAN, D.A., 2010. *Organizational Behaviour.* Harlow: Financial Times Prentice Hall /z-wcorg/. ISBN 9780273728597 0273728598 9780273728221 0273728229.

HUNT, D.M. and MICHAEL, C., 1983. Mentorship: A Career Training and Development Tool. *Academy of Management Review,* 07, vol. 8, no. 3, pp. 475–485 ISSN 03637425.

HYCNER, R.H., 1993. *Between Person and Person: Toward a Dialogical Psychotherapy.* Highland, NY: Gestalt Journal Press /z-wcorg/.

HYCNER, R.H. and JACOBS, L., 1995. *The Healing Relationship in Gestalt Therapy: A dialogic/self Psychology Approach.* Highland, NY: Gestalt Journal Press /z-wcorg/. ISBN 0939266253 9780939266258.

IGWE, A., 1997. personal communication.

ISAACS, W., 1999. *Dialogue and the Art of Thinking Together a Pioneering Approach to Communicating in Business and in Life.* New York, NY US: Doubleday /z-wcorg/. ISBN 0385479999 9780385479998.

JACKSON, Don D., 1968. *Communication, Family, and Marriage.* Palo Alto, CA US: Science and Behavior Books /z-wcorg/.

JACOBS, L., 1989. Dialogue in Gestalt theory and therapy. *The Gestalt Journal,* 12(1): 25–68.

JACOBS, L., 1995. The Therapist as "Other"; The Patient's Search for Relatedness. In R. HYCNER and L. JACOBS, *The Healing Relationship in Gestalt Therapy.* USA: The Gestalt Journal Press, Inc., p.215–234.

JACQUES, E. and TAVISTOCK INSTITUTE OF HUMAN RELATIONS, 1951. *The Changing Culture of a Factory.* London: Tavistock Publications /z-wcorg/. ISBN 0415264421 9780415264426.

JACQUES, E., 1955. Social systems as a defence against persecutory and depressive anxiety. In: M. KLEIN, P. HEINEMANN and R.E. MONEY KYRLE (eds), *New Directions in Psycho-Analysis: The Significance of Infant Conflict in the Pattern of Adult* Behaviour. London: Tavistock, pp. 478–498.

JENKINS, P., 2007. *Counselling, Psychotherapy and the Law.* Los Angeles; London: SAGE /z-wcorg/. ISBN 9781412900058 1412900050 9781412900065 1412900069.

JOINES, V. and STEWART, I., 2002. *Personality Adaptations: A New Guide to Human Understanding in Psychotherapy and Counselling.* Nottingham: Lifespace /z-wcorg/. ISBN 187024401X 9781870244015.

JUDGE, T.A., et al., 2007. Self-Efficacy and Work-Related Performance: The Integral Role of Individual Differences. *Journal of Applied Psychology,* 01, vol. 92, no. 1, pp. 107–127 ISSN 00219010.

JUNG, C.G., 1998. *The Psychology of the Transference.* London: Routledge /z-wcorg/. ISBN 0415151325 9780415151320.

KAMPA, S. and WHITE, R.P., 2002. The effectiveness of executive coaching: What we know and what we still need to know. In: R.L. LOWMAN and R.L. LOWMAN (eds), *The California School of Organizational Studies: Handbook of organizational consulting psychology: A comprehensive guide to theory, skills, and techniques.* San Francisco, CA US: Jossey-Bass. pp. 139–158 ISBN 0-7879-5899-9.

KAMPA-KOKESCH, S. and ANDERSON, M.Z., 2001. Executive Coaching: A Comprehensive Review of the Literature. *Consulting Psychology Journal: Practice and Research*, vol. 53, no. 4, pp. 205–228 ISSN 1065-9293; 1939-0149.

KAPUR, R., 1987. Depression: An Integration of TA and Psychodynamic Concepts. *Transactional Analysis Journal*, 04, vol. 17, no. 2, pp. 29–34 ISSN 0362-1537.

KARPMAN, S., 1968. Fairy Tales and Script Drama Analysis. *Transactional Analysis Bulletin*, vol. 7, no. 26, pp. 39–43.

KARPMAN, S., 1971. Options. *Transactional Analysis Journal*, vol. 1.

KAUFFMAN, C. and COUTU, D., 2009. The Realities of Executive Coaching. *Harvard Business Review*, vol. 87, pp. 1–24.

KAUFMAN, G., 1989. *The Psychology of Shame: Theory and Treatment of Shame-Based Syndromes*. New York, NY US: Springer Pub. Co. /z-wcorg/. ISBN 0826166709 9780826166708.

KENNEDY, D., 1998. Gestalt: A Point of Departure for a Personal Spirituality. *British Gestalt Journal*, vol. 7, no. 2, pp. 88–98 /z-wcorg/. ISSN 0961-771X.

KETS DE VRIES, M.F.R., 1980. *Organizational Paradoxes: Clinical Approaches to Management*. London: /z-wcorg/. ISBN 0422772801 9780422772808.

KETS DE VRIES, M.F.R., 1991. *Organizations on the Couch: Clinical Perspectives on Organizational Behavior and Change*. San Francisco: Jossey-Bass /z-wcorg/. ISBN 1555423841 9781555423841.

KETS DE VRIES, M.F.R., 2006. *The Leader on the Couch: A Clinical Approach to Changing People and Organizations*. San Francisco: Jossey-Bass /z-wcorg/. ISBN 0470030798 9780470030790.

KIEL, F., RIMMER, E., WILLIAMS, K. and DOYLE, M., 1996. Coaching at the Top. *Consulting Psychology Journal: Practice and Research*, vol. 48, no. 2, pp. 67–77 ISSN 1065-9293; 1939-0149.

KILBURG, R.R., 1996. Toward a Conceptual Understanding and Definition of Executive Coaching. *Consulting Psychology Journal: Practice and Research*, vol. 48, no. 2, pp. 134–144 ISSN 1065-9293; 1939-0149.

KING, K., 2004. Chapter 7: Relational Practice in Consulting. PhD Dissertation – University of Bath.

KING, P.M. and STROHM-KITCHENER, K., 1994. *Developing Reflective Judgment: Understanding and Promoting Intellectual Growth and Critical Thinking in Adolescents and Adults*. San Francisco: Jossey-Bass Publishers /z-wcorg/. ISBN 1555426298 9781555426293.

KIRKPATRICK, D.L., 1996. Evaluation. In: R.L. CRAIG (ed.), *The ASTD Training and Development Handbook* (4th ed.). New York: McGraw-Hill, pp. 294–312.

KIVLIGHAN, D.M. and SHAUGHNESSY, P., 1995. Analysis of the Development of the Working Alliance using Hierarchical Linear Modeling. *Journal of Counseling Psychology*, vol. 42, no. 3, pp. 338–349 /z-wcorg/. ISSN 0022-0167.

KLEIN, M., 1963. *Our Adult World, and Other Essays*. London UK: William Heinemann Medical Books /z-wcorg/.

KLEIN, N., 2000. *No Logo*. London: Flamingo /z-wcorg/. ISBN 0002559196 9780002559195 067697130X 9780676971309 0676972829 9780676972825.

KOFFKA, K., 1935. *Principles of Gestalt Psychology*. Oxford UK: Harcourt, Brace.

KÖHLER, W., 1969. *The task of Gestalt Psychology*, [S.l.]. Princeton University Press.

KOHUT, H., 1984. *How does Analysis Cure?* Chicago: University of Chicago Press /z-wcorg/. ISBN 0226450341 9780226450346.

KOHUT, H. and WOLF, E.S., 1978. The Disorders of the Self and their Treatment: An Outline. *The International Journal of Psychoanalysis*, 11, vol. 59, no. 4, pp. 413–425 ISSN 0020-7578.

KRANTZ, J., 1993. The Managerial Couple – Superior–Subordinate Relationships as a Unit of Analysis. In: HIRSCHHORN, L. and BARNETT, C. (eds), *The Psychodynamics of Organisations*. Philadelphia: Temple ISBN 1-56639-021-4.

KRANTZ, J. and GILMORE, T., 1990. Projective Identification in Organizational Consultation. (http://www.triadllc.com/pubprojective.html) In: KREITNER, R., KINICKI, A. and BUELENS, M., *Organizational Behaviour*. London: McGraw Hill /z-wcorg/. ISBN 0077098285 9780077098285.

KREITNER, R., KINICKI, A. and BUELENS, M., 2002. *Organizational Behaviour*. London: McGraw Hill /z-wcorg/. ISBN 0077098285 9780077098285.

KRISHNAKUMAR, S. and NECK, C.P., 2002. The 'What', 'Why' and 'How' of Spirituality in the Workplace. *Journal of Managerial Psychology*, 04, vol. 17, no. 3, p. 153 ISSN 02683946.

LAMBERT, 1992. Psychotherapy outcome research. In: J.C. Norcross and M.R. Goldfried (eds), *Handbook of psychotherapy integration*. New York: Basic Books.

LAMBERT, M.J. and BERGIN, A.E., 1994. The effectiveness of psychotherapy. In: A.E. BERGIN, S.L. GARFIELD, A.E. BERGIN and S.L. GARFIELD (eds), Handbook of psychotherapy and behavior change (4th ed.).Oxford UK: John Wiley & Sons. *The Effectiveness of Psychotherapy*, pp. 143–189 ISBN 0-471-54513-9.

LEE, R.G. and WHEELER, G., 1996. *The Voice of Shame: Silence and Connection in Psychotherapy*. San Francisco: Jossey-Bass Publishers /z-wcorg/. ISBN 0787902012 9780787902018.

LEIGH, P., 1997. The New Spirit at Work. *Training & Development*, 03, vol. 51, no. 3, p. 26 ISSN 10559760.

LEWIN, K., 1952. *Field Theory in Social Science: Selected Theoretical Papers*. London: Tavistock Publications /z-wcorg/.

LEWIS, C.S., 1978. *Till we have Faces: A Myth Retold*. London: Fount /z-wcorg/. ISBN 000625277X 9780006252771.

LEWIS, T., AMINI, F. and LANNON, R., 2000. *A General Theory of Love*. New York, NY US: Random House /z-wcorg/. ISBN 0375503897 9780375503894.

LINSTEAD, S. and PULLEN, A., 2008. Un-gendering Organization. In: D. BARRY and H. HANSEN (eds), *New Approaches in Management and Organization*. London: Sage.

LOCKE, E.A., 1977. The Myths of Behavior Mod in Organizations. *Academy of Management Review*, 10, vol. 2, no. 4, pp. 543–553 ISSN 03637425.

LOWMAN, R.L., 2005. Executive Coaching: The Road to Dodoville Needs Paving with More than Good Assumptions. *Consulting Psychology Journal: Practice & Research*, Winter2005, vol. 57, no. 1, pp. 90–96 ISSN 10659293.

REFERENCES

MACKEWN, J., 1997. *Developing Gestalt Counselling: A Field Theoretical and Relational Model of Contemporary Gestalt Counselling and Psychotherapy.* Thousand Oaks, CA US: Sage Publications, Inc ISBN 0-8039-7860-X; 0-8039-7861-8.

MACKINNON, D.P., LOCKWOOD, HOFFMAN, WEST and SHEETS, 2002. A Comparison of Methods to Test Mediation and Other Intervening Variable Effects. *Psychological Methods*, 03, vol. 7, no. 1, pp. 83–104 ISSN 1082-989X; 1939-1463.

MALONE, J.W., 2001. Shining a New Light on Organizational Change: Improving Self-Efficacy through Coaching. *Organization Development Journal.*, vol. 19, pp. 27–36 /z-wcorg/. ISSN 0889-6402.

MARODA, K.J., 1991. *The Power of Countertransference: Innovations in Analytic Technique.* Oxford UK: John Wiley & Sons ISBN 0-471-92626-4; 0-471-93041-5.

MARQUES, J.F., 2006. The Spiritual Worker: An Examination of the Ripple Effect that Enhances Quality of Life in- and Outside the Work Environment. *Journal of Management Development*, vol. 25, no. 9, pp. 884–895 ISSN 0262-1711.

MARTIN, D.J., GARSKE, J.P. and DAVIS, M.K., 2000. Relation of the Therapeutic Alliance with Outcome and Other Variables: A Meta-Analytic Review. *Journal of Consulting and Clinical Psychology*, 06, vol. 68, no. 3, pp. 438–450 ISSN 0022-006X; 1939-2117.

MASLOW, A., 1943. Psychology. In: J.A. SIMONS, D.B. IRWIN and B.A. DRINNIEN (eds), *The Search for Understanding.* New York: West Publishing, 1987.

MATHIEU, J.E., HEFFNER, GOODWIN, SALAS and CANNON-BOWERS 2000. The Influence of Shared Mental Models on Team Process and Performance. *Journal of Applied Psychology*, 04, vol. 85, no. 2, pp. 273–283 ISSN 0021-9010; 1939-1854.

MATHIEU, J.E. and MARTINEAU, J.W., 1993. Individual and Situational Influences on the Development of Self-Efficacy: Implications for Training Effectiveness. *Personnel Psychology*, Spring93, vol. 46, no. 1, pp. 125–147 ISSN 00315826.

MATHIEU, J.E., MARTINEAU, J.W. and TANNENBAUM, S.I., 1993. Individual and Situational Influences on the Development of Self-Efficacy: Implications for Training Effectiveness. *Personnel Psychology*, Spring93, vol. 46, no. 1, pp. 125–147 ISSN 00315826.

MAY, R., 1983. *The Discovery of Being: Writings in Existential Psychology.* New York: W.W. Norton.

MAYO, E., 1949. *The Social Problems of an Industrial Civilization.* Routledge & Kegan Paul /z-wcorg/.

MCCAULEY, C.D., VAN VELSOR, E. and CENTER FOR CREATIVE LEADERSHIP, 2004. *The Center for Creative Leadership Handbook of Leadership Development.* San Francisco; [Chichester]: Jossey-Bass /z-wcorg/. ISBN 0787965294 9780787965297.

MCGOVERN, J., et al., 2001. Maximizing the Impact of Executive Coaching: Behavioral Change, Organizational Outcomes, and Return on Investment. *The Manchester Review*, vol. 6, no. 1, pp. 1–8.

MCGREGOR, D., 1960. *The Human Side of Enterprise*. New York, NY US: McGraw-Hill.

MCNEAL, B.W., MAY, R.J. and LEE, V.E., 1987. Perceptions of Counsellor Source Characteristics by Premature and Successful Terminators. *Journal of Counseling Psychology*, vol. 34, pp. 86–89.

MEAD, G.H. and MORRIS, C.W., 1967. *Mind, Self, and Society: From the Standpoint of a Social Behaviorist*. Chicago [u.a.]: Univ. of Chicago Press /z-wcorg/. ISBN 0226516687 9780226516684.

MEHRABIAN, A., 1981. *Silent Messages: Implicit Communication of Emotions and Attitudes*. Belmont, CA US: Wadsworth Pub. Co. /z-wcorg/. ISBN 0534009107, 9780534009106.

MENZIES, I.E.P., 1960. A Case-Study in the Functioning of Social Systems as a Defence Against Anxiety: A Report on a Study of the Nursing Service of a General Hospital. *Human Relations Human Relations*, vol. 13, no. 2, pp. 95–121 /z-wcorg/. ISSN 0018-7267.

MICHOLT, N., 1992. Psychological Distance and Group Interventions. *Transactional Analysis Journal*, 10, vol. 22, no. 4, pp. 228–233 ISSN 0362-1537.

MILLER, J.B., 1986. *Toward a New Psychology of Women*. Boston: Beacon Press /z-wcorg/. ISBN 0807029106 9780807029107.

MILLER, S.D., et al., 2005. Using Outcome to Inform Therapy Practice. *Journal of Brief Therapy*, vol. 5, no. 1, pp. 5–17.

MILLER, S.D., DUNCAN, B.L., SORRELL, R., BROWN, G.S. and CHALK, M.B., 2005. Using outcome to inform therapy practice. *Journal of Brief Therapy* 5.1.

MILLS, J., 2005. A Critique of Relational Psychoanalysis. *Psychoanalytic Psychology*, vol. 22, no. 2, pp. 155–188 ISSN 0736-9735; 1939-1331.

MILNE, D., 2009. *Evidence-Based Clinical Supervision: Principles and Practice*. Malden Leicester UK: Blackwell Publishing; British Psychological Society ISBN 978-1-4051-5849-7.

MINDELL, A., 1995. *Metaskills: The Spiritual Art of Therapy*. Tempe, AZ US: New Falcon Publications /z-wcorg/. ISBN 1561841196 9781561841196.

MITCHELL, S.A., 1988. *Relational Concepts in Psychoanalysis: An Integration*. Cambridge, MA US: Harvard University Press.

MITCHELL, S.A., 2000. *Relationality: From Attachment to Intersubjectivity*. Mahwah, NJ US: Analytic Press ISBN 0-88163-322-4.

MITCHELL, S.A., 2002. *Can Love Last? The Fate of Romance Over Time*. New York, NY US: W.W. Norton /z-wcorg/. ISBN 0393041840 9780393041842.

MITCHELL, S.A. and ARON, L. (eds), 1999. *Relational Psychoanalysis: The Emergence of a Tradition*. Mahwah, NJ US: Analytic Press ISBN 0-88163-270-8.

MITROFF, I.I. and DENTON, E.A., 1999. A Study of Spirituality in the Workplace. (Cover Story). *Sloan Management Review*, Summer99, vol. 40, no. 4, pp. 83–92 ISSN 0019848X.

MOON, J., 1999. *Reflection in Learning and Professional Development: Theory and Practice*. London UK: Kogan Page /z-wcorg/. ISBN 074943452X 9780749434526 0749428643 9780749428648.

MOORE, R., 2008. *Group Supervision with a Multi-Disciplinary Trauma Resource Team in the North of Ireland: A Participative Inquiry into the Application of a 'Process Framework'*. D. Prof. ed. Middlesex University.

MORENO, J.L., 1945. *Group Therapy*. New York: Beacon House.

MORGAN, G., 1993. *Imaginization: The Art of Creative Management*. Newbury Park; London; New Delhi: Sage /z-wcorg/. ISBN 0803952996 9780803952997.

MOTHERSOLE, G., 1999. Parallel process: A review. *The Clinical Supervisor*, 18(2), 107–121.

MUELLER, W.J. and KELL, B.L., 1972. *Coping with Conflict: Supervising Counselors and Psychotherapists*. East Norwalk, CT US: Appleton-Century-Crofts.

MYERS, I.B., 1998. *MBTI Manual: A Guide to the Development and use of the Myers–Briggs Type Indicator*. Palo Alto, CA US: Consulting Psychologists Press /z-wcorg/. ISBN 0891061304 9780891061304.

MYERS, I.B. and MYERS, P.B., 1980. *Gifts Differing: Understanding Personality Type*. Palo Alto, CA US: Davies-Black /z-wcorg/. ISBN 089106074X 9780891060741.

NEAL, J.A., 2005. Spirituality in the Workplace. *Studies in Spirituality Studies in Spirituality*, vol. 15, pp. 267–281 /z-wcorg/.

NECK, C.P. and MILLIMAN, J.F., 1994. Thought Self-Leadership: Finding Spiritual Fulfilment in Organizational Life. *Journal of Managerial Psychology*, vol. 9, no. 6, pp. 9–16 ISSN 0268-3946.

NELSON, M.L. and FRIEDLANDER, M.L., 2001. A Close Look at Conflictual Supervisory Relationships: The Trainee's Perspective. *Journal of Counseling Psychology*, 10, vol. 48, no. 4, pp. 384–395 ISSN 0022-0167; 1939-2168.

NEUMANN, J.E., 1999. Systems psychodynamics in the service of political organisational change. In: R. FRENCH and R. VINCE (eds), *Group Relations, Management and Organisation*. Oxford: Oxford University Press, pp. 54–69.

NEUMANN, J.E., KELLNER, K. and DAWSON-SHEPHERD, A., 1997. *Developing Organisational Consultancy*. London; New York, NY US: Routledge /z-wcorg/. ISBN 0415157021 9780415157025 041515703X 9780415157032.

NHAT HANH and ELLSBERG, R., 2008. *Thich Nhat Hanh: Essential Writings*. London: Darton Longman & Todd /z-wcorg/. ISBN 9780232527353 0232527350.

NORCROSS, J.C., 1993. Tailoring Relationship Stances to Client Needs: An Introduction. *Psychotherapy: Theory, Research, Practice, Training*, vol. 30, no. 3, pp. 402–403 ISSN 0033-3204; 1939-1536.

NORCROSS, J.C., 2011. *Psychotherapy Relationships that Work: Evidence Based Responsiveness*. New York, NY US: OUP.

NORCROSS, J.C., BEUTLER, L.E. and LEVANT, R.F., 2006. *Evidence-Based Practices in Mental Health: Debate and Dialogue on the Fundamental Questions*. Washington, DC US: American Psychological Association /z-wcorg/. ISBN 1591472903 9781591472902 1591473101 9781591473107.

NORCROSS, J.C. and GOLDFRIED, M.R., 1992. *Handbook of Psychotherapy Integration*. New York, NY US: Basic Books /z-wcorg/. ISBN 0465028799 9780465028795.

NORCROSS, J.C. and LAMBERT, M.J., 2006. The therapy relationship. In: J.R. NORCROSS, L.E. BUETLER and R.F. LEVANT (eds), *Evidence-based practices in mental health: Debate and dialogue on fundamental questions.* Washington, DC US: American Psychological Association, pp. 208–218.

NUTTALL, J., 1974. Marketing Evolution in British Industry. *Marketing Forum*, vol. September.

NUTTALL, J., 2001. Psychodynamics and Intersubjectivity in Management Organisations. *Journal of Change Management*, 02, vol. 1, no. 3, p. 229 ISSN 14697017.

Ó MURCHÚ, D., 2010. *Adult Faith: Growing in Wisdom and Understanding.* Maryknoll, NY US: Orbis Books /z-wcorg/. ISBN 9781570758867 1570758867.

O'BROIN, A. and PALMER, S., 2006. The Coach-Client Relationship and Contributions made by the Coach in Improving Coaching Outcome. *The Coaching Psychologist*, vol. 2, no. 2, pp. 16–20.

O'BROIN, A. and PALMER, S., 2010. The Coaching Alliance as a Universal Concept Spanning Conceptual Approaches. *Coaching Psychology International*, vol. 3, no. 1, pp. 3–5.

O'NEILL, B. and GAFFNEY, S., 2008. Field Theoretical Strategy. In: P. BROWNELL (ed.), *Handbook for Theory, Research, and Practice in Gestalt Therapy.* UK: Cambridge Scholars Publishing.

OLIVERO, G., BANE, K.D. and KOPELMAN, R.E., 1997. Executive Coaching as a Transfer of Training Tool: Effects on Productivity in a Public Agency. *Public Personnel Management*, Winter97, vol. 26, no. 4, p. 461 ISSN 00910260.

ORANGE, D.M., 2008. Whose Shame is it Anyway? Lifeworlds of Humiliation and Systems of Restoration (Or "the Analyst's Shame"). *Journal of Contemporary Psychoanalysis*, vol. 44, no. 1, pp. 83–100 /z-wcorg/. ISSN 0010-7530.

ORANGE, D.M., ATWOOD, G.E. and STOLOROW, R.D., 1997. *Working Intersubjectively: Contextualism in Psychoanalytic Practice.* Mahwah, NJ US: Analytic Press ISBN 0-88163-229-5.

ORLINSKY, D.E., GRAWE, K. and PARKS, B.K., 1994. Process and outcome in psychotherapy: Noch einmal. In: A.E. BERGIN, S.L. GARFIELD, A.E. BERGIN and S.L. GARFIELD (eds), *Handbook of psychotherapy and behavior change* (4th ed.). Oxford UK: John Wiley & Sons, pp. 270–376 ISBN 0-471-54513-9.

OSWICK, C., 2009. Burgeoning workplace spirituality? A textual analysis of momentum and directions. *Journal of Management, Spirituality and Religion*, Vol. 6, No. 1, p. 15–25

PAGE, S. and WOSKET, V., 1994. *Supervising the Counsellor: A Cyclical Model.* London; New York, NY US: Routledge /z-wcorg/. ISBN 0415102138 9780415102131 041510212X 9780415102124.

PALMER, S. and WHYBROW, A., 2007. *Handbook of Coaching Psychology: A Guide for Practitioners.* London; New York, NY US: Routledge /z-wcorg/. ISBN 1583917063 9781583917060 1583917071 9781583917077.

PAMPALLIS-PAISLEY, P., 2006. *Towards a Theory of Supervision for Coaching – an Integral Approach.* D.Prof. ed. Middlesex University.

REFERENCES

PANKSEPP, J., 1998. *Affective Neuroscience: The Foundations of Human and Animal Emotions.* Oxford: Oxford University Press.

PARADISE, A. and MOSLEY, J., 2009. Learning in a Down Economy. *T+D*, 04, vol. 63, no. 4, pp. 44–49 ISSN 15357740.

PARLETT, M., 1991. Reflections on Field Theory. *British Gestalt Journal*, vol. 1, pp. 69–12.

PATTON, M.J. and KIVLIGHAN, D.M., Jr., 1997. Relevance of the Supervisory Alliance to the Counseling Alliance and to Treatment Adherence in Counselor Training. *Journal of Counseling Psychology*, 01, vol. 44, no. 1, pp. 108–115 ISSN 0022-0167; 1939-2168.

PELLING, N. and AGOSTINELLI, E., 2009. Supervisor development. In: N. PELLING, et al. (eds), The practice of clinical supervision. Bowen Hills, QLD Australia: Australian Academic Press. *Supervisor Development*, pp. 201–211 ISBN 978-1-9215-1331-2.

PELLING, N., BARLETTA, J. and ARMSTRONG, P., 2009. *The Practice of Clinical Supervision.* Bowen Hills, Qld.: Australian Academic Press /z-wcorg/. ISBN 9781921513312 1921513314.

PELTIER, B., 2001. *The Psychology of Executive Coaching: Theory and Application.* Ann Arbor, MI US: Brunner-Routledge, Taylor & Francis Group.

PERLS, F.S., 1951. *Gestalt Therapy; Excitement and Growth in the Human Personality.* New York, NY US: Julian Press /z-wcorg/.

PETERS, T.J., 1992. *Liberation Management: Necessary Disorganization for the Nanosecond Nineties.* London: Macmillan /z-wcorg/. ISBN 0333533402 9780333533406.

PETERS, T.J. and WATERMAN, R.H., 1982. *In Search of Excellence: Lessons from America's Best-Run Companies.* New York, NY US: Harper and Row. /z-wcorg/. ISBN 0060150424 9780060150426.

PETERSON, D.B., 1993. Measuring change: A psychometric approach to evaluating individual coaching outcomes. Anonymous. *Annual Conference of the Society for Industrial and Organizational Psychology.* San Francisco, CA, USA.

PETRIGLIERI, G. and WOOD, J.D., 2003. The Invisible Revealed: Collusion as an Entry to the Group Unconscious. *Transactional Analysis Journal*, 10, vol. 33, no. 4, pp. 332–343 ISSN 0362-1537.

PHILIPPSON, P., 2001. *Self in Relation.* Highland, NY US: Gestalt Journal Press /z-wcorg/. ISBN 0939266407 9780939266401.

PHILIPPSON, P. and UNITED KINGDOM COUNCIL FOR PSYCHOTHERAPY, 2009. *The Emergent Self: An Existential-Gestalt Approach.* London: Karnac /z-wcorg/. ISBN 9781855755253 1855755254.

PHILLIPS, A., 1998. *The Beast in the Nursery.* London: Faber and Faber /z-wcorg/. ISBN 0571192661 9780571192663.

PREACHER, K.J. and LEONARDELLI, G.J., 2001. *Calculation for the Sobel Test: An Interactive Calculation Tool for Mediation Tests.* Available from: www.unc.edu/~preacher/sobel/sobel.htm.

PROJECT MATCH RESEARCH GROUP, 1998. Therapist Effects in Three Treatments for Alcohol Problems. *Psychotherapy Research*, vol. 8, no. 4, pp. 455–474 ISSN 1050-3307; 1468-4381.

PUGH, D.S. and HICKSON, D.J., 1996. *Writers on Organizations.* London: Penguin /z-wcorg/. ISBN 0140250239 9780140250237.

RAGINS, B.R., COTTON, J.L. and MILLER, J.S., 2000. Marginal Mentoring: The Effects of Type of Mentor, Quality of Relationship, and Program Design on Work and Career Attitudes. *Academy of Management Journal*, 12, vol. 43, no. 6, pp. 1,177–1,194 ISSN 00014273.

RIZZOLATTI, G. and CRAIGHERO, L., 2004. The mirror-neuron system. *Annual Review of Neuroscience*, 27: 169–192.

ROBB, C., 2006. *This Changes Everything: The Relational Revolution in Psychology.* New York, NY US: Picador /z-wcorg/. ISBN 9780312426156 0312426151.

ROBBINS, A., 1994. *The Power to Reach Your Destiny.*

ROCK, D., 2009. SPECIAL REPORT: THE TALENT OPPORTUNITY – Managing with the Brain in Mind – Neuroscience Research is Revealing the Social Nature of the Human Brain and its Implications for Management. In a High-Performance Workplace, People's Social Needs – for Status, Certainty, Autonomy, Relatedness, and Fairness – Matter More than Money. *Strategy & Business*, no. 56, p. 58 /z-wcorg/. ISSN 1083-706X.

ROGERS, C.R., 1995. *A Way of being.* Boston: Houghton Mifflin Co. /z-wcorg/. ISBN 0395755301 9780395755303. ROGERS, C.R., KIRSCHENBAUM, H. and HENDERSON, V.L., 1990. *The Carl Rogers Reader.* London: Constable /z-wcorg/. ISBN 0094698007 9780094698000 0094698406 9780094698406.

ROSINSKI, P., 2003. *Coaching Across Cultures: New Tools for Leveraging National, Corporate, and Professional Differences.* London; Yarmouth, Me.: Nicholas Brealey Pub. /z-wcorg/. ISBN 1857883012 9781857883015.

ROTHSCHILD, B., 2006. *Help for the Helper: The Psychophysiology of Compassion Fatigue and Vicarious Trauma.* New York, NY US: W.W. Norton & Co ISBN 0-393-70422-X.

ROUSSEAU, D.M., SITKIN, S.B., BURT, R.S. and CAMERER, C., 1998. Not so Different After all: A Cross-Discipline View of Trust. *Academy of Management Review*, 07, vol. 23, no. 3, pp. 393–404 ISSN 03637425.

RYAN, S., 2004. *Vital Practice.* Portland, UK: Sea Change Publications.

SAFRAN, J.D., CROCKER, P., MCMAIN, S. and MURRAY, P., 1990. Therapeutic Alliance Rupture as a Therapy Event for Empirical Investigation. *Psychotherapy: Theory, Research, Practice, Training*, vol. 27, no. 2, pp. 154–165 ISSN 0033-3204; 1939-1536.

SAFRAN, J.D. and MURAN, J.C., 2000. *Negotiating the Therapeutic Alliance: A Relational Treatment Guide.* New York, NY US: Guilford Press ISBN 1-57230-512-6.

SAFRAN, J.D., MURAN, J.C., SAMSTAG, L.W. and STEVENS, C., 2001. Repairing Alliance Ruptures. *Psychotherapy: Theory, Research, Practice, Training*, vol. 38, no. 4, pp. 406–412 ISSN 0033-3204; 1939-1536.

References

SCHARMER, C.O., 2007. *Theory U: Leading from the Future as it Emerges: The Social Technology of Presencing.* Cambridge, MA US: Society for Organizational Learning /z-wcorg/. ISBN 0974239054 9780974239057.

SCHEIN, E.H., 1988. *Organizational Psychology.* Englewood Cliffs, NJ US: Prentice-Hall /z-wcorg/. ISBN 0136411924 9780136411925.

SCHNEIDER, S.C., 1991. Managing boundaries in organizations. In: M.F.R. KETS DE VRIES (ed.), *Organizations on the couch: Clinical perspectives on organizational behavior and change.* San Francisco, CA US: Jossey-Bass. *Managing Boundaries in Organizations,* pp. 169–190 ISBN 1-55542-384-1.

SCHÖN, D.A., 1983. *The Reflective Practitioner: How Professionals Think in Action.* New York, NY US: Basic Books /z-wcorg/. ISBN 046506874X 9780465068746 9780465068784 0465068782 0851172318 9780851172316 1856282627 9781856282628.

SCHÖN, D.A., 1987. *Educating the Reflective Practitioner: Toward a New Design for Teaching and Learning in the Professions.* San Francisco, CA US: Jossey-Bass ISBN 1-55542-025-7.

SCHORE, A.N., 2003. *Affect Regulation and the Repair of the Self.* New York, NY US: W.W. Norton & Co ISBN 0-393-70407-6.

SCHUNK, D.H., 1990. Goal Setting and Self-Efficacy during Self-Regulated Learning. *Educational Psychologist,* Winter90, vol. 25, no. 1, p. 71 ISSN 00461520.

SCHWARTZ, H.S., 1990. *Narcissistic Process and Corporate Decay: The Theory of the Organization Ideal.* New York, NY US: New York University Press ISBN 0-8147-7913-1.

SCHWARZER, R., MUELLER, J. and GREENGLASS, E., 1999. Assessment of Perceived General Self-Efficacy on the Internet: Data Collection in Cyberspace. *Anxiety, Stress & Coping,* 05, vol. 12, no. 2, p. 145 ISSN 10615806.

SCOTT-MORGAN, P., 1994. *The Unwritten Rules of the Game: Master them, Shatter them, and Break through the Barriers to Organizational Change.* New York, NY US: McGraw-Hill /z-wcorg/. ISBN 0070570752 9780070570757.

SCOULAR, A. and LINLEY, P.A., 2006. Coaching, Goal-Setting and Personality Type: What Matters?. *The Coaching Psychologist,* vol. 2, pp. 9–11.

SEARLES, H., 1955. The Informational Value of the Supervisor's Emotional Experience. In: H. SEARLES and R.P. KNIGHT (1965), *Collected Papers on Schizophrenia and Related Subjects.* London: Hogarth Press.

SEGAL, H., 1988. Notes on symbol formation. In: E.B. SPILLIUS and E.B. SPILLIUS (eds), Melanie Klein today: Developments in theory and practice, Vol. 1: Mainly theory. Florence, KY US: Taylor & Frances/Routledge, pp. 160–177 ISBN 0-415-00675-9; 0-415-00676-7.

SEXTON, W.P., 1970. *Organization Theories.* Columbus, OH US: Merrill /z-wcorg/. ISBN 0675093155 9780675093156.

SHARF, J., PRIMAVERA, L.H. and DIENER, M.J., 2010. Dropout and Therapeutic Alliance: A Meta-Analysis of Adult Individual Psychotherapy. *Psychotherapy: Theory, Research & Practice,* 12, vol. 47, no. 4, pp. 637–645 ISSN 0033-3204.

SHERER, M., MADDUX, J.E., MERCANDANTE, B., PRENTICE-DUNN, S., JACOBS, B. and ROGERS, R.W., 1982. The self-efficacy scale: Construction and validation. *Psychological Reports*, 51, 663–671.

SHERMAN, S. and FREAS, A., 2004. The Wild West of Executive Coaching. *Harvard Business Review*, 11, vol. 82, no. 11, pp. 82–90 ISSN 00178012.

SILLS, C., 2006. Contracts and Contract Making. In: C. SILLS and C. SILLS (eds), Contracts in counselling and psychotherapy (2nd ed.).Thousand Oaks, CA US: Sage Publications, Inc. *Contracts and Contract Making*, pp. 9–26 ISBN 1412920655; 9781412920650; 1412920663; 9781412920667.

SILLS, C. and WIDE, M., 2006. Making Contracts with Different Personality Types. In: C. SILLS, *Contracts in counselling and psychotherapy* (2nd edition).Thousand Oaks, CA US: Sage Publications, Inc. ISBN 1412920655; 9781412920650; 1412920663; 9781412920667.

SKINNER, B.F., 1957. *Verbal Behavior*. East Norwalk, CT US: Appleton-Century-Crofts.

SKINNER, B.F., 1974. *About Behaviorism*. Oxford UK: Alfred A. Knopf ISBN 0394492013.

SLUZKI, C.E. and RANSOM, D.C., 1976. *Double Bind: The Foundation of the Communicational Approach to the Family*. New York, NY US; London: Grune & Stratton; distributed in the United Kingdom by Academic Press /z-wcorg/. ISBN 0808909509 9780808909507.

SMITHER, J.W., et al., 2003. Can Working with an Executive Coach Improve Multisource Feedback Ratings Over Time? a Quasi-Experimental Field Study. *Personnel Psychology*, Spring2003, vol. 56, no. 1, pp. 23–44 ISSN 00315826.

SOBEL, M.E., 1982. Asymptotic Confidence Intervals for Indirect Effects in Structural Equation Models. *Sociological Methodology*, vol. 13, pp. 290–312 /z-wcorg/. ISSN 0081-1750.

SOLOMAN, B. and FELDER, R.M., 2005. Index of Learning Styles (ILS). Retrieved 27th January 1998, http://www.ncsu.edu/felder-public/ILSpage.html.

SOSIK, J.J. and MEGERIAN, L.E., 1999. Understanding Leader Emotional Intelligence and Performance: The Role of self–other Agreement on Transformational Leadership Perceptions. *Group & Organization Management*, 09, vol. 24, no. 3, pp. 367–390 ISSN 1059-6011.

SPAGNUOLO LOBB, M. and AMENDT-LYON, N., 2003. *Creative License: The Art of Gestalt Therapy*. Wien; New York, NY US: Springer /z-wcorg/. ISBN 3211839011 9783211839010.

SPEARS, L.C., 1995. *Reflections on Leadership: How Robert K. Greenleaf's Theory of Servant-Leadership Influenced Today's Top Management Thinkers*. New York, NY US: J. Wiley /z-wcorg/. ISBN 0471036862 9780471036869.

SPEARS, L.C., 2002. *On Character and Servant-Leadership: Ten Characteristics of Effective, Caring Leaders*. Available from: www.greenleaf.org.

SPINELLI, E., 1989. *The Interpreted World: An Introduction to Phenomenological Psychology*. London: Sage /z-wcorg/. ISBN 0803981155 9780803981157 0803981147 9780803981140.

REFERENCES

STACEY, R.D., 1992. *Managing Chaos.* Kogan Page /z-wcorg/. ISBN 074940681X 9780749406813.

STACEY, R.D., 2001. *Complex Responsive Processes in Organizations: Learning and Knowledge Creation.* London; New York, NY US: Routledge /z-wcorg/. ISBN 041524918X 9780415249188 0415249198 9780415249195 9780203361481 0203361482.

STACEY, R.D., GRIFFIN, D. and SHAW, P., 2000. *Complexity and Management Fad Or Radical Challenge to Systems Thinking?* New York, NY US: Routledge /z-wcorg/. ISBN 0203190157 9780203190159.

STAEMMLER, F.M., 1997. Cultivated Uncertainty: An Attitude for Gestalt Therapists. *British Gestalt Journal,* vol. 6, no. 1, pp. 40–48 /z-wcorg/. ISSN 0961-771X.

STAJKOVIC, A.D. and LUTHANS, F., 1998. Social Cognitive Theory and Self-Efficacy: Going Beyond Traditional Motivational and Behavioral Approaches. *Organizational Dynamics,* vol. 26, no. 4, pp. 62–74 ISSN 0090-2616.

STEIN, E., 1916. *On the Problem of empathy.* In: *The Collected Works of Edith Stein,* trans. by W. STEIN. 1989. Vol. 3. Washington: ICS Publications.

STEIN, E., 1989. *The Collected Works of Edith Stein, Sister Teresa Benedicta of the Cross, Disalced Carmelite.* Washington, DC US; [London]: ICS; Distributed by Kluwer Academic. /z-wcorg/. ISBN 0792304853 9780792304852.

STERN, D.N., 1998. *The Interpersonal World of the Infant: A View from Psychoanalysis and Developmental Psychology.* London: Karnac Books /z-wcorg/. ISBN 185575200X 9781855752009.

STERN, D.N., 2004. *The Present Moment in Psychotherapy and Everyday Life.* New York, NY US: W.W. Norton /z-wcorg/. ISBN 0393704297 9780393704297. STERN, S., 2010. A New Leadership Blueprint. *Management Today,* 10, pp. 38–41 ISSN 00251925.

STEVENS and HOLLAND, P., 2008. Counselling across a language Gap. *Counselling Psychology Review,* Vol. 23, No. 3, August 2008.

STEWART, L.J., PALMER, S., WILKIN, H. and KERRIN, M., 2008. The Influence of Character: Does Personality Impact Coaching Success?. *International Journal of Evidence Based Coaching and Mentoring,* 02, vol. 6, no. 1, pp. 32–42 ISSN 1741-8305.

STEYAERT, C. and LOOY, B.v., 2010. *Relational Practices, Participative Organizing.* Bingley, UK: Emerald /z-wcorg/. ISBN 9780857240064 0857240064.

STUART, I., 2010. The 'three ways out': escape hatches. In: R.G. ERSKINE (ed.), *Life Scripts: A Transactional Analysis of Unconscious Relational Patterns.* London: Karnac, pp.127–150.

SUE-CHAN, C. and LATHAM, G.P., 2004. The Relative Effectiveness of External, Peer, and Self-Coaches. *Applied Psychology: An International Review,* 04, vol. 53, no. 2, pp. 260–278 ISSN 0269994X.

SULLIVAN, H.S., 1953. *The Interpersonal Theory of Psychiatry.* New York, NY US: W.W. Norton & Co.

SUTICH, A.J., 1976. Emergence of the Transpersonal Orientation: A Personal Account. *Journal of Transpersonal Psychology,* vol. 8, pp. 5–14.

SUTTON, R.I., 2007. *The no Asshole Rule: Building a Civilized Workplace and Surviving One that Isn't.* New York, NY US: Warner Business Books /z-wcorg/. ISBN 0446526568 9780446526562.

TACEY, D.J., 2004. *The Spirituality Revolution: The Emergence of Contemporary Spirituality.* Hove, East Sussex; New York, NY US: Brunner-Routledge /z-wcorg/. ISBN 1583918736 9781583918739 1583918744 9781583918746 9780203647035 0203647033.

TAYLOR, F.W., 1911. *The Principles of Scientific Management.* New York, NY US: Harper and Brothers.

TENBRUNSEL, A.E., DIEKMANN, K.A., WADE-BENZONI, K.A. and BAZERMAN, M.H., 2010. The Ethical Mirage: A Temporal Explanation as to Why we are Not as Ethical as we Think we are. *Res.Organ.Behav.Research in Organizational Behavior,* vol. 30, no. C, pp. 153–173 /z-wcorg/. ISSN 0191-3085.

THACH, E.C., 2002. The Impact of Executive Coaching and 360 Feedback on Leadership Effectiveness. *Leadership & Organization Development Journal,* vol. 23, no. 4, pp. 205–214 ISSN 0143-7739.

THACH, L. and HEINSELMAN, T., 1999. Executive Coaching Defined. *Training & Development,* 03, vol. 53, no. 3, p. 34 ISSN 10559760.

THOMAS, F.N., WAITS, R.A. and HARTSFIELD, G.L., 2007. The Influence of Gregory Bateson: Legacy Or Vestige?. *Kybernetes,* vol. 36, no. 7–8, pp. 871–883 /z-wcorg/. ISSN 0368-492X.

THOMPSON, H.B., et al., 2008. *Coaching: A Global Study of Successful Practices.* Available from: www.amanet.org/research/pdfs/i4cp-coaching.pdf.

TRACEY, T.J. and KOKOTOVIC, A.M., 1989. Factor Structure of the Working Alliance Inventory. *Psychological Assessment: A Journal of Consulting and Clinical Psychology,* 09, vol. 1, no. 3, pp. 207–210 ISSN 1040-3590; 1939-134X.

TROMPENAARS, A. and HAMPDEN-TURNER, C., 1997. *Riding the Waves of Culture: Understanding Cultural Diversity in Business.* London: N. Brealey Pub. /z-wcorg/. ISBN 1857881761 9781857881769.

ULLMAN, D., 2009. *Cocreating the Field: Intention and Practice in the Age of Complexity.* New York, NY US: Routledge, Taylor & Francis /z-wcorg/. ISBN 9780415872591 0415872596.

URWICK, L.F., 1947. *The Elements of Administration.* London: I. Pitman /z-wcorg/.

VAN VELSOR, E., TAYLOR, S. and LESLIE, J.B., 1993. An Examination of the Relationships among Self-Perception Accuracy, Self-Awareness, Gender, and Leader Effectiveness. *Human Resource Management,* Summer, vol. 32, no. 2, pp. 249–263 ISSN 00904848.

VISSER, M., 2003. Gregory Bateson on Deutero-Learning and Double Bind: A Brief Conceptual History. *Journal of the History of the Behavioral Sciences,* Summer2003, vol. 39, no. 3, pp. 269–278 ISSN 00225061.

VISSER, M., 2007a. Deutero-Learning in Organizations: A Review and a Reformulation. *Academy of Management Review,* 04, vol. 32, no. 2, pp. 659–667 ISSN 03637425.

VISSER, M., 2007b. System Dynamics and Group Facilitation: Contributions from Communication Theory. *System Dynamics Review*, vol. 23, no. 4, pp. 453–463 ISSN 0883-7066; 10991727.

VISSER, M., 2010. Relating in Executive Coaching: A Behavioural Systems Approach. *Journal of Management Development*, 12, vol. 29, no. 10, pp. 891–901 ISSN 02621711.

VYGOTSKIĬ, L.S. and COLE, M., 1978. *Mind in Society: The Development of Higher Psychological Processes.* Cambridge: Harvard University Press /z-wcorg/. ISBN 0674576284 9780674576285 0674576292 9780674576292.

WACHTEL, P.L., 1977. *Psychodynamics and Behaviour Therapy: Towards an Integration.* New York, NY US: Basic Books.

WACHTEL, P.L., 2008. *Relational Theory and the Practice of Psychotherapy.* New York, NY US: Guilford Press ISBN 978-1-59385-614-4; 1-59385-614-8.

WAGNER-MARSH, F. and CONLEY, J., 1999. The Fourth Wave: The Spiritually-Based Firm. *Journal of Organizational Change Management*, 04, vol. 12, no. 4, p. 292 ISSN 09534814.

WAMPOLD, B.E., 2001. *The Great Psychotherapy Debate: Models, Methods, and Findings.* Mahwah, NJ US: Lawrence Erlbaum Associates Publishers ISBN 0-8058-3201-7; 0-8058-3202-5.

WANBERG, C.R., KAMMEYER-MUELLER, J. and MARCHESE, M., 2006. Mentor and Protégé Predictors and Outcomes of Mentoring in a Formal Mentoring Program. *Journal of Vocational Behavior*, 12, vol. 69, no. 3, pp. 410–423 ISSN 0001-8791.

WARD, W.A., 1999. *Leadership... with a Human Touch.* Chicago: Ragan Communications.

WASYLYSHYN, K.M., 2003. Executive Coaching an Outcome Study. *Consulting Psychology Journal: Practice & Research*, Spring2003, vol. 55, no. 2, pp. 94–106 ISSN 10659293.

WATZLAWICK, P., BAVELAS, J.B. and JACKSON, D.D., 1967. *Pragmatics of Human Communication; a Study of Interactional Patterns, Pathologies, and Paradoxes.* New York, NY US: Norton /z-wcorg/. ISBN 0393010090 9780393010091.

WEICK, K.E., 1979. *The Social Psychology of Organizing.* Reading, MA US: Addison-Wesley Pub. Co. /z-wcorg/. ISBN 0201085917 9780201085914.

WEICK, K.E., 1995. *Sensemaking in Organizations.* London: Sage Publications /z-wcorg/.

WERTHEIMER, M., 1944. *Gestalt Theory,* New York, NY US: Hayes Barton Press /z-wcorg/.

WEST, L. and MILAN, M., 2001. *The Reflecting Glass: Professional Coaching for Leadership Development.* Basingstoke: Palgrave /z-wcorg/. ISBN 0333945298 9780333945292.

WESTERMAN, M.A., 1998. Reconceptualizing Defense as a Special Type of Problematic Interpersonal Behavior Pattern: A Fundamental Breach by an Agent-in-a-Situation. *Journal of Mind and Behavior*, vol. 19, no. 3, pp. 257–302 ISSN 0271-0137.

WESTON, M., 1994. *Kierkegaard and Modern Continental Philosophy: An Introduction*. London; New York, NY US: Routledge /z-wcorg/. ISBN 0415101190 9780415101196 0415101204 9780415101202.

WHEATLEY, M.J., 2006. *Leadership and the New Science: Discovering Order in a Chaotic World*. San Francisco, CA US: Berrett-Koehler /z-wcorg/. ISBN 1576753441 9781576753446.

WHEELER, G., 2000. *Beyond Individualism: Toward a New Understanding of Self, Relationship, & Experience*. Cleveland, OH US: Gestalt Institute of Cleveland Press ISBN 0-88163-334-8.

WHEELER, G., 2002. The developing field model: Toward a Gestalt developmental model. In G. Wheeler and M. McConville (eds), *The Heart of Development: Vol 1: Childhood*, NJ: Gestalt Press, p.37–82.

WHEELER, G., 2003. Contact and Creativity. In: M. SPAGNUOLO LOBB and N. AMENDT-LYON (eds), *Creative License: The art of Gestalt therapy*. New York: Springer Wein.

WHEELER, G., 2009. *Cocreating the Field: Intention and Practice in the Age of Complexity*. New York: Routledge, Taylor & Francis.

WHEELER, G. and MCCONVILLE, M., 2002. *The Heart of Development: Gestalt Approaches to Working with Children, Adolescents, and their Worlds*. Cambridge, MA US; Hillsdale, NJ US: Gestalt Press; Distributed by Analytic Press /z-wcorg/. ISBN 088163350X 9780881633504 0881633402 9780881633405.

WHITTINGTON, J.L., et al., 2009. Transactional Leadership Revisited: Self—other Agreement and its Consequences. *Journal of Applied Social Psychology*, 08, vol. 39, no. 8, pp. 1,860–1,886 ISSN 0021-9029.

WHITWORTH, L., KIMSEY-HOUSE, H. and SANDAHL, P., 1998. *Co-Active Coaching: New Skills for Coaching People Toward Success in Work and Life*. Palo Alto, CA US: Davies-Black /z-wcorg/. ISBN 0891061231 9780891061236.

WILLIAMS, L. and PLAGENS, C., 2009. Dynamic Co-Presencing: A Creative Approach to the Gestalt of Curiosity. *Gestalt Review*, vol. 13, no. 2, pp. 173–185 ISSN 1084-8657; 1945-4023.

WINNICOTT, D.W., 1965. *The Maturational Processes and the Facilitating Environment; Studies in the Theory of Emotional Development*. London: Hogarth /z-wcorg/.

WITTGENSTEIN, L., 1922/1961. *Tractus, Logico-Philosophicus*. Trans. D.F. PEARS and B.F. MCGUINNESS. London: Routledge and Kegan Paul.

WORTHEN, V. and MCNEILL, B.W., 1996. A Phenomenological Investigation of 'good' Supervision Events. *Journal of Counseling Psychology*, 01, vol. 43, no. 1, p. 25 ISSN 00220167.

WYCHERLEY, I.M. and COX, E., 2008. Factors in the Selection and Matching of Executive Coaches in Organisations. *COACHING*, vol. 1, no. 1, pp. 39–53 /z-wcorg/. ISSN 1752-1882.

YALOM, I.D., 1970. *The Theory and Practice of Group Psychotherapy*. New York, NY US: Basic Books /z-wcorg/. ISBN 0465084451 9780465084456.

YALOM, I.D., 1980. *Existential Psychotherapy*. New York, NY US: Basic Books /z-wcorg/. ISBN 0465021476 9780465021475.

REFERENCES

YONTEF, G.M. and YONTEF, G.M., 1993. *Awareness, Dialogue & Process: Essays on Gestalt Therapy.* Highland, NY US: Gestalt Journal Press /z-wcorg/. ISBN 0939266202 9780939266203.

Many books on coaching have focused more on what the coach does than on the client. *Coaching Relationships* is different. It places relationship, to self and to others, including the coach, at the heart of the coaching activity. This involves a major change of emphasis, from a focus on coach techniques and interventions, goal-setting and action planning, towards an appreciation of and engagement with patterns of relating. This 'relational turn' mirrors similar movements in all fields of psychological work as well as in organisational theory, sociology and the arts. Further, it recognises that today executive coaching relationships in organisations will mirror and reflect the wider executive relationships that exist.

Coaching Relationships: The Relational Coaching Field Book presents a compelling account of the 'drama' of the relational turn in executive coaching. The book describes the evolution of this radical view of coaching and explores how this view expands our understanding of relationships. The editors focus on the importance of here-and-now relating as it evolves during the coaching process, and also on the relationships in the 'material' that the client brings.

All five parts of the book consider executive coaching practice as it really happens. It starts with an exploration of what relational coaching means in practice and goes on to explore what the relational perspective means for such issues as contracting and the supervision that coaches undertake as well as opening our eyes to deeper vulnerabilities within the relationship. Finally, *Coaching Relationships* presents a new way of doing research into coaching effectiveness, based on the descriptions of robust pieces of research into what works in coaching, carried out in three different countries, the US, Canada and the UK.

Coaching Relationships: The Relational Coaching Field Book is edited by two internationally recognised experts, leaders of the key Executive Coaching programmes at the Ashridge Business School, UK.

Erik de Haan is the Director of the Ashridge Centre for Coaching and programme leader of Ashridge's Master's (MSc) in Executive Coaching, and its Postgraduate Certificate in O.D. – Consulting and Coaching Supervision. He is also Professor of Organisation Development and Coaching at the VU University of Amsterdam.

Charlotte Sills is a coach and coach supervisor and co-director of the Coaching for Organisation Consultants programme at Ashridge Business School, UK. She is a visiting professor at Middlesex University and was for many years head of the Transactional Analysis Department at Metanoia Institute, UK where she is still a senior tutor and supervisor.

Ashridge is one of the world's leading providers of executive education. Established in 1959, it has acquired an outstanding international reputation in helping to make a difference to both individuals and organisations through its combination of executive development, research and consultancy expertise. Its activities include open and tailored executive education programmes; MBA, MSc & Diploma qualifications; organisation consulting; applied research; and online learning. Clients include leading organisations in the private and public sectors in the UK and across the globe.

LIBRI
PUBLISHING

ASH

ISBN 9781907471285

US $40.00
CAN $40.00
54000

9 781907 471285